# The Afterburner Advantage

How a small team of fighter pilots
transformed 3,500 companies and
helped an NFL team win the Super Bowl

## By Christian "Boo" Boucousis
### CEO, Afterburner, Inc.

Happy About

20660 Stevens Creek Blvd., Suite 210
Cupertino, CA 95014

Published by Happy About®
20660 Stevens Creek Blvd., Suite 210, Cupertino, CA 95014
**https://HappyAbout.com**

First Printing: March 2025
Paperback ISBN (1st Edition): 1-60005-290-8 978-1-60005-290-3
eBook ISBN (1st Edition): 1-60005-291-6 978-1-60005-291-0
Place of Publication: Silicon Vally, CA
Paperback Library of Congress Number: 2025901568

## Trademarks

All terms mentioned in this book that are known to be trademarks or service marks have been appropriately capitalized. Neither Happy About, nor any of its imprints, can attest to the accuracy of this information. Use of a term in this book should not be regarded as affecting the validity of any trademark or service mark.

## Warning and Disclaimer

Every effort has been made to make this book as complete and as accurate as possible. The information provided is on an "as is" basis. The author(s), publisher, and their agents assume no responsibility for errors or omissions. Nor do they assume liability or responsibility to any person or entity with respect to any loss or damages arising from the use of information contained herein.

## Dedication

To Lulu, Fletch, Sadie, and Joshua, who give me the leeway to pursue my passion.

# Contents

# Foreword

*By Jeff Sutherland, Co-creator of Scrum and Scrum@Scale*

I first learned the value of a disciplined process in the cockpit of an RF4C, flying at supersonic speeds over North Vietnam. During those harrowing missions, any small oversight could spell disaster in a matter of seconds. There wasn't time to second-guess; there was only time to observe, orient, decide, and act. John Boyd would codify that approach into the now-legendary OODA Loop—one that I embedded into the DNA of Scrum and Scrum@Scale to help teams stay ahead of fast-changing conditions.

Years later, my time coaching companies on Agile ways of working proved that the very same iterative mentality that saved my life in the air could transform organizations on the ground. *Adapt quickly, respond intelligently, focus on what matters,* and do it all over again. In this book, *The Afterburner Advantage*, Christian "Boo" Boucousis distills that same proven mindset and methodology—originally forged in the intense world of fighter aviation—into a practical formula that leaders in any field can adopt. Boo has flown some of the world's fastest jets. He has built businesses from scratch and collaborated with thousands of people across industries. Every story in these pages is steeped in that unbreakable discipline that made him (and me) successful in circumstances where the margin of error is razor-thin

Here's what makes *The Afterburner Advantage* more than just another leadership book:

## 1. Plan–Brief–Execute–Debrief = Build–Measure–Learn

In Scrum, we continuously iterate: we plan in short sprints, execute rapidly, and then inspect and adapt in retrospectives. Fighter pilots do the same: they plan meticulously, brief the team, execute the mission, then debrief to extract lessons learned. Boo reintroduces this Plan–Brief–Execute–Debrief loop in a refreshing way to help teams achieve "Flawless Execution" (FLEX). Anyone who has tried a Scrum sprint will appreciate how naturally the fighter pilot cycle aligns with Agile thinking: smaller increments, faster feedback loops, and consistent continuous improvement.

## 2. Nameless–Rankless = Blameless Retrospectives

One of the most powerful features of Scrum is the retrospective—an opportunity to reflect on what went well, what didn't, and what to change next time. Fighter pilots have done something very similar for decades, but they call it "the nameless–rankless debrief." Regardless of rank or seniority, every pilot and crew member has permission—and responsibility—to discuss what actually happened. By stripping away titles and hierarchy, the focus is on improvement, not blame. This is exactly what we mean by a "blameless retrospective." Boo's stories on how the New York Giants used this principle to elevate accountability and morale illustrate how such simple rules can flip a team's trajectory from average to Super Bowl champion.

## 3. OODA Loops in Everyday Business

The OODA Loop's power is in its speed, simplicity, and repeated iteration. Observe your environment, Orient to what matters, Decide on a path, and Act before it's too late. Then do it all over again. It turned out to be the backbone of mission success in Vietnam, the beating heart of Scrum, and the operating principle of thousands of successful organizations. *The Afterburner Advantage* offers concrete techniques—developed in the cockpit—that ensure your team sees problems clearly, takes decisive action, and never stops adapting, even under pressure.

## 4. Turning Theory into Muscle Memory

Pilots train and rehearse until every maneuver, every checklist, and every emergency procedure is second nature. That's how they stay calm when the unexpected hits. In business, you want that same muscle memory. Repetition should never be about boredom; it's about mastery. Boo explains how to compress learning cycles, reduce the noise from distractions, and ingrain new habits so that your team's reactions become both swift and correct—especially when the stakes soar.

## 5. High-Performance + High-Purpose

Make no mistake: no methodology can flourish if it's purely mechanical or robotic. People need a reason to care. One of my favorite reminders comes from my own time coaching companies on Scrum: "If your team doesn't know *why* they're doing something, they'll either do it poorly or not at all." By bringing real-life fighter pilot stories, Boo keeps us focused on mission, not mere tasks. The result? You build teams that not only execute *fast* but execute with *passion*, forging a culture that's as human-centric as it is results-driven.

Over half a century ago, half the pilots flying RF4Cs in my wing didn't return from missions over North Vietnam. We owed it to each other to execute flawlessly, to communicate fearlessly, and to continuously refine our approach. In modern business, the stakes may not be life or death, but they can feel just as high for your dreams, your career, and your company's survival. *The Afterburner Advantage* shows how the same relentless discipline that helps fighter pilots come back in one piece can help you build teams that thrive under pressure.

If you're ready to debrief your own ways of working and consistently hit your goals—even under the stress and complexity of our hyperconnected world—this book will show you how. Boo's framework is immediately applicable, whether you're leading a billion-dollar enterprise, coaching a sports team, or simply trying to cut through organizational inertia.

I'm excited you're picking up this book. As someone who's lived through dogfights in the air and corporate battles on the ground, I see *The Afterburner Advantage* as both a validation of universal principles and a blueprint for success in an age where agility and discipline must coexist.

Read on, and let Boo show you how to Plan, Brief, Execute, and Debrief your way to better business outcomes, stronger teams, and a winning culture.

**—Jeff Sutherland**
*Co-creator of Scrum and Scrum@Scale,*
*Vietnam War Veteran and RF4C Pilot,*
*Agile Pioneer and Author*

# Introduction

An interest in applying combat disciplines to the battlefield of business is not new. Sun Tzu wrote *The Art of War*, the first breakout book, nearly 2,400 years ago. Since then, dozens if not hundreds of books have appeared, each with their own take on this basic concept filtered through the author's particular lens.

Christian "Boo" Boucousis is unique in two vitally important ways. First and foremost, Boucousis was a world-class fighter pilot flying the super-advanced F/A-18 Hornet. He was that highly trained man-machine interface sitting in a cockpit surrounded by a dizzying array of insistent data inputs all feeding him information that he had to process and act on in milliseconds. He was given that jet only after three years of unforgiving training, then flew for another six or seven years before he was asked to take his toolkit to the national war college and train the generals—meaning he was a top-of-the-top fighter pilot in a top-of-the-top community of pilots who then climbed up another notch and trained the leaders.

But that's not what makes Boo—and this book—unique. In fact, Boucousis would be the first to tell you that it's not being a fighter pilot that defines him, but rather his last 20 years in business at the helm of major global projects to which he applied his skills and training. In 2010 he got a call from a group of investors who were financing the construction of a major hotel property that was stalling and perilously close to collapse. Boo came in and threw out the book, replacing the countless to-do lists with a simple but inflexible focus on *outcomes*. What are we trying to *accomplish*, he would ask, then we'll see what we need to do—never realizing that this management style of his was in fact a reflection of his decades of training as a pilot. The application of these disciplines paid off; the hotel was built ahead of time and below budget and has been one of the most successful of its kind. Nicely, it was also a jumping off point for a series of his successes in industries as diverse as publishing, logistics and health care.

It was in 2014 that the seeds for this book were planted. That year, he went to see a seminar put on by a fellow fighter pilot. He arrived at the venue loaded with a heavy dose of skepticism and was ready to brand the seminar a gimmick—but after walking into a room filled with more than 1,000 expectant attendees, and 20 or so former fighter pilots training them, he knew something was very right about it all. 10 years later he bought the company.

As I said in the beginning, this book is unique in several ways, each of which seriously matters in the world of business books. First, it brings forth the exacting discipline of a fighter pilot and why they work in life, but that's not enough. What makes it so endlessly spot on and applicable to anyone building a career is how Boo used these exact same techniques in the real world. It's not enough to be a great pilot and give advice. Instead, what you are about to read has been modeled, tempered, tested, applied, and shaped by 20 years of successful leadership in the art of business. And that's something no one else can say.

I wish you well.

DLK

Author

*The Eleventh Hour: How Great Britian, the Soviet Union, and the U.S. Brokered the Unlikely Deal that Won the War* (Wiley)


Founder

The Military Channel

# A Note from the Author

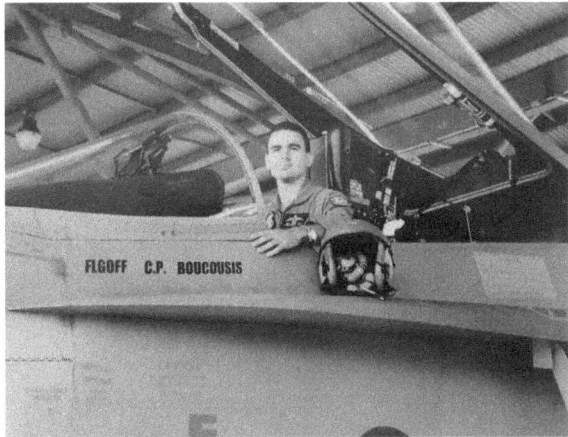

*Figure 1. Boo as a fighter pilot in the Royal Australian Air Force*

I'm a fighter pilot. I was 22 when I started flying the F/A-18 Hornet—a flying machine capable of flying at over 1,260 miles per hour, where I was trained in the art of how to consistently complete complex missions successfully, while processing hundreds of data inputs from three digital screens, a helmet, four radios, a wingman, and my own internal biases, doubts, and beliefs.

Inside my cockpit, I see and hear data.

Inside my helmet, I see and hear data.

Inside my mind, I see, hear, and *feel* data.

Data comes at me as lights, tones, voices, digital readouts, symbology, and physical inputs.

Data comes to me from a dozen other fighter jets simultaneously connected to my jet via a real time data link. It comes as fast as the airspace I'm flying through, and I have to process it and distill it, make a whole bunch of split-second decisions, and do it fast. I mean, it's very fast—utterly fast—and each data point is absolutely important. And yet, in that cockpit, inside my helmet, when I do all the fighter pilot stuff you'll read about in this book, it all feels like it's in slow motion, like a John Wick movie with Keanu Reeves dodging bullets in slow-mo.

While all this is happening, I'm utterly alive and engaged in the moment. I'm aware of my environment and the situation around me "in the now" (where I am and my impact on those around me). I'm also trained to sense and process what's likely happening in the near future (where my jet and I will be in a few seconds). I see where I'm headed in the far future (what's happening at my destination, the target). I have been trained in a unique cognitive model to create what fighter pilots call "SA," which is short for situational awareness. Not only am I alert to my situation—we all are to some extent—but because of my training, I'm hyper-alert and can comprehend the impact of my thoughts and actions on the environment around me. My SA feels like a superpower, and to some extent, I guess it is. I'm trained to do the hard things at 1,260 miles per hour in a cockpit sitting in a swarm of data streams—and yet, when I, or any other fighter pilot, are on our game, in the zone, it can feel effortless. When's the last time you finished a day, walked in the door to your family, and felt like you had an effortless day? You can if you're trained to create an environment to operate in "the zone" once or twice a day.

The fact is, I wanted to be a fighter pilot from the age of five. Actually, that's probably not the right way to frame it, but from the age of five, I completely *believed* that I was going to be a fighter pilot, no matter what. I've learned over the last 31 years, since I joined the Air Force, that there is a HUGE difference between wanting something and believing something. I had just finished high school when I was selected for pilot training as a scrappy, wiry 18-year-old. I was a very ordinary kid with a big dream, to be a single-seat fighter pilot, a knight of the air, even though I knew absolutely nothing about the jets I would ultimately fly. There was no digital age when I grew up; I bought one of the very first cellphones when I started officer training! The jet, though, the McDonnell Douglas F/A-18 Hornet, my dream jet, was the first digital age aircraft of the digital era, and I was an analog kid—nothing special—on the precipice of a new high-speed, loud, intensely competitive, digitally powered world.

I was also what they called a "repeat," meaning I did my final year at high school twice as I missed the grades I needed for college on my first attempt. Academics had always been something I struggled with. A diagnosis of ADHD at the age of 48 helped me finally put my lack of academic prowess into perspective, and I was able to finally shrug off this life-long nagging self-doubt that I was somehow always a little "dumber" than average. I didn't have any special talents, I wasn't a genius, and I didn't even go to college—well, I did, for six weeks, until I walked out of the middle of a calculus lecture in my math degree (I did a math degree because I watched a video of a fighter pilot in a recruitment video say they did one. When I sat in that calculus class, I felt stupid and out of my depth). All I wanted to do was fly. So here I was, scraping through school as a B+ student (the second time around), and I wanted to fly the most advanced fighter jet in the world? Maybe I can frame it this way: I was facing this enormous gap between where I was and where I wanted to be, and even though I knew where I wanted to go, I had no idea what I was doing. Sounds a lot like your life, right? You have dreams and aspirations; you know where you want to go. So, how's that going? Are you there yet? If not, I can show you how to get there (I did, by accident!).

I don't fly the Hornet anymore. In some ways I wish I still did; there's a story coming as to why my career was cut short, so hang in there if you've ever had a dream ripped from your fingers due to no fault of your own. Today, I'm the CEO of Afterburner, Inc. This company has become my new cockpit. Along with a small team of retired and serving fighter pilots, I travel the world training, speaking, and teaching professionals at some of the world's largest corporations, as well as at some of the newest, most exciting and driven VC-backed start-ups. I've helped thousands of individuals set their goals; explore the gaps between desires, strategies, dreams, and reality; and through willpower and training, and following an incredibly simple and elegant process, get to the other side with flying colors.

Like that 5-year-old who ultimately became a fighter pilot. Just like I believed I was going to be a fighter pilot, I believe Afterburner and the fighter pilot mindset will allow you to surprise yourself and turn what you want into what you have. If you dream of playing in the NBA, NFL, or MLB; if you're in the NBA, NFL, or MLB, and want to win the Super Bowl, NBA Finals, or World Series; if you want to own your own business, get promoted, earn more, or run the best school in the country, you can.

Today, I ask myself how I turned my dreams and ambitions into reality. And by that, I mean not just the dream of becoming a fighter pilot but also becoming a business founder, becoming financially independent, and, most importantly, discovering an incredible wingman, a life partner, with whom I have built a beautiful family and a life that fills my cup each day.

As I reflect, I see with crystal clear clarity that the same tools and processes that made a fighter pilot out of a 19-year-old are the same tools that any entrepreneur, salesperson, corporate citizen, or baseball coach could use to bridge their gaps. And they weren't just tools in a conventional sense. Rather, they crafted a unique way of thinking, a different cognitive model from the one we use every day, a mental model that gave me a unique mindset, a fighter pilot mindset. And that stays with you.

The founder, someone who has become a very dear friend of mine, Jim "Murph" Murphy, an F-15C fighter pilot, started Afterburner in 1996 and grew it into a multimillion-dollar business. I have so much respect for Murph's intellect and drive. He turned a shattered dream of playing Major League Baseball into a career as a fighter pilot, then created the bridge between the fighter pilot world and business, and a bridge between my business life and fighter pilot career. He is the OG of bringing a military (fighter pilot) mindset to business. He had the insight to bring the same fighter pilot tools, processes, and our fighter pilot mindset, and adapt them to the corporate world, the sporting world, and any organization really that had a passion for winning.

The fact that it worked is obvious from the data. Since that first day 28 years ago, we've become a bedrock in the leadership development and training industry. We've sold over 250,000 copies of our books, trained more than 2,200,000 people, and worked with countless companies on the INC 500—plus no less than 94% of the Fortune 1000. Our clients include iconic brands like American Express, Marriott, NFL, IBM, McDonald's, and Microsoft, but also the newest, hardscrabble startups funded by Silicon Valley. Home Depot was our first client in 1996; they're an awful lot bigger now than they were then, and we like to think we had something to do with their scaling so effortlessly. So changed were they by the processes that they had us train every new store manager and deputy for many years in what we called then "Flawless Execution." IHG, the hotel group that includes the Intercontinental brand and Holiday Inns, has had us training their hotel general managers worldwide. We've trained IHG people in Dubai, Spain, Australia, France, Japan, and Canada. Today, 3,500 companies later, we get letters from successful men

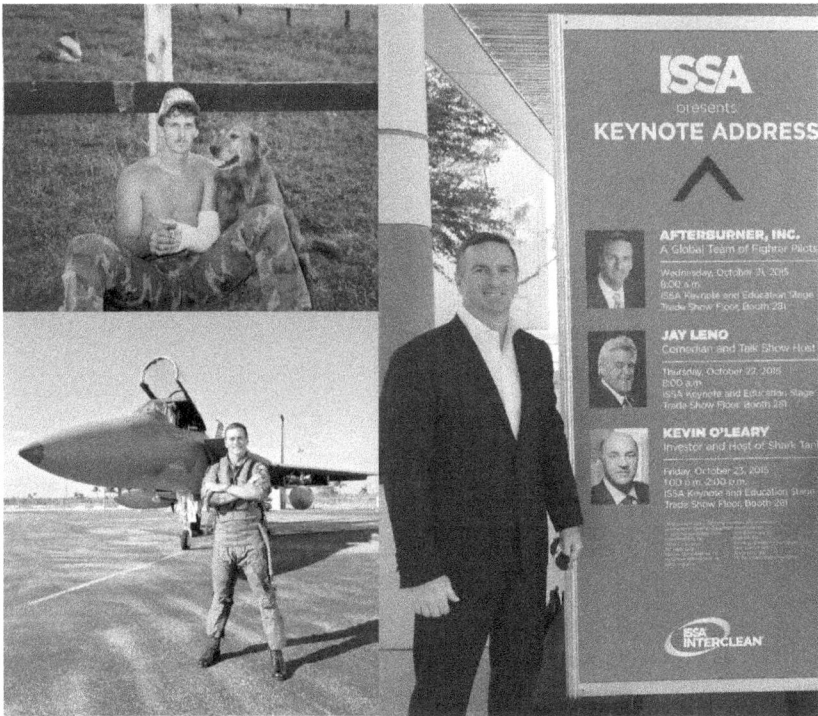

*Figure 2. Afterburner Founder James "Murph" Murphy*

and women worldwide who credit the fighter pilot mindset for their companies' success and the success they're experiencing in life.

And, like Home Depot, 85% of our clients are repeat customers.

Ten years ago, I first saw an Afterburner keynote at a small vineyard in rural Australia. The topic was "Flawless Execution"—how to go about your life doing things better, doing things flawlessly, actually delivering on dreams, strategic goals, and the most audacious aspirations. Well, my brain exploded, my synapses were firing, and it was like two completely unrelated and independent parts of my life fused into synchronicity. I was hooked, I was a believer; this fighter pilot stuff really works in life AND business. It resonated with everything I knew as a fighter pilot, and here it was expressed in terms the ordinary businessperson could use. It took nearly ten years, but when it came time, Jim and I talked and I bought into the company and now run it.

Murph wrote the first edition of this book decades ago. It was titled *Flawless Execution*, and it laid out the roadmap and explained how our fighter disciples, the way we think, and, importantly, the way we work together can deliver a profound change in the corporate world. Back then, however, our jets were a far cry from the fifth-generation human-machine-fused digital wonders they are today. Now it's time to take this company into the next stage, a stage molded by our new team and our fifth-gen jets, our fifth-gen pilots, and a new generation of thinking for you.

**Figure 3. Fifth-Generation Fighter Pilot and Aircraft, the F-35B Lightning. UK MoD.**

How on earth could a fighter pilot mindset help you? Look at your world. You're overloaded with data, your world is moving fast, and you're motivated. You're always learning from your mistakes and from your victories. You're growing as a person, and you're doing a great job. But like anyone with ambition, there's always more. Maybe you're on the flip side of that coin? You're a little lost, struggling with motivation, and each day feels like scaling a mountain without a summit. It doesn't matter who you are, there is always a future you want to get to from the place you are today. That is life, and you don't need any special talents to close that gap.

**A Note from the Author**

But what if I said to you that you could do it all faster and with less effort? Learn faster, grow faster, hit your targets faster, hit bigger goals, get promoted quicker, become a better leader faster, create more time in your life for the things you want to do, and maybe, if the stars align, live the purposeful and meaningful life you've dreamed of. If you think that's impossible, stay with me, let me help you believe it is possible. More so, if you believe you're already a high performer and you think you've already got it all hacked, do what fighter pilots do—stay curious. I'll share my personal insights on how I turned the dream of becoming a fighter pilot into the reality of having the best job in the world. I had no awareness of it at the time, it felt pretty hard; however, with the benefit of age and maybe a little wisdom, I'm able to reflect and drill down on the elements of my journey that added disproportionate value to my life.

It's certainly not all about me! This book shares a few case studies and stories from our team, in addition to folks who demonstrate a fighter pilot mindset to dominate their industries and build companies and products that never existed into billion-dollar behemoths. Not many, though. I want to focus on the *how* in these pages; I think there's more value in that.

That's the Afterburner Advantage. Our mission is to build high-impact leaders and teams that get the hard stuff done. Business is hard, life is hard, and personal growth is hard. Let's get it done!

Blue skies.

**Christian "Boo" Boucousis**

CEO

Afterburner, Inc.

# 1 Introduction to the Fighter Pilot Mindset

The **Introduction to the Fighter Pilot Mindset** in *The Afterburner Advantage* introduces the core principles that define how fighter pilots operate and why these concepts are relevant to business and leadership. It emphasizes **situational awareness (SA)**—the ability to process data in real-time and make rapid decisions—along with **iterative thinking**, represented by the ORCA loop Objective, Result, Cause, Action which allows pilots to stay agile in dynamic environments. Boo highlights how belief, discipline, and adaptability drive success, explaining how these same principles can help leaders and teams in any field achieve high performance and continuous improvement.

# 1 The Afterburner Advantage, from Flawless Execution to FLEX, 27 Years

> "It takes 20 years to build a reputation and five minutes to ruin it. If you think about that, you'll do things differently."
> **Warren Buffett, CEO of Berkshire Hathaway**

We've been building credibility in the fighter pilot mindset and ways of working ever since we introduced the business world to Flawless Execution— and what a success it has been. We've trained CPAs, salespeople, investment bankers, customer service reps, CEOs, forklift drivers, entrepreneurs, first responders, and countless others. Since 2019, even the Blue Angels have been using our "Plan–Brief–Execute–Debrief" model—talk about full circle! We've been with companies in the hotel industry, franchising, finance, packaged goods, food service, energy, construction, and airlines. We've worked with companies that had just a handful of people, VC-backed start-ups, and global behemoths. We've even been called in to work with over 18 NFL teams and their high-performing athletes. Our first team, the NY Giants, went from a so-so season to winning the Super Bowl against the dynastic Patriots in 2012! Little wonder, then, that 17 other teams promptly hired us. Did those 17 listen or commit to the process? Well, the Broncos did, and look what happened in 2015!

We started this company on Apple Valley Road in Atlanta, Georgia, on the ground floor of a two-story condominium. What should have been our living room was the packing department. What should have been our kitchen was a break room. The pantry was storage. The garage was so full of our presentation tools that our cars lived on the street. Our laptops weighed a ton, if not more. A cellphone was attached to a 6-lb. battery by a cord. The point is, when we started Afterburner, Inc., we knew how effective the training would be in the business world. We believed then, as we do now, that our mindset—the way we think, our systems, the way we work—would apply to virtually anyone willing to have the courage to listen and the curiosity to keep an open mind. We started with a small handful of fighter pilots spreading the good word, and since 1996, we've employed 100s of fighter pilots to bring the fighter pilot mindset into organizations. We knew it would "take off" in the real world, and it has. We've repeatedly helped leaders, teams, and corporations deliver optimum results in the minimum amount of time and with the least effort. Who wouldn't want that?

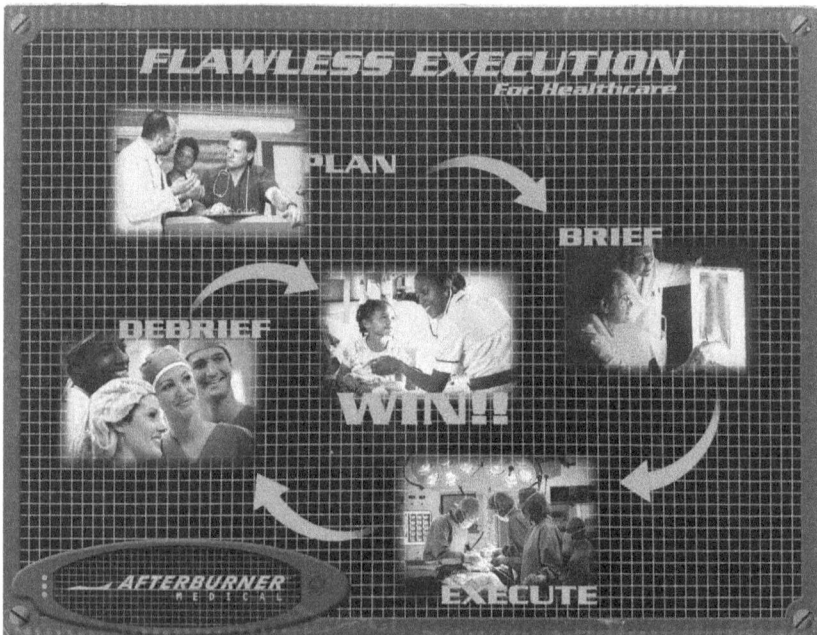

*Figure 4. The first iteration of Flawless Execution*

Becoming a fighter pilot is not the end state, just like being a great basket-ball player isn't the finish line. Once a person becomes a "bograt," "noob," "FNG," or "punk,"—aka ego-killing terms of endearment we adorn new fighter pilots with—we have to get them combat-ready, build them into consistently great leaders and mentors, and make sure each follow-on mission is flown flawlessly. That is the heart of the Flawless Execution™ method. Flawless Execution is the sum total of every fighter pilot mission flown: every breakthrough in strategy, tactics, speed, aerobatics, performance; every accident; every lesson learned; every successful mission; each upgrade in aeronautics, software, weapons, avionics and sensors; and every flying experience on a mission since Day One. Flawless Execution is transformative and ever-evolving and ever-present, and with it, a fighter pilot stays on top of their game in the most complex environment on the planet. They achieve their mission, and they get home safely.

Pilots are not particularly different from anyone else. Murph hadn't so much as flown a Cessna when he walked into flight school—he was swinging baseball bats. Three years later, he was a flight lead in an F-15C single-seat frontline combat fighter jet. I was a high school grad who didn't have any desire to go to college, I was so hopeless at academics that I didn't "believe" I could graduate. I did start flying at 15, flew solo at 16, started the recruitment process when I was 17, and at 18, I started IFS—Initial Flight Screening. Three years later, I was a squadron "bograt" flying the next generation of Hornets, and years later, Tornados in the UK as a "B-Cat" full-up mission commander and flight lead, with the responsibility of leading billions of dollars in high-tech assets on multi-national missions of up to 100 aircraft anywhere in the world, at the age of 26. I'm just one fighter pilot. There are 100s, if not thousands who've done the same, thanks to the mindset and the system we operated in.

From nothing, I began a fantastic eight-year stretch before having my wings clipped, thanks to an auto-immune disease called Ankylosing Spondylitis, ejected as a "Med-cat" medical abnormality on a $3k-per-month disability pension... Talk about bummed out. Now here I am, writing this book as the co-owner and CEO of Afterburner, sharing my experience as a fighter pilot and a business founder of two multi-million-dollar businesses. Now I'm bringing the two worlds together—not only the theory but also the practice of Flawless Execution.

It takes about three years and $15 million to transform the average Jane or Joe into a high-performing fifth-gen base-level fighter pilot—and around six to seven years to become a "Top Gun" instructor, or what we call a "patch wearer." We call them that thanks to the unique patch these instructors wear on their flight suits in recognition of the incredibly Intensive program they've completed. These pilots are our Yodas, the highest of our high performers, and the wisest of our sages. This was another dream of mine, by the way, a dream cut from underneath me due to a medical condition I had no control over. I'll talk more about that later, about dreams and why they can present a bounty of opportunity for you when they shatter. Sometimes, your dreams just aren't big enough, and they shatter for a simple reason: to bring the bigger ones into your view.

Before we get into the meat of FLEX, let's unpack the term "high performance." Believe it or not, those words can be misconstrued, misunderstood, and misrepresented. When I use the words high performance in this book, I'm talking about high performance within a high-performance environment. It's easy to look good in the sandlot. You're always a star in your own backyard. Rather, think about the Chicago Bulls, the New England Patriots, Serena Williams, Ray Dalio, Elon Musk, Bill Gates, Steve Jobs, Warren Buffett, Roger Federer, or any team and individual who consistently outperforms the rest in high-performance environments. Now add consistency. Think of outperforming the others year after year, as in building a dynasty. What I like to call "dynastic performance." We pilots have to be dynastic-performing individuals, leaders, and teams. It's not because we are exceptionally talented or remarkable people. It's because we've learned and follow a winning process. We have to, because if we don't, we don't just lose on the scoreboard, we may lose a friend or leave a family without a mom or dad. You get the rest of my point. For ease, I'm going to stick with "high performance" throughout the book, because it's a term you're likely familiar with. When you read it, think dynasty!

But nothing stays the same, particularly with technology, and even more so in the air. The major milestone in the Flawless Execution process occurred over 25 years ago with the advent of the digital, hyper-fast, hyper-instrumented F-15, F-16, F-18 fighters. The origins of the fighter pilot mindset have roots in something called the "OODA" loop—the first time fighter pilots transitioned from linear thinking to iterative thinking.

You're about to read the first AI Sidebar in the book. What's the AI Sidebar? I think of AI as a wingman. For my ADHD brain, it's a force multiplier and allows me to catch up with my more academically-minded friends! I once heard an AI expert on the speaker circuit refer to AI as the most informed idiot in your business. I wanted to demonstrate that AI is just a member of the team, maybe not an idiot, more book smart than street smart, and AI certainly requires a great deal of oversight, or what we call "Red-Teaming." I asked our Afterburner AI, engineered using ChatGPT and configured explicitly for FLEX organizations, many questions while writing the book. The AI sidebar answers these questions, so I just cut and pasted them into the book! OK, no, I didn't; I used it as a starting point, then found various supporting articles and journals before having the results peer-reviewed. I'll be honest with the correct prompts, and once you "train" your GPT and build your knowledge base AI, you get a 95% solution.

# AI Sidebar: The Origins of Iterative Thinking in the Air Force – The OODA Loop

John Boyd, considered one of the world's greatest strategic military thinkers, was a U.S. Air Force Colonel and military strategist. He developed the OODA Loop as a cognitive framework for decision-making for fighter pilots to win in air combat. The OODA Loop stands for Observe, Orient, Decide, and Act, and it represents a continuous cycle of gathering information, processing it, making decisions, and taking action. Boyd created this model in the mid-20th century based on his experiences as a fighter pilot and his deep study of systems theory, thermodynamics, and biology.

# The Importance of Iterative Thinking

Iterative thinking, which involves repeatedly going through cycles of action and reflection, is central to the OODA Loop's power. Rather than relying on a static plan, iterative thinking promotes FLEXibility and adaptability. During his time as a fighter pilot, Boyd realized that the speed at which a pilot could process and act on information often determined the outcome of a "dogfight," or when two fighter jets are locked in an aerial joust. A pilot who could observe the enemy, orient themselves to the situation, make a decision, and act faster than their opponent was more likely to win. This ability to adapt quickly and adjust to changing conditions gives iterative thinking its strength.

Iterative thinking allows decision-makers to learn from each cycle of action. After each round of the OODA loop, they can assess what went well and what didn't, incorporating new information into the next round of decision-making. This constant refinement leads to better decision-making, better systems, and more capable people over time, enabling faster responses to changes in the environment.

# Why the OODA Loop Is a Powerful Cognitive Model

The OODA Loop's power lies in its focus on speed, adaptability, and constant reevaluation. It doesn't just encourage swift action; it encourages the right kind of action based on continuously updated information. The model forces leaders and decision-makers to remain "situationally aware" of their surroundings, avoid complacency, and adjust to real-time changes.

In military and competitive contexts, Boyd emphasized the advantage of completing the OODA Loop faster than one's opponent. This disrupts the opponent's decision-making process, creating confusion and allowing the faster actor to dictate the terms of engagement. In turn, this translates to outpacing competitors by responding to market shifts or customer needs more quickly and effectively.

Overall, the OODA Loop "is a powerful cognitive model because it promotes agility, learning, and adaptability, all of which are crucial in rapidly changing, high-pressure environments."

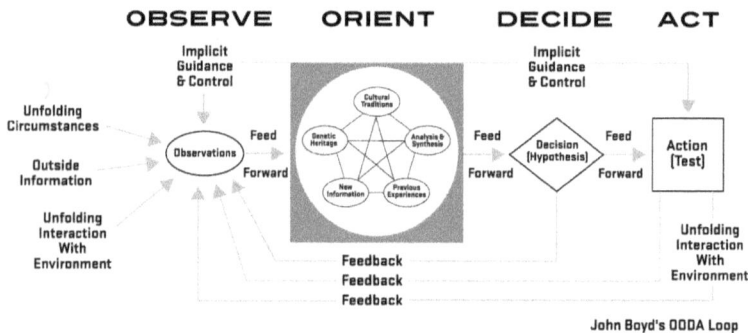

*Figure 5. John Boyd's OODA Loop*

OODA's not perfect, though; there is no perfect system. We champion three core principles when it comes to Flawless vs. Perfect Execution.

1.  Perfection is unattainable, as Vince Lombardi famously said, "We will chase perfection, and we will chase it relentlessly, knowing all the while we can never attain it. But along the way, we shall catch excellence." Fighter pilots don't let the fact we'll never fly a perfect mission stop us from trying to get as close to the perfect outcome as possible.

2.  Flawless, as we define it, is attainable. It's investing in the things we can control, adapting to those we cannot, and asking, "How can I do that better tomorrow?"

3.  Make the complex simple and the simple compelling. As part of my personal development, I was in a program designed to help folks with conference speaking. One of the very successful speakers on the course said to me that "every book must have a quote from Einstein," so here's mine: "If you can't explain it simply, **you don't understand it well enough.**" When it comes to leadership and building high-impact, results-driven teams, we speak simply yet comprehend deeply.

Pilots needed a daily process for execution excellence when operating at the limits of the human brain, the human body, and an aircraft's tolerances in an ultra-high-speed environment. Pilots needed a process to perform their missions in a cockpit containing a complex array of data sources, data links, GPS signals, and multifunction information displays that required them to be exceedingly skilled in switchology and finding the right information at the right time to make split-second decisions.

But no more. No more switchology. We are in an era of human/machine fusion, a change from switches to technology immersion, from the fourth generation to the fifth iteration of the fighter pilot's operating environment in what we call fifth-generation aircraft. A jet now has sensors that operate across multiple frequencies and spectrums and super-computers that feed integrated data streams into the cockpit. No longer are key functions a matter of switches and physical devices that require manual action by the pilot. Human and machine have been fused into one operating system to speed up reaction times and reduce workloads. When we breathe, our jet breathes; when we struggle to breathe under the crushing pressure of high G-force, our jet forces air via our oxygen masks, into our lungs to keep us conscious and alive. When we talk, our jets respond to our voice prompts. The modern fighter pilot's $400,000 helmets are marvels of technology that even Hollywood couldn't imagine.

*Figure 6. The Fifth-Generation F-35 Lightning II Helmet – Human and Technology Fused*

The digital information fed into an F-35 helmet would take up most of the instrument panel in an older jet. It turns roughly 11 million lines of code into decision-supporting knowledge and wisdom, all presented to make a $4,000 Apple VR Headset look like a tinker toy (try and use it upside down while your friend spins you around by your feet). Indeed, fitting a helmet to a pilot takes about two days and starts with the jet learning the voice of their pilot, mapping the ear canals to support three-dimensional sounds and alerts, and "boresighting" the pilot to the aircraft, so wherever the pilot looks, the jet's systems will follow, and wherever the jet senses a threat or opportunity, it immediately cues the pilot's vision. The F-35 and its fifth-gen design have introduced us to fused technologies to deliver the most important information to the pilot at just the right time to support a decision; it creates "Situational Awareness." We do a deep dive into this concept throughout this book.

So, why FLEX? People make mistakes. Companies make mistakes. Sometimes a mistake works its way into a complex system and a hidden flaw brings down people and companies who had little or nothing to do with the company or the people who caused it. Mistakes, errors, and omissions can hurt you; mistakes can hurt others, others' mistakes can hurt you, and it can be a vicious cycle if we don't break the loop. Mistakes cost lives and money, and far too many of them are avoidable. One has to go no further than to remember the flawed update to CrowdStrike's Falcon platform that, in the summer of 2024, caused widespread BSOD (Blue Screen of Death) to bring down airlines, hospitals, banks, government agencies, and any other organization using Microsoft Windows. Look at the fallout from the Boeing problems of 2018 and 2019 that continue today; we've dedicated a chapter to this. Consider the countless spin doctors who have the unenviable task of correcting the mistaken words uttered by political candidates. The list goes on and on.

But look what happens when we cut down on our mistakes, when our leaders are more efficient, more effective, and more successful, and when a company is more efficient, more effective, and more successful. We all benefit. We have a world with less waste, fewer errors, and more personal successes. Dynasties are created. High performance becomes a way of life. Think Home Depot, Microsoft, Google, Apple, Nvidia, all of whom have been through our programs and to which we have contributed to changing the way leaders and their teams think and act.

We fighter pilots can't afford too many mistakes. When we climb into our jets, there is a moment of respect, even a healthy fear, for the machine we're about to fly. After all, we will sit on top of one or two fire-breathing engines that can lift 40,000 lbs. straight up in the air like a rocket ship with exhaust nozzles reaching 1500-2000 degrees and wings hung with air-to-air missiles and 500 lbs. of highly explosive bombs. Mistakes in a jet like that take a nanosecond—and in a nanosecond, you're what we indelicately call "a smoking hole in the ground." That's why we lean into a process and a mindset that helps keep us safe and helps us take corrective action before a mistake evolves into something worse. In the most recent year that data are available, we had a 99.998% safety record and a 98.99% success rate in combat missions. In your world, that would be comparable to driving a car around town for 300 years with only one fender bender, or making around 99 sales calls without a "no."

And your world is no different from mine.

Today is a new day. Just as the fourth-generation fighters are slowly heading to the boneyard, so are the old skill sets. Today there are data streams, VR helmets, AR, and AI. Today, a single jet is connected to six, maybe 12 other jets and an entire battlespace ecosystem that spans the globe and works together against 20 hostile aircraft far beyond where the human eye can see. As it has been with our jets, it was time for a change at Afterburner. And it was never too soon. Today we teach an upgraded version of our processes, a version we call **FL**awless **EX**ecution, or **FLEX**. FLEX is a new layer built on the base layers, which integrates with today's digital world and discards some of the old switchology.

This book will speak to leaders and soon-to-be-leaders in the same voice. Great leaders were once great followers, and great followers are ready to become great leaders, so the voice in this book speaks to both as one.

Finally, once you ingrain the process, FLEX becomes an excellent baseline for whatever you stack on it—even improvisation works. If your company uses Agile, stack Agile on FLEX or Six Sigma or any other management process. Either way, the Afterburner Advantage gives you the underlying processes that are proven to help you become a high-performing individual and your company a high-performing company. It brings to your existing processes high-level situational awareness, or the "Big Picture," the glue that holds you all together.

So, bring us a burning desire to *be* a high performer, a willingness to buckle down and learn *how* to be a high performer. FLEX a competitive spirit that drives you to be the best, and the desire to constantly improve. Bring us that, and FLEX will transform you into the realm of dynastic performance—to be the successful person and business you want to be.

# 2 The Missing Piece— Debriefing with the New York Giants

Deon Grant,
Free Safety

*Figure 7. Afterburner Founder James "Murph" Murphy with NY Giants Deon Grant Superbowl XLVI*

Never in our wildest dreams did we foresee training NFL athletes in our fighter pilot methods. How could they even relate to us? Football players throw passes, block and tackle, run post patterns, and kick field goals. They need coaches diagraming plays with "X's" and "O's" and nutritionists to fuel their finely tuned bodies. We fly jets and turn and burn. We use our FLEX process to transform people into high-performing individuals like us, but NFL players are already high-performing individuals. Moreover, NFL teams were already using three of the four steps in our FLEX process. We start our process with planning, and the NFL teams are superb at it. They have a half dozen coaches who spend countless hours building a game plan and assembling a playbook. They know the competition, they have contingency plans, check downs, and last-minute adjustments at the line of scrimmage. At that level of planning excellence, why would they need us?

Briefing is the second step in our FLEX process, and they were already masters at that. They take this massive playbook and have in-depth team meetings to brief the team on the game plan. Then they break it down by specialty and brief it again, unit by unit, until it's drilled into everyone's head. Do they do a good job briefing? We think so.

What about execution? Execution is the third step in our FLEX process, and we all know they're good at it. Look at any NFL team and you'll see the best of the best on the field and a cadre of coaches making dynamic adjustments as the game unfolds. Pardon the pun, but that's right out of our playbook, too.

So, again: Why Afterburner? They're good at planning. They brief. They execute. It seems like they had everything they needed.

But there was one piece missing, a critical piece, a piece that tied it all together, a piece that in its absence was hurting the rest.

Coach Tom Coughlin is the consummate perfectionist. He drills down on every detail. His life's mission is to give his teams a competitive edge. Coach Coughlin read our first book, *Flawless Execution*, and liked what he read, particularly the section on our nameless-rankless debriefs, which intrigued him. In his world, the post-game debrief was more or less as it had been for years. It was called something different though; it was a "review" or re-view, to watch something again. His coaches would call in the players, show the game films, mistakes would be called out, players would grumble, and that was that. Nothing magical about it, but nothing really clicking, either. Communication was breaking down. "We gotta do XYZ better!" a player would shout. Then a second player yelled something a little louder, and then a third, and so on. It was clear to everyone that if they were going to execute better on the field, they had to communicate better off the field. There's a big difference between watching something again, a "re-view," and a debrief. One is watching, using the passive structures of the brain, and the other is learning, unlocking the cognitive structures of the brain.

In 2011, when we came in, the New York Giants were six games into the 2011-12 season with a 4-and-2 record. That was a so-so season, which was very frustrating for Coach Coughlin because he had anything but so-so talent. He had Eli Manning at quarterback, Victor Cruz in his receiver corps, and players like Justin Tuck on defense. The Giants had won the Super Bowl title four years earlier, and they were every bit the players today as they were then. Except they weren't performing to their potential. The team sensed it, and the coaching staff sensed it. Unless something changed, they weren't going to the Super Bowl this year.

That's where Coach Coughlin made a connection. In truth, he thought fighter pilots and football players were very similar, at least in one crucial aspect. We both lived in a binary world, a black-and-white world, a pass-fail world. In football, you either won or lost. That's binary. In our world, we either won the battle or lost. That's also binary. Plus, in both of our worlds, the smallest detail could be the difference. Coughlin read our book and decided that our people were exactly what his team needed. "I thought the players would relate to fighter pilots," he explained in an interview with *The Wall Street Journal*. And they did. But what did the coach want of us? He called us in and asked us to train his players on the fourth step of our FLEX process, the debrief.

Our debriefs were different. First of all, we don't let the coaches into the room. Only the participants in a mission get to debrief the mission. In the fighter pilot community, we get everyone together who flew a mission, we throw away rank at the door, we ditch our names, and we focus on the facts. We call this process the nameless-rankless debrief. Did "X" stay on my wing, as planned? Yes or no, and if no, why not? Did "Y" release the HARM missile 10 clicks out? Again, yes or no, and if no, why not? We close the door and openly talk about our mistakes. If I was leading a formation of four jets and the pilot on my left was out of position, they'd self-identify that, and if they weren't aware of it, I'd say so in the debrief. It doesn't matter if he's a colonel and I'm a lowly lieutenant; a fact is a fact, and we state the facts so we won't make that mistake again.

Now, there's a lot more to this than that and we'll get to it in Chapter 9, but in the end, nameless-rankless is designed to get people talking, and that was important with the Giants. Their post-game debriefs had become a noisy room filled with aimless talk. Moreover, we know that people hold things inside. It could be because of low self-esteem, confusion, embarrassment, pride, or fear, and fear is the worst. Fear of judgment. Fear of failure. Fear of being cut from a team. The nameless-rankless debrief process provides a framework for a psychologically safe environment for open and frank communication. We don't attack when we debrief. We look for ways to do better next time. How do you get better if you don't have an effective method of self-analysis?

So, they called us and we sent in three of our best trainers and we turned their system upside down. We threw out the coaches and gathered the players in the meeting room. We had Eli Manning pick 30 plays and put them on the screen. If you made a mistake, it was your job to call it out. If you didn't own up to it, the others would call you out for you. But nobody called anybody out. When a Brandon Jacobs play came on the screen, he immediately said, "I should've hit that hole harder." On a pass play, a lineman yelled, "I need to knock that end's hands down so you've got a clearer path to throw, Eli." Receivers said they needed to catch balls and block safeties better. Instead of the coaches coming down on the players, we forced the players to critique themselves. No matter their skill position, their celebrity status, or how fat their paycheck was, in that room, at that debrief, the players were all equal with equal voices, and that created a safe environment to talk and improve. "It takes away from the coach calling us out," said one of the players. "Guys can stand up and talk," said another. "It's not about who's right," said Coach Coughlin of the process. "It's about what's right." Which was exactly the point. Identify the strengths and weaknesses. Do it in a non-threatening, non-judgmental way. Loop the lessons learned back into next week's game plan. Win.

And so it built, one week after the next. Better communication flourished, robust and honest feedback, and a stronger team. Players started to identify what had to be done to plan better, execute better, what help they needed from others. They were learning from themselves, taking responsibility for their own performance, improving the small things, aligning better as a team. The FLEX debriefs built energy and purpose. The team was coming together in a new way, from the inside out. They were communicating in a new way. From a culture where things were being held back, we showed them how to create a culture where people felt comfortable talking. The Giants were not only learning a new process, they were tweaking their culture, and that stays with you long after we've left. A positive culture and a desire to learn are two of the payoffs of doing Flawless Execution debriefs. Do them often and do them well, and they did.

Which means, at some point, we knew it would all come together.

Well, the Giants were supposed to have a rough year, and it was far from clear sailing after we left. We trained them and worked with them, but learning is always up to the individual. I think most of them got it, but it was still jelling as the season went on. They finished the year with a 9-and-7 record. They ranked dead last of 32 NFL teams in rushing offense for the season. In fact, they were the first team in NFL history to reach the Super Bowl with a negative point differential (394 scored versus 400 against).

But underneath the numbers was a team that was talking, growing, and improving 1% per day, talented players who had the will to be champions, and sure enough, they went on to win four sudden-death playoffs in a row.

Maybe that's when it all came together. The FLEX debrief was far from the only reason that it happened that year, but to cap off the 2011-12 season, the New York Giants won Super Bowl XLVI, and they defeated a dynasty to do it: Brady, Belichick, and the Patriots.

And we fighter pilots will never forget that.

# 2 The FLEX Process Overview

In the **FLEX Process Overview,** *The Afterburner Advantage* introduces the Plan–Brief–Execute–Debrief (PBED) framework, a structured approach adapted from fighter pilots to enhance decision-making and performance. This process, rooted in discipline and adaptability, is designed to guide teams and leaders through clear planning, effective communication, execution, and continuous growth. By laying out this cognitive framework, Boo provides readers with a mental map for applying the FLEX process in both business and personal contexts, ensuring efficient operations, accountability, and long-term success.

# 3 The FLEX Process— Software for Your Brain

**"The mind that perceives limitation is the limitation."**
**Buddha**

The media, or more accurately, Hollywood, has us wrong. Fighter pilots are not turn-and-burn mavericks, nor are we any-landing-is-a-good-landing cowboys. They mistake self-assuredness, self-worth, and confidence for cockiness. The pilots who come in to be the personification of "Maverick" are usually washed out of the program pretty quickly. One of our Afterburner team's wives said it best. Her first impression of fighter pilots was the movie *Top Gun*; however, after leaving a fighter pilot bar for the first time, she said it was like hanging out with a bunch of nerds. So, she walked out with a new perspective on fighter pilots and the man who ultimately became her husband!

We're meticulous planners. We like to add value to our communication through a briefing. We value the people in our team and teamwork. We like data, the kind of data that enhances our decision-making. We strive to lead boring missions (because it means no surprises and nothing went wrong because we were prepared for everything). Does that sound like a shoot-from-the-hip, someone-get-me-my-spurs cockiness? Not to me.

The fact is, we don't get into our jets until we're confident we can successfully execute the mission we're about to fly. We get that confidence through the process we call Flawless Execution or FLEX. The process isn't just words and lines on a page, it's a cognitive process too. FLEX comes from our years as fighter pilots operating in a demanding environment where mistakes were terribly costly and outcomes so vitally important. We sincerely believe in the discipline and awareness that we learned flying jets as part of a combat squadron. We and our colleagues have relied on what we learned until it became second nature in all our endeavors—in the Air Force, in business, and in our personal lives. We use it, mentor it, and cultivate the behaviors it modifies because we all have a friend who isn't with us today because of an honest mistake that put them and their aircraft into the ground. The FLEX process has allowed us to stay safe and consistently achieve our goals. They are the processes that originated in the U.S. Air Force and they are common to all of the air forces that fly alongside them: the Royal Australian Air Force, the Royal Air Force of the United Kingdom, the Royal Canadian Air Force, and the fighter pilots of Brazil, Chile, Malaysia, Singapore, Thailand, India, Israel, Italy, Greece, France, the Netherlands, Argentina, and any others involved in joint military exercises and campaigns with the U.S. All of these pilots would recognize and use the principles in this book, though they may have their own terms for them. But this is how fighter pilots think, act, and win. We plan a mission. We brief a mission. We execute a mission. We debrief the mission. These tried-and-true processes, developed and tested over decades of experiences, both good and bad, have resulted in predictable, repeatable outcomes with a 99.998% success rate.

FLEX is a deeply human and people-centric process. In the Air Force, we have taken literally 1,000s of average Janes and Joes and, in three years, turned them into razor-sharp, high (dynastic) performing fighter pilots. FLEX taps into the human need to survive and excel simultaneously. We humans are a cognitive species. We are wired to learn, to adapt, to modify our behavior if our behavior is thinning out the herd. Let's put it another way, it doesn't matter who you are; you want to survive, thrive, and excel. Our DNA is wired to find ways to excel. Because of that, our FLEX process can be used by almost anyone who has a willingness to learn. If you have a goal and you're receptive, they work. If you hope to be a CEO or want more from your people, our processes work. I'm proof of that. I was a pimply-faced 19-year-old with no college education. Three years later, I was flying the F/A-18 Hornet.

The long and the short of it is this. After hanging up our flight suits and transitioning to a business where we have trained more than two million people across 3,500 companies, every one of us here at Afterburner would say the same thing—our world is no different than yours. Your competition wants to beat you out. Your buyer is tough and well-informed, and your world is exceedingly fast and demanding. Immersed in today's fast-paced digital world with near-instant information updates and immediate decision-making, you can literally have a really bad day before you even get into your car. In a nanosecond, external factors can turn you into a bewildered, confused, and failed executive, just as my dynamic environment at 1,200 miles per hour can turn me into a smoking hole in the ground.

But it doesn't. Here's why.

In my fighter pilot world, we fly missions. We have an objective, we assemble the right team to accomplish the objective, we plan it, we brief it, and we execute it, then we unpack the results in what we call a debrief. We then go our separate ways, build our individual skills and knowledge, then come back and do it again in a different team, day after day, week after week, year after year. We don't expend effort without defining the intended impact that results from the effort; we aren't in the business of "wasted effort." You and I waste effort, though, in business, a lot of effort!

We spend an average of 31 hours per month in unproductive meetings.

We switch tasks every 3 minutes, and it takes up to 23 minutes to refocus!

We spend about 11 hours per week reacting to unnecessary emails and digital messages.

We waste around 2.5 hours per day due to non-work-related distractions.

It's why you need a "mission mindset," or what fighter pilots call a "mission bubble," dedicated time during the day to focus, with zero distractions, on the mission objective. In your world, your mission is called a sales call, a portfolio review with a client, or a new product launch. It might be a campaign for public office, a line extension of an existing product, or a new marketing campaign. For a few of you, it may be a Super Bowl win!

Whatever your mission, you'll start with a high-definition picture of the desired outcome; Jim Collins may call it a BHAG, Simon Sinek your "why," or just your run-of-the-mill "great idea." We would like a little more detail; we want to know you, the leaders, your personal intent, AND the organization's strategic objective. Unlike my generation, fifth-gen fighter pilots love face cream, so let's start there. Your mission might be to introduce a new age-defying face cream to retailers, but the overall intent is to help your company reach its goal of becoming a leading manufacturer in the health and beauty space. The face cream is your mission and the objective is to launch it, and that aligns with the larger overall future for your company.

You'll start by assembling your team of at least two people, and together with your team, you will create a believable, achievable, and measurable goal collaboratively; this is called intentional collaboration, and it is far superior to ordinary collaboration and brainstorming. To keep the complex simple, moving forward we'll be using the word "objective" in place of goal, target, outcome. It's a simple term that implies "objectivity" and defines your destination. It's the future you want.

Next, you'll create the mission plan. It will cover every step in a sequence of events that starts the moment you arrive at the office, from the first words you utter when you start the meeting to the purchase order and your return home.

You'll go in to meet the buyer with the right mentality. You will expect things to happen fast, move quickly with sudden twists and turns. You will be ready to embrace confusion and chaos and rapid-fire information and even a little fear. Some of the "what-ifs" in your contingency planning will materialize, but you've thought through how to react, so you will handle it and move forward.

You'll read the room; that is, you will pick up as many verbal and visual cues as you can to maximize your situational awareness and adapt as needed.

You'll be prepared—you'll communicate in the context of the buyer and, what *their* objectives are, and you'll be enhancing *their* situational awareness and defining the value you bring to help them achieve *their* own objectives. It's not win/win; it's even better, it's consistent alignment of mutual expectations. You'll never be alone. You'll have a wingman. If you get caught up in the weeds, you have someone to bail you out. And you won't take that as a failure. Letting the wingman pick up the slack is not a setback; it's a planned response to a possible contingency, and they save your ass and turn a buyer sitting on the fence into a buyer sitting on your porch sharing cocktails.

In the end, when you get to the negotiating phase, you'll be on the sure ground because you know your customer's intent and your company's intent—you're not bound hand and foot by a specific number or a glossy brochure. Your company wants to get into the beauty space and this new SKU is part of that, so the details are up to you. Twenty pieces? Five sizes? Sell-in allowances? So long as you achieve the overall intent of the mission, your sales call will be a success, and the details will be worked out later.

Afterward, you dial into your daily debrief, and you and your team will immediately debrief the sales call. What went right, what went wrong? Did we have the right attitude and approach? You, as the leader, will set the tone and self-assess first, then the rest will follow. Somewhere, somehow, there will be something that will improve the next sales call by 1%. And the next by another 1%. Or more. And so on. It's an iterative process that feeds back into the loop any and all lessons learned from each and every call and feeds forward actions that deliver results.

That's the FLEX engine at work, accelerating you to your destination.

## Remember, Flawless Does Not Mean Perfect

I'm not expected to be perfect, and I won't be, and neither will you, and before you and I meet, know I know that. Because if you pretend to be, or tell stories, I'll see right through you, as will any FLEX practitioner, and that puts you on the back foot immediately. Flawless Execution does not mean perfect execution. Flawless Execution is executing within the plan's parameters—and every mission has issues. The Navy's Blue Angels are one of the world's most dedicated precision aerial performance teams, and they will be the first to tell you that there is no perfect airshow. But built into my plans—and theirs—are safety rails, guideposts, contingency plans, and all sorts of cues that tell me when I'm off track and give me the responses and actions I need to get back on track.

Look at our mission data. During a recent campaign, fighter pilots were sent against more than 80 drones and missiles and completed their missions with a 98.92% success rate. That's a high-risk mission with a very small object, both of us moving at maximum speed—and, still, the success rate was nearly 99%.

FLEX is the distillation of decades of rigorous pilot training, hundreds of thousands of hours of flying the most advanced fighter jets in the world in peacetime, in combat. In FLEX we have all the processes and systems that kept us alive and winning, distilled and sharpened and poured into a platform that can be easily learned by individuals, small teams, and corporations alike. It is true that we say that the debrief is the ultimate payoff, but FLEX is an integrated whole. Without the front end of the system, the backend doesn't work, and without the backend there is no front end at all. It's all about balance and speed.

# Method

The secret to FLEX is our circular execution engine that has four stages: Plan – Brief – Execute – Debrief. It is a process that starts the minute you have a mission. Let's say I'm tasked to take out a facility two hours from my base. That's a mission. Perhaps orders come down to fly relief supplies to an earthquake-torn community. That's a mission. How about a meeting with your client? Yep, that's a mission. A family trip to the Outer Banks? That's a mission. A field trip for your students. FLEX it first. Before I fly any mission, I prepare myself and my team using FLEX: Plan – Brief – Execute – Debrief.

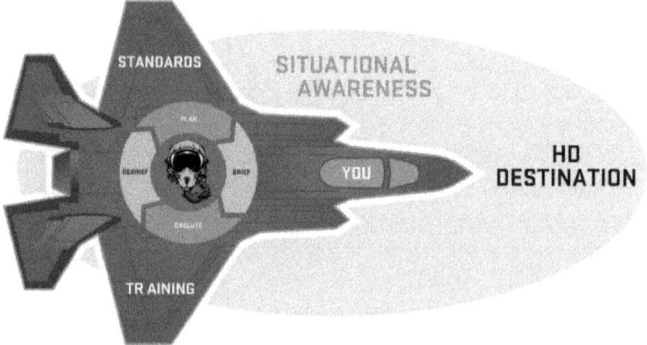

*Figure 8. FLEX – The Method that Drives a Mindset*

# Start With the End in Mind – The High-Definition Destination

I'm going to call you out on this straight up. You're not winning because you don't know what winning looks like. You have a vague idea, you may have won a few things here and there, and I'm not talking about gambling, I mean things you really tried to win. If you are winning, it's likely inconsistent or you're telling yourself you are, when in fact, you're probably not. Winning to you looks slightly different to the team members working with you, and that slight difference amplifies as more people get involved in the execution of your big dream. You are programmed as a human, focusing on winning for yourself, not the team. Unless, of course, the team win equals a personal win. It's a "survival of the species" thing, well beyond the scope of this book and a field of work that fascinates me.

So the first step in FLEX is to articulate a clear collective mission objective and to do that in absolute detail—something we call a High-Definition

Destination (more on that in Chapter 4). Where are you going? After that, you begin planning the mission. What are you doing? The plan itself could be a dozen pages or it could be just one—it doesn't matter, it is whatever the mission requires. Both of these steps are collaborative; that is, you do these steps with your team, not in some ivory tower or a dark room setting a world record for the densest PowerPoint strategy presentation.

Once the mission is planned, you brief the plan to your team to confirm their understanding, then you execute the mission, and finally, you compare the plan vs. its execution in the debrief. From beginning to end, you're thinking, intuiting, and calculating. You're balancing creativity with tried-and-true routines. You're fully engaged, but you're not lost in the details. FLEX draws upon your cognitive skills and creativity while offering a repeatable, foundational routine that covers all the bases and thus helps minimize mistakes and maximize your execution excellence, all of which increase your odds of true success. In the debrief, you're being iterative; against the preset goals, you're looking for mistakes and lessons learned so you can constantly improve.

The following chapters go into these steps in depth, but it is helpful to have a quick frame of reference to see how they work.

**Plan**. It's important not to miss anything when planning, so we have a process called the Six Steps to Mission Planning. The Six Steps start with the Mission Objective. You will state your objective (or multiple objectives, if you have more than one). It may be a strategic plan (outcome-focused) where we will be using a High-Definition Destination (again, more on that in a moment), or action-focused, in which case it will simply be an "objective" supported by actions. That done, you will identify threats to achieving your mission. After that, you will identify resources to draw on for your mission, and then you evaluate lessons learned from similar missions and fold them into your plan. That done, you can assign a course of action to every member on your team and confirm contingency plans so the unexpected doesn't derail you. The six-step plan answers these six critical execution questions:

1. What's the point? Why are you doing this and expending effort and resources?

2. What's in the way and what's going to stop you from success?

3. What resources do you have to get the job done?

4. What have you learned in the past that you can use today?

5. What is every leader and team member going to do?

6. What if something goes wrong? And it will...

**Brief**. Next comes a thorough briefing with the team. The briefing connects the future (the plan) to today (action). It IS the mission, so as a leader you have to be across the details and be there in front of the team to communicate it directly, personally, and concisely on the day of the mission. This is your last chance to ask questions, and to ensure the team understands expectations and their roles in the mission. To keep you on track, we have a useful mnemonic so you don't forget anything, and one inviolate rule—when you leave the briefing, there are no unanswered questions. Tip: I often call out and pose a question, pause for a response, and then pounce on one person for the answer, usually the disengaged or distracted team member! "Pose, pause, pounce" shifts our team from passive information receivers into engaged knowledge seekers. The brief is how the mission will be flown, so we brief it until there are no more questions, period, end of sentence.

Execute. Execution is all about rhythm and decision-making, where we seek or create situational awareness as a priority, where we do the right things at the right time. We will show you that every mission has a set of measures that demonstrate your effectiveness, or often, your ineffectiveness! These measures align you with your objectives and help you determine if your individual and collective actions are effectively moving the organization in the right direction. In our jets we need to keep our team focused on the priorities for each discreet mission, so we have clear-cut ways to measure our progress. We will give you those measures and indicators as well as mechanisms to keep people focused, to bridge the gaps between the plan and the results of your actions, the execution gaps (X-Gaps, more on that in Chapter 11), and to identify and dynamically correct sub-optimal performance.

**Debrief**. The Debrief is one of our most powerful tools. This is our feedback loop. It is a process by which you and your team analyze the results of a mission in a safe environment and identify lessons learned, then feed those lessons learned back into the plan for the next mission. A good debrief is like having a million-dollar consulting firm at your fingertips, but it's even better than that because the process guarantees nearly instant buy-in from the team, minimizes emotions and friction, and nearly always eliminates cognitive disapprovals. Layer in AI through effective debrief prompts, and suddenly you turn your data and information into execution wisdom! During our time with the Giants, Quarterback Eli Manning led the offensive team debriefs. "I wasn't coaching anybody," he said. "I was just coaching myself, looking at what I needed to do better, and telling everybody. Then everybody would talk about what they needed to do to improve."

Debriefing is easily the most important step in the entire process, one that significantly improves your next mission, sales call, product iteration, AI prompt, social impact, and one that makes a meaningful contribution to your corporate knowledge base. However, it is the one step that is rarely incorporated in today's business environments; no one from Afterburner has walked into an organization that has a debrief culture. Zero. Flawless doesn't mean perfect, so, even after a successful mission, we look for mistakes and any deviations from the plan. We do that using a highly structured process that encourages free and frank dialogue in a nameless-rankless environment. The leader starts the debrief, the rest sit and pay attention—one up, one down, as we say in our world. Then we use a structure called the ORCA engine: **O**bjective. **R**esult. **C**ause. **A**ction. What learning points have we identified? What action will we take tomorrow? We get 1% better after each debrief. Or more.

# Tip: People

The New York Giants illustrate another point. The overall FLEX process doesn't require any particular skillset, background, or profession. Fighter pilots come from all walks of life. We have pilots who grew up on farms, pilots who came out of universities, pilots who never went to a university. We have pilots who bounced around for a few years in sales or computer programming or construction before they saw the light. Men and women, Asians, Africans, Europeans, Russians, and even Australians like me. Pilots arrive in pilot training with different reflexes, IQs, cognition, aptitudes and attitudes, lung capacities and other physiology, and even goals. Some want to fly fighters, some want to drive our flying gas station, the new KC-46 tanker. But they all go through the same two-to-three-year process that takes their human physiology and innate cognitive abilities, tweaks them, molds them, and educates them until a pilot is minted. The point is, I did it, our people here at Afterburner did it, we have over 2,200,000 corporate people who've done our training, and, football player or farm girl, you can do it, too. Like fighter pilots, high-performing individuals come from all walks of life; you're not born a high performer, you become one, and the fighter pilot mindset and FLEX are the simplest template you can find to accelerate your journey to being a high performer. All you have to do is bring the commitment and effort.

The second point is like the first. Great coaches don't try to change the extraordinary skills of great athletes. They build on those skills, tweak them, polish them. Rather than change the player, they'll change their game plan and build plays around the player. If you're a rollout quarterback, a great coach will design rollout plays.

We are the same. You don't have to walk on coals to adopt FLEX. FLEX makes high-performing individuals out of you irrespective of what you bring to the table, so long as you bring a willingness to learn and a desire to succeed. Our guinea pig was Home Depot. We did an Afterburner Day with them. We trained their people. Did it work? Was it relevant to their business goals? I think so. They have had us back multiple times over 27 years, and by any measure, they are significantly larger now than 27 years ago.

FLEX is a baseline. It magnifies the asset you bring us, it becomes a foundation upon which your creativity—and your success—takes off.

Third, FLEX is an iterative process; that is, it gets better and better with each use, and you get better and better—1% better every iteration.

Importantly, FLEX takes on the hard stuff and plows through it. That's part of our fighter pilot DNA—we take on the hard stuff, so we adapted that to FLEX, to be there when you take on the hard stuff. And through open dialogue, peer critiques, and by incorporating new learning points, each iteration builds on the previous one and results in continuous improvements.

Call it an operating system for your high-powered brain. We don't compete with other systems; we help you use them more effectively. We have codified the fighter pilot processes and formatted them into a comprehensible, teachable process that you can learn in hours—one on which you may comfortably stack any system or process you like.

All of this has become increasingly important, and it will continue to be that way. Getting things done these days is rarely easy, and we rely more and more on technology doing the doing, which is great, as it frees us up to do more thinking! Sure, we have more opportunities, but with them come greater expectations, responsibilities, and risks. We have more people to keep happy—all those stakeholders—with more demands. The digital world means our decisions are dissected and parsed in slow time after the event. We face more uncertainty because the changes are more frequent, and changes bring with them things we've never encountered before. We need to build for the future, and at the same time we need to deliver results today. So, it's harder to do the things that really matter, personally and professionally, and to do them well.

The NFL team's use of FLEX is a high-profile example of FLEX in action, but it's also typical. The debrief used our classic FLEX process: simple yet deliberate, exhaustive yet efficient, direct yet empowering. It's elegant in its simplicity and compelling in its results. And, although the debrief was where the Giants focused, FLEX is a lot more than that. FLEX is an end-to-end way of getting the right things done right. It helps you set your objectives and your ultimate destination, decide a path to reach it, and complete the actions along that path—even if the ground beneath you shifts. All the time, it makes you a better leader and a better follower while helping you build a better team.

FLEX is deliberately simple. As you work with it, you'll find it sharpens your team's awareness, focuses your impact, and builds a supportive peer group. Each part of the FLEX process reinforces your confidence so that your strategy is on track, that each person has a clear and critical role, and that you and your team will be a success.

# AI Sidebar: The Fighter Pilot Mindset Is a Growth Mindset

If the FLEX method is about getting things done, a Fighter Pilot Mindset is about framing the future through the right lens. FLEX connects the art of strategy (tomorrow) to the science of execution (today). The Fighter Pilot Mindset helps us create strategies that have a high probability of success, and supports the decisions we make as the real world impacts our desired strategic outcomes.

Remember, the DNA of FLEX is the system used to train and fight in arguably the world's most complex, high-speed, information-saturated, three-dimensional environment. It has evolved for use in business and successfully delivered from simple, repeatable to complex, and audacious strategies. It's a way of working together to create high-speed, frictionless organizations helmed by impact-focused leaders and powered by highly engaged teams. It harnesses the lessons from our world to build purpose-driven teams.

Carol Dweck is one of the world's preeminent thinkers on mindset. In her breakthrough book *Mindset*, she introduces the concept of "fixed" and "growth" mindsets. To use a little fighter pilot mindset here, I'll simplify the core concept: she defines two mindsets.

Fixed Mindset. People with a fixed mindset believe that their abilities, intelligence, and talents are fixed traits. They think that they have a certain amount of intelligence and ability, and that's it; their potential is predetermined. Individuals with a fixed mindset are likely to desire to appear smart but may avoid challenges, give up easily, feel threatened by the success of others, and see effort as fruitless when one isn't naturally skilled or talented.

Growth Mindset. Individuals with a growth mindset believe that abilities and intelligence can be developed with time, effort, and dedication. They think of the brain as a muscle that gets stronger and more capable with use. This mindset fosters a love of learning and resilience that is essential for great accomplishment. People with a growth mindset view challenges as opportunities to grow, they value effort as a path to mastery, they learn from criticism, and find lessons and inspiration in the success of others.

FLEX is a methodology that creates a growth mindset even in the most stubborn and fixed of thinkers. It was born out of years of taking hundreds of thousands of everyday pilot candidates and turning them into growth-minded fighter pilots. The process is centered on thinking, planning, and teamwork on two levels—quick thinking and deep thinking. We do our slow, deep thinking before and after a mission: planning and debriefing.

We do our quick thinking during the mission. This is when we need to be agile, adaptive, and decision-focused, based on real-world situational awareness. Our deep (slow) thinking takes place before a mission and, again, after a mission, and that ends our day-to-day execution.

This combination creates the time and space to think ahead of a mission so we have the extra headspace we need to process and react to the unexpected around us during the mission. We have a wingman, two jets, two pilots, two brains. One is busy doing, working the systems in the now, while the other is keeping tabs on the "Big Picture," or maintaining situational awareness of the space we're operating in, thinking one step ahead. We call it battle space, you'd call it your market. Both of us work in demanding environments. As I said, fighter pilots and high-performing individuals have a lot in common.

# Aviator Sidebar: The Blue Angels

Whilst the Plan–Brief–Execute–Debrief method was documented first by Afterburner, conceptually, culturally and philosophically, the Blue Angels use Plan–Brief–Execute–Debrief as their way of planning and executing all their airshows, training flights, and transits; it's how they run the entire operation. There is good reason for that. The Blue Angels fly a high-speed airshow in a small airbox using jets that go several hundred miles per hour. They fly their demonstration in formations as tight as 18 inches wingtip-to-wingtip. That leaves little room for errors, so they need an airtight process. FLEX is a system that lets them evaluate themselves in a way that is both comprehensive but not complex.

They start the FLEX process with slow thinking—defining and believing their purpose and the vision of the demonstration—then they kick into their fast-thinking mode with our Plan–Brief–Execute–Debrief cycle. They use the FLEX process so they don't overlook anything. The framework drives consistent, effective results in a complex environment while helping the team go over the details of the show without missing any step along the way. It is compact and precise, quick and to the point.

With their typically intense focus and discipline, they methodically work through the FLEX framework. By being thoroughly briefed, a pilot is thoroughly in the moment, which creates time to think. As the pilots execute the routines, they can balance the simplicity of the plan with dynamic outcomes in the air, balance the reliability of the plan with creativity as needed, balance the flow of the process with high situational awareness.

After the demo, they go directly into a dedicated room and have an open dialogue, using the nameless-rankless debrief. "Rank or experience doesn't come into play," said one of their pilots. "Those things are good, but you have to set those things aside when the critiques start to come because that's the only way you're going to learn." Using video from multiple angles and whiteboards, they try to identify the tiniest mistake and then they summarize any learning points so they can feed them into the brief for the next airshow. As a result, each debrief is exhaustive. Any deviation is called out, all of which results in continuous improvements. "We examine our mistakes so we get the very best information," said another of their pilots about our debrief process. "We even debrief the march out to the airplane and the march back at the conclusion of the show." Not a bad idea when you're about to fly six high-speed $48-million jets mere inches apart in front of 100,000 spectators.

## Mindset and Methodology

When we put on our flight suit, we put on a very specific mindset. That's the first ingredient of our FLEX process. Just as professional athletes put on their game faces before they go onto the field, and actors and actresses walk behind the curtain and go over their lines and get pumped up before they perform. We all get into the right mindset. Next comes methodologies. We want a toolset of methodologies that enables us to achieve consistent, high quality, and repeatable results in a highly dynamic environment. We weren't born with this mindset or these methodologies—no one is—but we learn them and train them until they are second nature. Mindset and methodologies are the key to our mission.

## The FLEX Mindset Is a Fighter Pilot Mindset

The FLEX mindset is a way of thinking and working for high-impact leaders, teams and individuals who turn their future intentions into day-to-day purposeful actions that deliver results. Simply put, it's the operating system of a fighter pilot where intentions deliver impact.

The Mindset is built on four essential elements: Impact, Iteration, 3B's (Biases, Beliefs and Behaviors) and Action.

### 1. Impact – Set the future

Set your intention with HDDs, then deliver on your mission objectives: Success begins with clarity. Setting a clear and committed intention is the foundation of the Fighter Pilot Mindset. When you know precisely what impact you want to achieve, your focus sharpens, and your actions align to create meaningful results.

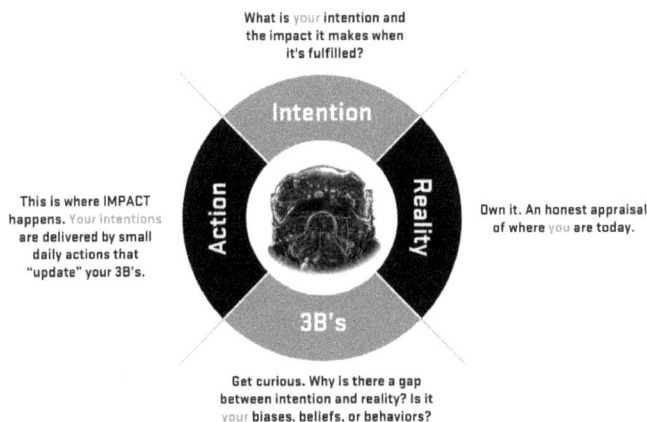

What is your intention and
the impact it makes when
it's fulfilled?

This is where IMPACT
happens. Your intentions
are delivered by small
daily actions that
"update" your 3B's.

Own it. An honest appraisal
of where you are today.

Get curious. Why is there a gap
between intention and reality? Is it
your biases, beliefs, or behaviors?

*Figure 9. The Fighter Pilot Mindset*

## 2. Iteration – Results vs. Intentions

The key to evolving your biases, beliefs, and behaviors and ultimately making better decisions, what some call becoming "self-aware," is the habit of intentional reflection or iteration. It's thinking in a circle, where we grow from who we are (today) to who we want to be (tomorrow), getting curious as to the journey so far, and asking the question of why there is a gap between the two (yesterday).

The Fighter Pilot Mindset uses an iterative ORCA approach to refine actions and achieve impactful outcomes. The O in ORCA is Objective, or in fighter pilot speak, a very clear and measurable intention. R is Result, the reality you are in right at this moment. The gap between the two is the execution gap, and we iterate to close it.

## 3. The 3B's. Understand that your biases and Beliefs Drive Your Behavior

Your biases and beliefs guide your behaviors and decisions. By understanding and aligning these beliefs with your intentions, you create a pathway to evolve your habits and behaviors, forming a foundation for consistent success. If you do it, your team will follow.

The C in ORCA is "Cause" or "Curiosity"; it's an open and honest conversation, usually with yourself or within a peer group, where we discover the cause of the gap between our objectives and results. When we apply the mindset to ourselves, it's usually a bias, belief or behavior. When we apply the mindset across a team, it's likely the same or something with the culture or system you're operating in.

### 4.   Action – Build Your Micro-habits with ORCA

We start with intention and end with action, accountable action. It's these actions, taken daily, that create contextualized micro-habits, or the habits tailored to you, your personality and characteristics to deliver the impact you've set.

We do a deep dive on debriefing and ORCA in Chapter 9; what's important though, is you understand that a simple methodology delivers a very useful FLEX mindset.

ORCA stands for:

- **Objective (O):** This is your intention in the context of time, and you can measure it; it has to be a number that defines the impact you want to make.

- **Results (R):** Measure your current results against your objective.

- **Cause (C):** Investigate the root cause of your results through curiosity, reflection, and a "nameless and rankless" philosophy.

- **Action (A):** Take a small, focused action within 24 hours to evolve your and your team's biases, beliefs, and behaviors to be a future fit.

Because it's only intentions actioned that deliver an impact.

# The FLEX Biases

The key to FLEX, from a human-centric perspective, is the evolution of your "operating system." Just like a smartphone, you have an autopilot, an automated way of thinking; they're called biases, and they simplify and accelerate your decision-making and situational awareness. Here are some key biases of fighter pilots:

- <u>We are action-biased. We are intentional, action-driven and impact-focused</u>. Before we expend energy or commit an ounce of brain power to a task, we ask, "What is the impact this mission will deliver and is it worth it?" Too often our intentions go unrealized in business and life, so we run a simple equation: Intention + Action = Impact. So you can see that work without purpose or intent is busy-ness, intent without action is dreaming, but when you master the art of translating big intentions into small daily actions, you're guaranteed to make an impact.

- <u>We are biased to preserve momentum. Speed is life</u>. Have you ever been in a presentation that puts you to sleep? The pace is soooo sloooow. We expect and embrace a rapidly changing environment. In fact, we view fast-paced challenges as assets and opportunities. The sign on the wall says it all: "Speed Is Life." Jets need speed. Pilots need speed. Speed gives us room to check down through our options. Speed gives us room to maneuver, to find solutions if we have problems. We want to be the quick thinkers in the room. We not only embrace a good, crisp, fast-paced meeting, we try to engineer one. Some people are knocked down by speed. Speed doesn't throw us off. Rapid-fire change doesn't surprise us. We expect it. We move with it. We feed off it. But what would you rather have? The opposite of speed is boredom, stalled out, stopped, or the end of a meeting.

- <u>We are biased towards low risk. There's healthy fear</u>. Getting into a $90-million jet and riding on top of one or two fire-breathing engines has its moments. We're human. We expect fear to be part of our mission, so we channel it, we convert it to energy, we want to be right in the middle of the peak stress curve, not under or over aroused, just right. At some point something will send a surge of adrenaline through our veins. Scientists call this the fight-or-flight syndrome. Most people let it take control of them, or they overreact. We don't. We expect it, and when it hits, we channel it rather than letting it paralyze us or letting it force us to react the wrong way. We feel that fear, we channel it, our focus intensifies. Everyone has it. Professional athletes. Actors. Businesspeople when they open the door and walk into a boardroom and see 14 faces turn to them, expectant.

- <u>We're biased towards confidence</u>. Some people hate structure. Some people like to wing it. And in some situations that works. Think of a quarterback that likes to roll out of the pocket. I get it. But that's a high-risk maneuver. Maybe it has a 50% success rate, maybe a little more or less. That's great in football or baseball, but not good enough for us. 99.998%. We know a good process leads to success, which leads to confidence, which is where our skills are at their best. We go out feeling like a winner, walking with a sure step, confident in our ability and that of our team.

- <u>We are biased to focus on what we can control</u>. The fighter pilot mindset is to focus on the things we can control and forget about the rest. You're not going to change the weather, but you're ready for it. A flight is delayed, so it's delayed. Move on to your contingency plan. The power is out; get out the printed version of your pitch, the leave behind. In our mission mindset, we don't waste time on things we can't control. We keep ourselves focused on things we can control.

# 3 Deep Dives into FLEX Components

In **Deep Dives into FLEX Components**, *The Afterburner Advantage* thoroughly examines each stage of the FLEX process—Plan, Brief, Execute, and Debrief—providing actionable insights and real-world examples. Boo begins with setting a clear, measurable goal (the High-Definition Destination) and guides readers through the **Six-Step Mission-Planning Process**. He emphasizes the importance of detailed planning, effective briefings to ensure alignment, disciplined execution, and thorough debriefs for continuous improvement. Through stories and practical examples, this section shows how each component works together to drive consistent, high-level performance in dynamic environments.

# 4 The High-Definition Destination—From Idea to Reality with Flawless Execution

> "To me, ideas are worth nothing unless executed. They are just a multiplier. Execution is worth millions."
> Steve Jobs

## FLEX Planning

FLEX planning is like a good novel. We write the story of our future: chapter, line, and verse. Like all good novels, that story is compelling, it has some mystery and some unknowns, but it has an ending, something we call a "future picture," a view of what success looks like when the story ends.

Like all good stories, it includes things we can control and things we can't. Told right, it prepares us to execute what we can control and adapt to the things we can't control.

## HDD – The High-Definition Destination

The path from strategy to execution is direct and easy. There's the future, and today. That's it. What we do to paint the future is create objectives. If your strategy is a collection of objectives, we call those HDDs. If your objectives define action, we call those mission objectives. HDDs define objectives. Mission objectives define action. Period. Don't allow yourself to overcomplicate it any further, as it becomes a difficult strategy to execute; simplicity is the guiding principle.

Here's an example of an HDD. I've used OpenAI's publicly available strategic plan and run it through our Afterburner AI platform to demonstrate how a strategy may be articulated as HDDs.

# OpenAI's HDD (Example Only)

## THE HDD:

"To ensure that artificial general intelligence (AGI) benefits all of humanity."

## The Intent:

By 2030, OpenAI will be the global leader in advancing safe and ethical artificial intelligence technologies, ensuring that AGI aligns with human values and serves the collective interests of humanity. We will prioritize accessibility, fairness, and collaboration to maximize AI's societal benefits while mitigating risks.

# Vision HDD

## Vision HDD:

"To create and shape AGI that uplifts humanity, empowers individuals, and fosters equitable societal progress."

## The Intent:

By 2040, OpenAI envisions a world where AGI seamlessly integrates into every aspect of human life, solving complex global challenges such as climate change, healthcare inequities, and education gaps. Our AGI will act as a trusted partner, empowering individuals and organizations to reach their full potential in a safe, sustainable, and equitable manner.

# Strategic HDDs

### 1. Advance Safe and Ethical AGI Development

- By 2025, OpenAI will establish industry-leading research frameworks for developing safe and ethical AGI, incorporating human alignment, transparency, and interpretability into every AI model.

- Success metrics: Publishing 100+ safety-focused papers and deploying models with built-in ethical safeguards.

## 2. Democratize AI Access

- OpenAI will ensure that AI technologies are accessible to individuals, small businesses, and underserved communities by offering affordable tools and transparent APIs.
- Success metrics: 1 billion active users on OpenAI platforms and partnerships with 100+ global nonprofits by 2030.

## 3. Collaborate to Foster Responsible AI Innovation

- By 2026, OpenAI will form partnerships with governments, academic institutions, and industry leaders to co-create global standards for ethical AI development and deployment.
- Success metrics: Participating in drafting global AI regulations and leading at least 10 industry-wide AI governance initiatives.

## 4. Accelerate Societal Progress Using AI

- OpenAI will focus on deploying AGI to address humanity's greatest challenges, including climate change, healthcare, and education disparities.
- Success metrics: 10 major AGI deployments directly impacting global problems by 2035.

## 5. Build Trust and Transparency

- OpenAI will maintain an open communication approach by publishing regular updates on research, safety, and ethical considerations.
- Success metrics: Establish a global Trust Index showing that 90% of OpenAI users believe the organization's values align with the public good.

It is clear, (somewhat) measurable, and achievable, establishing the North Light and guiding principles for the entire organization. Some of the strategic HDDs could use a little more numerical detail; however, I'm not going to be presumptuous and fill those out. It's 80% there, and we humans (or OpenAI's humans) can work out the details.

There's an old sailor's adage that applies here. It doesn't matter how good the wind is if you don't know where you're headed. We fighter pilots always start a mission with the endpoint in mind, and we get very, very specific about it. We describe our endpoints in high definition, something we here at Afterburner call a High-Definition Destination or HDD. Where are we headed, what are we trying to accomplish, what tools do we have, how do we quantify it, and how do all the different strategic objectives come together to paint a single big picture? We write the answers to those questions using words and terms that are clear, concise, and simple—no buzzwords or I'm-smarter-than-you words. The important part is thinking and describing the end point in HDD, that is, describing our goal in detail as sharp and clear as an HDTV. Once we know our HDD, it becomes our North Star, it answers Simon Sinek's "Why." It's how we know we're on the right path, moving in the right direction, on time, on target.

Example #1. Let's say you want to book a hotel room in Dallas. That's a pretty simple task, right? But there are hundreds of hotels in Dallas, so you have to add a little detail. You want a Marriott hotel in Dallas. Still not HDD—too much ambiguity. How about this: a ground level room in a Courtyard by Marriott on the west side of Dallas for three nights from 21 March that accepts pets and has a conference room that's not booked up

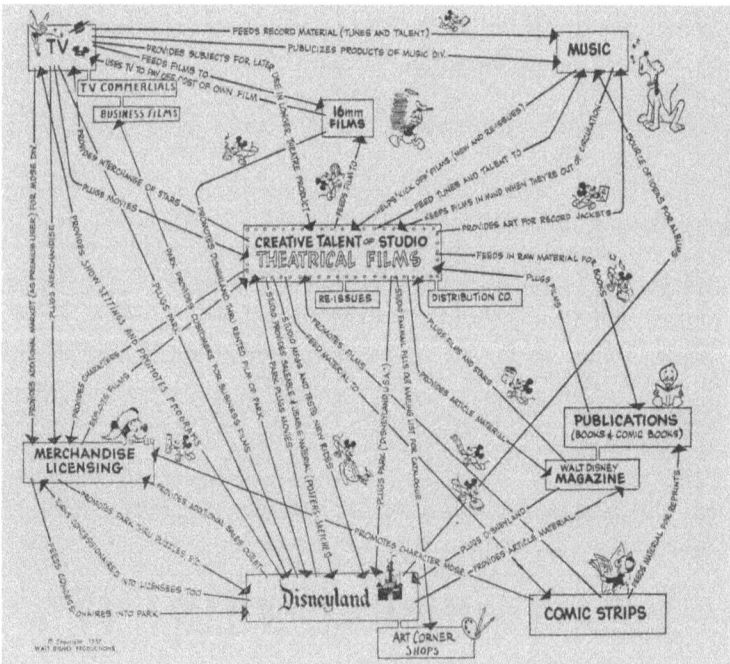

*Figure 10. Disney HDD Map Circa 1957*

because you have a meeting that you are hosting and because the dog you're taking can't go up in an elevator. That is a detailed, concise yet plain-worded description of the desired end point. That's an HDD. Put it on a piece of paper, give it to your team members, and they'll get the job done with minimum intervention from you.

Example #2. Let's say you want to break a new product into a new retail chain and you're presenting the new SKUs to the buyer next week. For brevity's sake, let's focus on the sell-in. Of course you want the buyer to take your new SKU; that's a given. But that's not an HDD. Here it is in HDD: The end state you want is an opening order (distribution) for the entire family of three SKUs for two pieces each that will be placed on-shelf at eye level in the analgesic section with shelf talkers promoting a BOGO50 (buy-on-get-one 50% off) during a November launch. That's an HDD. It has detail. Clarity. Yet, it uses simple words. If the buyer refuses the shelf talker, swap it for a store coupon. A good HDD is flexible. If they offer you two SKUs, not three, take two SKUs. But if they want to put your item in the shoe department, you say "no." It's not your HDD. HDD is your North Star. It guides everything you do.

Let's say my squadron of fighter pilots gets a call to provide cover for a relief mission. That happens, we're trained to do it, so we say "yes." We're told that there will be six C-130s flying in with 12 Red Cross vo-lunteers and a security ground team landing on a military runway two miles from a potentially hostile air base operated by a sabre-rattling dic-tator to offload and deliver 14 pallets of vitally needed food. Our job? Protect the volunteers until the mission is over. But how? Against what? Why? The HDD we write is a little clearer. Our mission is to create and enforce a no-fly zone over the activity area to neutralize hostile drones during the six-hour operation so that nothing interferes with the relief mis-sion. You get the idea. We want the HDD to be a future picture that can be expressed in simple terms so that anyone in the organization can play it back in living color. The HDD defines the fundamental goals, yet it's not so detailed that it limits people's creativity, nor is it so fuzzy that it allows for spurious interpretations that might prejudice performance. We want that vision to be clear so that it is not confusing or difficult to implement. Set a clear HDD, and people will rally round it. Leave it vague and people will draw their own conclusions and fill in the blanks because you intro-duced ambiguity to the mission, the A in VUCA—Volatility, Uncertainty, Complexity, and Ambiguity.

# AI Sidebar: What Is VUCA?

The term VUCA is an acronym for Volatility, Uncertainty, Complexity, and Ambiguity—first coined by the U.S. Army War College in the late 1980s. It emerged in response to the chaotic and unpredictable post-Cold War world, where traditional military strategies were less effective due to rapidly changing global dynamics. The term was adopted as a way to understand and navigate this new environment, emphasizing that strategies need to account for rapid, unpredictable changes in circumstances.

# Why VUCA Is Useful for Business

VUCA is a valuable mnemonic because it encapsulates the challenges modern organizations face. Each component addresses a different facet of the business environment:

Volatility refers to the speed and unpredictability of change.

Uncertainty highlights the difficulty in predicting future outcomes and trends.

Complexity acknowledges the intricacy of multiple interconnected forces affecting decisions.

Ambiguity points to the lack of clarity or "unknown unknowns" in interpreting situations.

By framing the external business world with these four dimensions, VUCA helps leaders develop adaptive, resilient, and flexible strategies. It encourages them to prepare for unexpected changes and create systems that can quickly respond to disruptions, making it a powerful tool for decision-making and risk management in the era of automation.

The HDD is designed to give the team leader the basis and the confidence to make good decisions, to keep their mission on track, or to even abort the mission if it's no longer headed for the HDD. When a movie tanks at the box office, how often have you heard actors say, "We knew it would be a bad movie from the start." Abort!! Cut your losses and re-invest in something with ROI; this movie isn't delivering on the HDD.

The components of each HDD statement should be absolute and internal, not external, aka relative to a market or an economy. This is important; the fighter pilot mindset is focusing and measuring the things you can control and adapting those to the things you can't. You want $XX million in sales, not #3 in the marketplace. Markets, like the world in which fighter pilots operate, are not zero-sum games: company performance is in part dependent on industry performance, which is in part dependent on macroeconomics and geopolitical forces. You could be #1 in the market and fall short of your sales goal—or last in the market and sweep past that goal by 200%. All we care about is you and your absolute numbers. How they rank is irrelevant to everything save ego. Put a stake in the ground with your objectives, specify numbers rather than calling for "more than last year," and adjust those numbers in each year's strategic cycle, as need be.

Set a realistic vision, but don't be afraid to set some stretch targets for your high performers. We want the HDD to express a sense of purpose that compels us rationally and practically, as well as emotionally and inspirationally. We want a vision of the future that people can get behind. Such a vision helps to "direct, align, and inspire actions on the part of large numbers of people," as John Kotter said, and that's exactly what we want.

Note that we avoid the "how" in an HDD. How I take off and land my jet, what route I fly to get to the no-fly zone—that's up to the team.

# Creating Your HDD

A good HDD stands at the very peak of the company and its mission and cascades through every leader to the execution layer. It is the target and destination to which all the other objectives are aimed. If establishing a colony on Mars is Elon Musk's HDD, then each Falcon rocket Space-X launches is a supporting HDD, aligned with that vision, and is an absolute, discrete success on the pathway to that destination.

Writing an HDD requires a fine balance. Too much detail and it becomes a task list and not a vision. On the other hand, generalized, heavily inspirational visions can drive the purpose of a company or community, but that's not enough. Consider these two great HDD visions that, different as they are, would both inspire us, and would be standards against which we can test everything we do:

"I have a dream that my four little children will one day live in a nation where they will not be judged by the color of their skin, but by the content of their character."

"At the Coca-Cola Company we strive to refresh the world, inspire moments of optimism and happiness, create value, and make a difference."

These visions give us identity and purpose, and they are invaluable both for the people pursuing them and for the communities they serve. Yet pure as they are, would they be enough to guide decision-making on important operational matters at all levels of your company or community? We need a little more context and detail.

# The HDD Toolset

<u>Get the right team in place.</u> You create your HDD through open planning, so make sure you have everyone you need in the room. First and foremost, get the people who will be tasked with achieving the HDD in there. Are there others who have the situational awareness you need to assess the trends and threats that will affect the company over the next three years or more? Get them in the room. If specialists are needed to fill in that situational awareness, get them in the room. Don't make assumptions on behalf of others; if you need details, find the experts.

<u>Ensure the HDD dimensions are clear, measurable, achievable, and aligned to each other.</u> Decide what words and descriptions are most important, and test them. Are they clear, measurable, and achievable? When strung together, are the words and descriptions aligned with each other? That is, are they mutually consistent, and can they support each other? Weed out any conflicting words or destinations in your HDD.

<u>Is your HDD and your organizational identity a unified vision?</u> Stand back and consider your organizational identity and your HDD together. Do they fit as one? Will they mutually guide and inspire? Are they something your team can achieve? Who will be happy if you achieve it? Who may not be happy, and does that matter?

<u>Connect it to your organizational purpose, vision, and values.</u> Why does your company exist? Is it to create wealth or offer existential fulfillment for your

owners and employees? Is it to give customers a unique experience and be part of a fabulous industry? Is it to do something valuable for the community or the world? The Coca-Cola Company may want to "refresh the world and inspire moments of optimism and happiness," but it needs an HDD for what it will be as a company to do that. You won't have an actionable HDD unless you have a clear purpose or mission to connect with.

<u>Tap into your situational awareness.</u> Think broadly. Sweep your mental knowledge banks for information. Consider not just how the company has recently fared, but the trends and threats on the horizon. What's out there? What do you see? The team has to have a common view of its position and possibilities. This is a great place to look at the horizon—and beyond—as a group.

# Keep It Simple – Clear, Measurable, Achievable

The HDD captures your story, or the art of your strategy, and outlines the plot and characters for the team. Write that story in words that flesh out the roles people play and do it in some detail. If you're a numbers person, get help from a creative; if you're creative or a natural storyteller, bring in someone from accounting. Even at the highest level of strategy development, we want diversity in our team. Use words that are clear and definitive, against an outcome that is measurable and achievable. That's what we mean when we say, "a good HDD stands at the very peak of the company and its mission. It is the target and destination to which all the other objectives are aimed." The HDD is your story. Make it clear, measurable, and achievable.

# AI Sidebar: The Hype Cycle

Everyone has ideas. An annual strategy is in itself an idea. But in reality, an idea is a dream, a hope, a "maybe"—a best guess as to what the future looks like. There is always an enormous gap between an idea and an idea becoming reality. Gartner conceptualizes the execution of ideas as "Hype Cycles." Hype Cycles offer a snapshot of the relative market promotion and perceived value of innovations. They highlight overhyped areas, estimate when innovations

# Gartner Hype Cycle

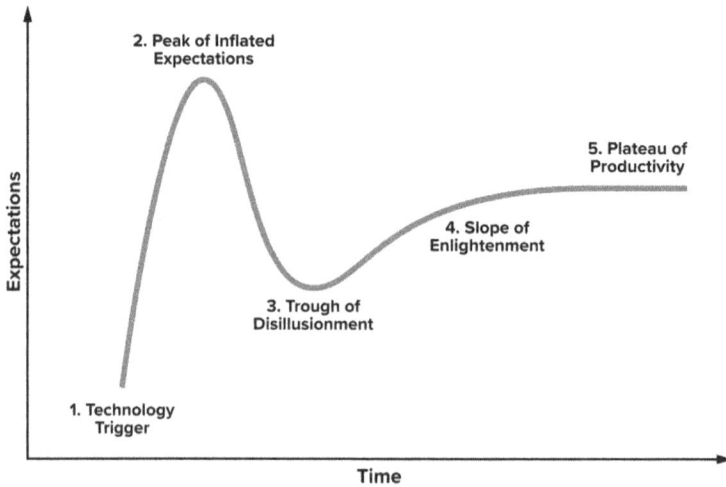

*Figure 11. The Gartner Hype Cycle*

and trends will reach maturity, and provide actionable advice to help organizations decide when to adopt. You can replace "expectation" with "motivation" on the graph too; it's directly proportional to fresh intention untainted by action!

As you can see in the adjacent graph, the hype or excitement around an idea peaks significantly at its inception, only to fall away into a "trough of disillusionment" as the reality of execution takes hold. Only the very best ideas survive this disillusionment, and unfortunately, even the best ideas can fail if the team loses its mojo.

The Gartner Hype Cycle is further reinforced by the esteemed Harvard Professor Clayton Christensen seminal study into failed product launches. His research discovered that only 1,500 products from 30,000 product launches succeeded in the market, a paltry 5%.

Let's unpack what's going on here and maybe learn why we consistently fall into this trap. A simple way to conceptualize ideas or innovations is to consider an idea as an expansive thought or "art" and execution as laser-focused thoughts and action, or the "science" of the process. "Art" and "science" are two mental paradigms involving two different parts of the brain that really don't play well together, and perhaps that's why delivering audacious strategy and innovation is so hard.

Perhaps true innovators have a foot in each camp, those we view as bipolar or ADHD-equipped. They find conviction and commitment in the compelling story of an idea and a hyper-focus driven by the sense of achievement we feel during the science of its development and ultimate release.

With FLEX we consider both. An idea or innovation that feels good is driven by what we believe, not what we do. We see it as purposeful, and ultimately, we're convinced it's achievable, and that fuels our drive. We have to win though, too; desire without success quickly turns into despair. The art of strategy is engaging the heart; the science is the detail to engage the mind and body.

# Final Thoughts – Successful Missions Deliver Your HDD

It's likely that the HDD you've set for your company, or your strategy, is not a simple set of tasks. It's likely that achieving your end results will take time, effort, and many teams to achieve. If it's a capital-intensive strategy, reaching an HD Destination may take five to 10 years. If it's service or product-based, your HDD may be as tight as a quarter, as Nike has recently demonstrated with a shift to quarterly planning product cycles, or Lego, where the product cycle is compressed to 14 days. Either way, a single team can achieve so much in a day, a week, a month, or even five years.

That said, we learned from COVID that planning too far into the future is futile. One day you're serving dinner in your trendy restaurant thinking about opening a second location, the next, the tables are empty and you're near bankruptcy. Consider the transformative speed of Artificial Intelligence. In our AI-powered markets, everything has been vastly accelerated. Most business owners think artificial intelligence will benefit their businesses. A substantial number of respondents to a recent McKinsey survey (64%) anticipate that AI will improve customer relationships and increase productivity, while 60% expect AI to drive sales growth. Increased productivity = increased speed = faster decision-making! Same caution, though: Be wary of planning too far into the future—plan small, plan often, and plan together.

Second, because of its importance, your HDD will be created by senior executives, or the owner of a business, or you, but not by the legions of people who do the day-to-day work of an enterprise. That's a mistake. The HDD is a very essential document, it needs contributions and perspectives across the business. The leaders deliver on the plan and they own it; creating by themselves is setting the plan up to fail. It's that North Star for nearly everything you and your company will do, so it will guide more than one mission. Little wonder that it will likely be the responsibility of a corporation's most senior executives. From that point on, however, these higher-level missions will rely on other missions to be completed by executives on the next level down, and then the next level down, and so on, until we reach our high-performing forklift operator in the distribution center. The HDDs need to cascade down through the organization, each owned by a leader, until we hit the execution layer, when they turn into objectives that drive action, which we explore in Chapter 6.

That means that missions need to be launched up and down the company. Distinguishing between a strategic mission and a tactical mission, for instance, is misleading. A strategic mission for one level of management is a tactical mission for the next level down. That's just the way organizations are structured and why they are so powerful—when all those missions are aligned. There is no "strategic" or "tactical" level. There are all just objectives (the future), teams (the people), and actions (the getting things done).

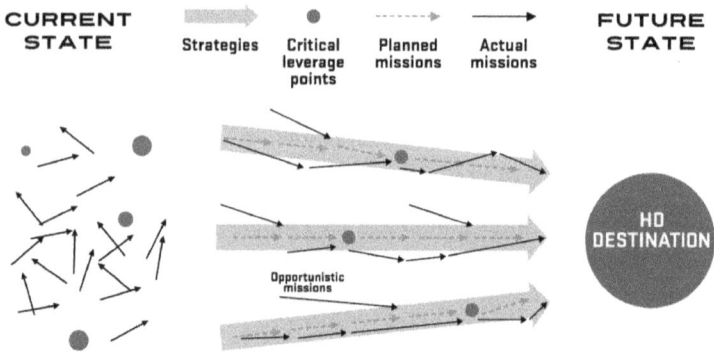

*Figure 12. Mission Alignment vs. Tactical Focus: HDD, Objective and Actions*
*Source: Afterburner, Inc.*

Third, as would be suggested by the preceding, all mission objectives have one thing in common. They're aligned with the HDDs. Every discrete mission has a clear line of sight to the ultimate HDD of the organization. There is an immediate, measurable, and achievable objective for a mission, yes. But in the planning and conduct of that mission there will be choices to make. To help make them, the team has to keep an eye on the objectives, all the way up to the top, to the HDD. That's the guiding light.

Don't be hung up on what you call those missions either. They may be projects, programs, launches, events, sales cycles, work packages, or just plain "missions." They may be standalone, they may be interconnected. But no matter the word, for the team planning and carrying them out, they're just missions, discrete packages of work with clearly defined and measurable outcomes. And the teams will FLEX them in exactly the same way.

"Mission alignment." On the left is the current state of far too many organizations. Teams are doing things, but most are doing their own things, they are busy. But are they somehow aligned? They might be. Will the impact of a particular action help the organization achieve its objectives, directly or indirectly, one, two, or three levels down? If it does, go for it. If it doesn't, tread very carefully.

# Aviator Sidebar: HDD in Action

It is not easy to paint a vision of something as complex as an organization, with all the uncertainty of the future, and all the possibilities. What would you include, and what would you leave out? Some companies have great visions. Amazon's vision is "to be Earth's most customer-centric company; to build a place where people can come to find and discover anything they might want to buy online." We now know what that vision looks like—it's what we see every day, that is, Amazon.com.

Dan McAtee found himself in need of an HDD when he became president of a major international steel company that had operations in 35 countries including the U.S., Colombia, England, Pakistan, and Vietnam. His challenge was to align these diverse groups of facilities and employees with clear goals. That was never going to be easy, so the Afterburner Team helped Dan beat complexity with simplicity.

He got everyone he needed into one room—people representing the different countries, functions, levels, and specialties inside and outside the firm—to create a shared HDD. Everyone, in one room! And it was not just the Board, not just the C-suite, not just the VPs, not just the mill managers, but everyone with a lever to pull to influence and drive the business.

It took them two days, and at the end they had an HDD that they owned, collectively and individually. McAtee called it a 75 percent plan, and that was enough. "Working with other methodologies, I've spent too much time trying to get perfect data. You just can't do it or do it expediently. And I'm a Six Sigma black belt! So we all came up with a simple plan together. It got us moving together in a common direction, accountable to one another. And the process builds in feedback and adjustment, so we'll figure out the remaining 25 percent as we go. The important thing is that we're moving forward together. We started allocating limited resources in an effective way and avoiding fights! Our alignment vastly improved decision-making because we could test options against our agreed HDD."

The real test came, though, when the financial markets melted down in 2008. "When the financial crisis came, this process kept the company above water," said McAtee. "Our demand dropped by 20 percent, but we still grew at 5 percent, even in that environment. Our people could execute against our plan and make needed adjustments locally, since they were empowered and understood the HDD."

# A New Factory

Consider a mission to build a factory to a set of clear specifications. That's a mission with a measurable objective. But it is not an end in itself—you are not building a factory for its own sake. You are building the factory because the company wants to increase its production, or to shift its production, or to make a different product. That's the intended impact you're looking for, and it's the objective of the team that desires the factory to be built. But that's not an end in itself either. Why increase production? Because it will help fill orders, which thus meets the goal of increased revenue, which is the mission and objective of the team that ordered the increased production. Why increase revenue? Because the revenue objective is part of the HDD, one of the company's performance goals, which is why the CEO asked for it. Why a revenue goal? So investors will continue to invest in the company, which in turn provides jobs for its people and serves the needs of its customers.

Is that the end of the story? No. The people designing the factory need situational awareness of the other missions that are pushing towards the HDD. They may relate to the culture (open sight or silo), business model (made-to-order or commodity), or product quality. Choices in factory design have to take into account these market objectives just as much as their immediate "build a concrete slab" objective.

Some missions are completed quickly, and some are longer-term. You won't be surprised to read that the FLEX engine is designed to power both, with some important differences. Essentially, the longer time frame means changes in the situation, the team and other resources, and the objectives over that time. Over a longer period, the surrounding environment changes. Competitors or investors may come and go. Crises may arise elsewhere in the business to take away people and resources. Changes in regulations may demand more or less compliance cost. The world may change—wars in Ukraine, the Middle East, and impending financial system collapse. People may leave for other pastures. All of this means that a mission objective and plan will need to change, or more accurately, evolve. The original measure may become too easy due to breakthroughs elsewhere or in its own missions, or too hard. A better way of reaching objectives may be discovered as new resources become available. The Execution Gap or X-Gap meeting is a tool to keep your execution and plans aligned no matter what the world throws at you. These regularly scheduled meetings are discussed in more detail in the next few chapters. Don't get me wrong. At Afterburner, we know how complex organizational strategy and change can be: we've seen them in action countless times. However, to deal with change, we also need to adopt a fighter pilot mindset—change is the game, the constant, so we need to be willing to evolve, to drive evolution.

# Tip: The Six Steps for HDD Building

This was the most challenging part of writing this book, it's a little like the circular formula in excel! I had to find a place to explain the system to build an HDD. You need to know about HDDs to understand mission planning, and you need to know how to build HDDs, too! It's really simple. Use the same process and methodologies you'll read in Chapter 6, except for Step 5. Instead of Courses of Action, you're creating Supporting

HDDs. If you find your supporting HDDs look more like actions (binary measures), then stop. Your HDD is a mission objective now, so time to build your mission plan.

Remember, HDDs define the future; objectives define action.

That probably doesn't make a lot of sense right now, but it will once you finish Chapter 6.

# 5 | FLEX Planning—Plan the Way You Plan

"An idiot with a plan beats a genius without one." Warren Buffet

We, fighter pilots, hate surprises. It's hard enough to hang onto a jet at 1,000 miles per hour with static electricity arcing across the cockpit while threading thunderstorms with 4,000 lbs. of explosives strapped to your wings, or going "blind" on our leader while pulling 9G to maneuver into a position of advantage in an air combat mission, simultaneously trying to get eyes on the bandit (Bad Guy) and the lead (our Boss) in a three-dimensional virtual fishbowl. It's hard enough to fly in a disciplined formation, while working the radar, managing a data link, listening to radio calls, and monitoring the stream of data on the display that come at us both in the aircraft and the helmet. It's harder still in combat, when you're tracking multiple targets, coordinating with other air assets, or dodging through an integrated air defense system bristling with surface-to-air missiles and you're avoiding getting shot down.

There's no time to think in that environment. Thinking clogs our headspace just like junk clogs a drain. The time for thinking is on the ground. The time for a clear headspace is while we're executing our missions. That's why we thoroughly plan a mission. The last thing we need is something to come at us out of nowhere, something unexpected that we really have to think about. It's not enough to know what to do when it's going well, or even what to do if something goes wrong. We have to plan for as many threats and opportunities and contingencies as we can think of. We want to cut short the list of things that could take us by surprise. Said differently, we want to so thoroughly plan our mission such that in most situations, our responses are intentional, scripted, and preplanned. The last thing you want to be thinking is "What's this button do?" when you're in the heat of air combat!

That's not to say things are ever perfect. They're not. In Australia, fighter pilots call fighter pilots "knucks," which can either be interpreted as a "knucklehead" or "knuckledragger," all equally ego-deflating terms. We knuckleheads are the first to admit that planning as a tool for execution is inherently flawed. A plan looks ahead, looks into the future, and who has a 100% perfect crystal ball? No one does. A plan builds a set of actions for a future that doesn't yet exist, and no matter how effective we are or how much information we have, we are always walking into the unknown armed only with a few likely outcomes and a lot of possibilities. By definition, that means there can't be such a thing as a perfect plan.

But we know that. We know the other team wants to surprise us, to get inside our decision-making loop, and that they'll use every tool in the toolbox to do that, so we get very good at looking into the "threats to success" to deny us the success of the mission we're about to fly and at preparing to counter as many of them as we can. How do we do that? We start with the end in mind, what effect we are looking to have as a result of the mission, or more specifically, what **impact** we are trying to make. Define the "HDD" or "Mission Objective," then work backwards to create the actions to deliver the impact. Planning is also a mindset, and that mindset is centered around an unshakeable belief that your plan is for a 100% committed, must-win execution. That mindset halos out to the other members of the team and shapes their own mindset. You exude the confidence of a winner, they exude the confidence of a winner. You walk the walk and talk the talk, they walk the walk and talk the talk. Together, they're ready to climb in the jet and fly the mission. Together, you and your team are impossible to beat. You want to inspire and engage your people? Plan and execute "must-win missions," and people will gravitate to you like a moth to a spotlight.

Does that sound like the planning you put into your latest project, negotiation, or presentation? Planning is the first stage in the plan–brief–execute–debrief FLEX cycle. It sets both the tone and the direction for the rest of the cycle. It's the future you desire planned in detail, it's the story you want to tell, one that is compelling and believable. Unlike a story, though, you're going to be the central character and execute each page;

it's not just a figment of your imagination, which is unfortunately where many strategies start and end. In a word, the plan is everything, and everything rotates around the plan. The mission plan is adaptable, so plan small, plan often, and stay grounded in reality.

You create a plan. You brief a plan. You execute a plan—execution is the plan in action; the execution of the mission is doing what you've briefed. Finally, you debrief the execution against the plan. You measure your results against the objectives of the plan.

It always comes back to the plan—the plan sets the tone for the entire FLEX process.

# I. There's a Method to Our Planning. There Is Also a Mindset to Our Method.

You may think this is overkill, but we have entrenched habits when we start planning a mission. Why is that? No matter the mission, there are countless variables in play that if our planning wasn't highly structured, we'd never get out and actually do something. It's easy to succumb to paralysis by analysis or get lost in a whiteboard filled with word salad, so over the last 27 years, we've fine-tuned what works and what doesn't work in the process of creating a tight, achievable, winning plan.

## 1: FLEX Planning Is Fast, It Has a Bias for Action

The difference between fighter pilot planning and business planning is a bias towards action vs. analysis and assumption. For example, technology companies hire graduates well versed in accessing, manipulating, and analyzing data, but less so in making the decisions on which that data is based. These analysts are rewarded for spending hours—even days—on the data. We can't wait that long.

By bias to action, we don't mean an impulsive, knee-jerk response to information. We mean an appreciation that planning time is finite, that you can't just go on and on about things, that the mission is upon us and it's time to go. The team leader has to make that call. The planning stage has gone on long enough. We're building a collective consciousness, not necessarily a consensus or a majority vote. The leader calls for action; they have the 51% vote once all the data has been reviewed and the subject matter experts in the team consulted.

So, how can FLEX planning be fast yet still consider all the data it needs for an effective plan? How do we keep it moving while getting all the data we need? No one wants to be bogged down for days. Planning is not an end in itself. The trick is to start the process with the right tone, and the tone should be biased toward action to fulfill your intentions.

## 2: FLEX Planning Is a Known, Shared, Time-Limited Process

Your team is a team because of the expertise each person brings to the table. Your members have skills specific to the mission. We're pilots, and we're about to fly a mission. Our experiences are the reason we're in the room, and that defines the possible actions the team can take and the possible paths forward to achieve the mission objectives. A good team knows its stuff, sees how it applies, and knows the steps in the plan that are needed and what each step will accomplish. That's the "shared" part: We're going to grind out our plan on that basis, rather than throwing a million ideas up on a whiteboard and creating time-consuming distractions. That means the discussion is focused, it's intentional, and we must achieve the objective and make an impact. We work through what we need to work through in a brisk, timely fashion. There aren't a million ideas to throw on the whiteboard, and we all intuitively know that. We plan our plan, and we get going.

## 3: Acknowledge Planning Is Dynamic vs. Static

We pilots have trained skillsets that get us through the unknowns. You do too. So, rather than spending hours on analyzing and planning for situations that will, in the end, be dynamic and unknowable, we make decisions, lock down the plan, get out the door, and allow things to be dynamic in execution, trusting in our skills and standards to navigate these unknowns. By acknowledging that things will be dynamic or VUCA, we reduce the time spent planning for unknown outcomes, which is, in the end, an extra and largely needless planning segment that can box you in when you need flexibility. Your plans should never cut down your future options to act. A FLEX plan assumes that once you're out the door, the team will be making some decisions on the fly, dynamically, once the action starts. We embrace that. It's the nature of our business. A bias to action gets us into the game, which in turn allows events to unfold, which in turn removes uncertainty, complexity, and ambiguity. The fuzzy haze of "the future" becomes the crystal-clear reality of the "now."

# II. FLEX Planning Is Fully Considered

The FLEX planning process needs to be fast, but your FLEX plan itself needs to be fully considered to be effective. Four elements will make sure it is:

1. You embrace open planning
2. You use our Six-Step Planning Process in Chapter 6
3. You stay focused on the impact of the actions vs. the actions themselves
4. And you have your plans independently reviewed by a Red Team

## 1: You Embrace Open Planning

Open planning means that all the right people are in the room and take part in the planning. To that end, "the right people" consist of three different groups. First, bring in all the people responsible for executing the plan—the pilots who are going to fly the mission. That's a given. That's how we get buy-in, that's how they own the plan—blunt any resistance that would come as a result of the plan originating from some unknown group in a white castle. Every person who is part of the mission is part of the planning.

Second, bring in a mission champion, a person senior enough to resolve resource issues and conflicts.

Finally, bring in the experts or the specialists. When I plan a mission, I bring in specialists from intelligence, maintenance, weather, weapons, and battlespace management. Each one of them has in-depth knowledge in their area. Each one helps me build the picture by using their unique knowledge and their unique situational awareness on specific unknowns. If you need more specialists, bring them in. The more diverse the group, and the more perspectives, the better. That's how we deal with complexity—we include people, we build understanding across departments, we engage people with different specialties, even different generations. Open planning is a disciplined collaboration that makes FLEX work.

Tip: In business, if the plan includes how you deliver what your client wants, think about including your client in the planning. Nothing beats that for improving the quality of the plan, the client buy-in, and the overall client relationship.

## 2: Use the Six-Step Planning Process

It's a given in life that people forget things, leave things out, and jump around from one topic to the next; we can be all over the shop. The Six-Step Process prevents that. It's a checklist of things to consider in a specific order. It is designed so that all contributions are captured in an orderly fashion and that each item in the plan leads to a clear course of action. This is a time-limited process, but it's rigorous.

The Six Steps start by identifying the team's objective and end with a watertight plan for achieving it. They consider the threats to success, your available resources, lessons learned from previous missions, and any execution shortfalls. They lay out a clear course of action, and when used as a roadmap, they're airtight and ready to be briefed and executed.

## 3: Focus on Impact-based Planning

The leader has to lay out the impact of our actions and the intent of the mission before asking the team to plan it. The mission objective will follow, and it will flesh out the details and measurements to deliver on the intent. Maybe I can frame it a little better: Our impact can be measured once we achieve our objectives; the intention tells the story. You may have heard the phrase, usually after a mistake or when someone's feelings were hurt, that the other party was "well-intentioned." Their intentions were good, but their impact was poor. Most people end up in an argument, fight, or even a war because both sides have "good intentions." The impact of these well-intentioned wars is devasting; many of our fighter pilots have seen that impact up close on a screen with an image from a targeting pod, and it's horrific.

So, what is intent? The intent is intent, no impact! It's a broad statement of what the leader wants the mission to accomplish; it's the art of the strategy, and it lacks detail. On the other hand, an objective (or HDD) is specific and delivers an impact. It states what you have to do to achieve the leader's intent; it's pure science. Bring these together and we define our why, conceptually and literally.

Intent is an essential step and where we start our planning process. From that, every step in the plan leading up to this end point is impact-based, meaning the resulting impact of a specific action will take the team and its organization one step closer to its intended destination. Intent shapes impact, and the impact of our mission may reshape our intent; it's like everything in FLEX, yin and yang, striking a balance between cause and effect.

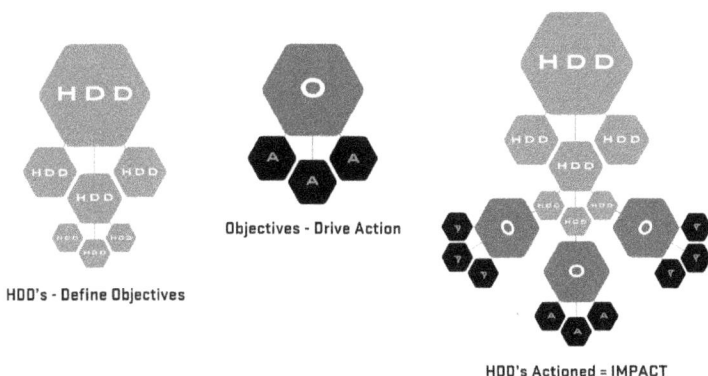

*Figure 13. How HDDs, Objectives and Actions align*

## What's the Difference Between an HDD and an Objective?

An HDD is a destination supported by other HDDs; it's all about the future. Eventually, an HDD is supported by an Objective. An objective is different because it is supported by action. HDDs define the future, while objectives define the actions we take to get there.

## 4: Conduct a Red Team Review

The Red Team is where we invite external challenges to our plan. A Red Team Review is the final stage of our planning process. The Red Team Review is a break-it-down, find-the-flaws, stress test of the plan conducted by a totally fresh set of experienced eyes. If a key specialist cannot be included in the planning team, make sure they're in the Red Team. Red-teaming manages one of the biggest threats to planning: our cognitive biases and beliefs, those things that prevent us from seeing our own flaws, flaws that may be embedded in the plan, flaws that will kill us, someone on our team, or worse still, an innocent bystander.

The FLEX plan for planning works because it offers the right balance between speed and deliberation. It bridges the gap between "close enough is good enough" and "100 percent certainty."

What's left is the final ingredient in the planning stage, the point where it's time to move on, to act, to execute the mission, and that call is the leader's, which is what leadership is all about.

# III. FLEX Plans Are Simple. Plan Small. Plan Often.

The more complex a plan, the more likely it will fail. The more steps it has, the more detailed the instruction, thus the greater the risk of human error. That's just a fact of life. Plan small. Plan often. Keep it simple.

A simple plan also names names. *Who* does *what* and *when* is core to a simple plan. To that you must add a measure of their progress. That ensures that the people accountable for something are absolutely clear on who does what, when, and how we measure their progress. There can be no ambiguity around small steps. Who. What. When. And the measure of progress/success. Why is this so important? If your strategy is to pick your daughter up from school at 3:45 p.m. and you're ambiguous about which route to take, toll roads (fast) or no toll roads (slow), there's a risk that subconsciously you may plan to leave later for toll roads, yet you take the slow route, finding yourself 12 minutes late. This happens often, your subconscious autopilot isn't as reliable as the one in our jet!

But that's not all. FLEX calls for a little more, and that little bit more makes all the difference in the world. A FLEX plan asks why, answers who, what, when. . . and then adds the what-if. Those simple questions carry a lot of weight.

## The "Why" of a Mission Is a Powerful Motivator

The "why" of a mission must align with your organization's reason-for-being; that is, the impact of your mission should achieve the why of your organization. It confirms your organization's reason for being and clarifies the deeper meaning of the discreet mission's objective (BOGO50 product launch, for example), the "why" of that objective. People don't just execute a mission. They have to *believe* in the mission. Consider a pharmaceutical company. Why do you work for a pharmaceutical company, and I fly jets? The answers reflect our personal missions in life, what we want to do with ourselves. Perhaps your life goal is to reduce world suffering caused by rare diseases. Developing a cure for a new disease would align with your sense of purpose. The "why" of a major project to develop a new drug for a new pandemic would certainly work for you but would be alien to me.

## The "What-If" of a Mission

The world is an imperfect place. Things go wrong. We need to test a plan against the things that might go wrong, and that makes the "what-ifs" hugely important, and they get everybody's attention. What if the engines seize up halfway to the target? What if our sensors go on the fritz? I have a friend who packs an umbrella even on a sunny day. That's a "what-if." I have another friend who brings her back-up battery pack to the office. That's another "what-if." (We actually had a rare power outage in the center of the city; she felt redeemed that day.) As they say in the squadrons: "Plan for perfection, prepare for the worst."

We go through the "what-if" phase of planning to make sure we've thought through the threats and all those things we can't control but that have a very real chance of happening. So important are these that we keep the "what-if" as a separate action item right at the end of the process because we don't want the planning process to get derailed by the 1000s of random things that "could" go wrong. A deep desire to stay alive keeps you focused.

These two questions—the "why" and the "what-if"—are what make your plans dynamic, that is, able to respond to changing conditions and the realities you encounter as you execute the mission. It makes the plan both threat-sensitive and time-sensitive. If a team has situational awareness and knows why they're on the mission, they can adjust their plan and still deliver what's needed. And if it's not possible, they can abort. In short, these two questions, why and what-if, engage your people at the earliest point, and as they work through the answers with you, you'll get buy-in and clarity around their own objectives, and they become superstars. All of this "what-if" thinking is essential if your operating environment is in any way complex or unpredictable. A FLEX plan calls on your team to be absolutely engaged in their mission from the heart, the brain, and right down to the soles of their feet, not just robotically. These two questions top and tail your plan.

## Focus on Action, Standardize the "How"

The FLEX plan sets out what each person needs to achieve. But if it tries to answer how they're going to do it, it's at the wrong level and should not be part of your plan. That's for the individual team member to decide. When we fly a mission, we fly the plan, and that's it. We draw on checklists, procedures and standards—fixed routines that we know work, routines that keep things calm, routines that free up our minds for the decisions that matter—but for the basics, we rely on our company standards and procedures that are by now automatic. This includes techniques that we've developed and come to trust and shared experiences that we've codified. But these are not part of the plan—they're our wings, they are the things we rely on when we're in action. And every company, every individual, has wings too. The "automatics" are the best practices for you and your company.

AI Sidebar: Creating standards or procedures has never been easier with AI. Simply use your AI platform of choice and type "I would like a standard procedure to [Insert outcome/objective here]" and you'll have the 80% solution in 25 seconds. Upload your existing standards and procedures into the knowledge base, add additional prompts like "best practice," and refine them over 20-30 minutes until you have something fit for purpose. Once it's done, upload and save it in the knowledge base for next time and for the entire team to use!

# Less Is More, Only Include What's Needed

A FLEX plan does not go into the detail of how every task is to be done, nor does it restate standards. The mission is defined by its intended effect: the impact we want. Similarly, each action in the plan is defined only by its intended impact: what by when by whom, i.e., clear, measurable, achievable. How that result occurs is up to the team (for the mission/project/product launch or event) or the individual (for the actions).

Example: If your plan calls for Tom to have a car outside 1135 North Street at 11 p.m., it's Tom's task to get it there. You don't tell him how to get there. You don't plan the route taken, the speed driven, the need to obey traffic laws, the need for fuel or how to push the start button. You don't worry about the way Tom drives. Your team will have standard operating procedures. It's obvious the car needs gas in the tank and air in the tires. That is Standard Operating Procedures (SOP). More than that, these are "breathing" steps: steps so obvious it's like telling people to remember to breathe. Beyond that, leave it up to Tom to drive the car his way, using whatever techniques and preferences he likes consistent with the SOPs. If you go into too much detail, if you belabor the obvious, it's an insult to people, and you are micro-managing. They're on the team to do the things they do—let them work it out. As Charles Duhigg said in *The Power of Habit*: "Giving employees a sense of agency—a feeling that they are in control, that they have a genuine decision-making authority—can radically increase how much energy and focus they bring to their jobs." Or, remember how General Patton put it: "Don't tell people how to do things. Tell them what to do, and let them surprise you with the results."

# Tip: Not Your Typical Planning Process

Many companies have planning and project management specialists who use complex, degree-demanding software to create "the project plan." These specialists stand apart from the operating division, which means that most of the planning is done by people other than the team that's going to execute it. These specialists will work long into the night to figure out exactly how their team will execute a plan, generally without including the team in the planning process. This creates a gap between the planners and the execution teams, a gap that only gets bigger the more complex the plan.

We're uncomfortable with that gap. In FLEX planning, the people executing a plan are always in the planning meetings, or their leaders or representatives are. FLEX plans are created by the teams who are responsible for executing them. By being part of the team, people have signed up to the team's plan. They are making commitments to their team, and once committed, those commitments hold. It's social and methodical; the planning process sets the bedrock for engagement and ensures we cover each other's blind spots, establish clear roles and responsibilities, and help leaders understand when to lead from the front and when to stand shoulder-to-shoulder during execution.

Second, most planners start their work by looking back, by rolling out a new plan using the last plan. That's understandable. It gets you to a first draft fast and lets you start tweaking it, but that's wrong. By rolling out the last plan, you're also rolling out all its assumptions about the context, threats, and resources available. Those assumptions may or may not be valid today, may or may not be threats today. Instead, FLEX planning starts with the future and always looks forward to the mission objective.

The third difference is the amount of analysis that goes into FLEX planning. If you're updating the last plan and then rubber stamping it, you're giving dangerously little consideration to new data and current affairs. You're just handing out a list of tasks that has been updated and, no doubt, swollen over the years. Indeed, oftentimes a task is on a list long after one remembers why it's on that list, which, generally, comes down to the fact that no one has been brave enough to remove it for fear of unknown consequences. Importantly, FLEX plans set objectives to STOP doing the things that aren't working and remove the bloat. FLEX teams know the purpose of each step in a plan because they put it there specifically to get one step closer to the mission objective. We learn from our previous missions, yes, but we don't roll forward one plan into the next. Rather, we extract lessons learned (nudge nudge, AI is your friend here) and roll those forward. That's iterative, not rubber stamping, and, by definition, each plan gets smarter.

Finally, there is a section in most corporate plans called "risk assessment and management." In it, the planners list the ordinary risks to the business and note that they're aware of them and that they have situational awareness, but rarely are these risks—or their mitigation—integrated into the plan.

Rather, they are there as window dressing. It's as if by mentioning them, they've absolved themselves of the true impacts. Either way, they have this section as additional planning considerations held apart from the main flow, often written by the lawyers. The point is, they stand apart and are not integrated into the actions detailed in the plan to achieve the objective. It's, as a fighter pilot would say, tin-plating your ass if something goes wrong.

That's a mistake. Risk management is different for us. It's serious. We don't give it lip service; the whole point of the plan is to mitigate risk and win. This is where we really, really deal with threats—with weaknesses, blockers, information gaps, or challenges—in short, any threats to the plan. In FLEX planning, if a material threat can be controlled in any way, that control is captured as an action item in the plan. If the threat is uncontrollable, then a contingency plan will come into play at a decision point with a known trigger. There's no point worrying about a risk unless it's real and unless you can do something about it.

Nothing is tossed into the plan as CYA (Cover Your Ass) boilerplate. We list risks, review them, and plan actions for them while we're on the ground. We never wait to do this. It's too late in the air, so we do it now. All risks are contextualized within the plan. We are respectful of the risks rather than afraid of them. In the end, we know the plan will go forward, with or without those threats appearing and trying to stop or impede us. In the end, there are no floating risks left out there that we haven't put into context.

Finally, FLEX planning only stops when the mission is over. Remember, planning is your best guess as to "what's next," so it stands to reason that you're always planning what to do next until there is no next, even whilst in the air. Let's say the weather changes while en route, we re-plan, or the tanker that was giving us gas had a mechanical problem and didn't launch, we re-plan. We pilots are continuously adapting to the realities up to and through the moment of the brief, pausing only to start the mission and then continuing again right to the end. We go out on a mission loaded with options and loaded with trigger points and driven by a mentality that centers on a bias for action, that centers on an unshakeable belief that we will win.

# AI Sidebar: Apollo 13 – A Two-Minute Planning Lesson

Not everyone is able to sit in on a fighter Squadron planning session. Instead, have another look at the scene from the movie *Apollo 13* known as "A New Mission" (you'll find it on YouTube). It happens pretty quickly, but it's all there. Shortly after Tom Hanks beams in with "Houston, we have a problem," all the flight engineers at Mission Control are brought together. Ed Harris, as mission commander Gene Kranz, switches to "failure is not an option" planning mode. He needs everyone there: it's open planning.

"OK people, listen up! I want you all to forget the flight plan. From this moment on, we are improvising a new mission." The objective is to get the astronauts home. The threats are many and obvious. They identify the only engine capable of keeping the spacecraft going and revisit what they know about it. Ideas are tossed up and thrown aside, and it starts looking impossible. The urgency adds pressure and makes it look more impossible.

Kranz ignores the fuss and the overhead projector that inevitably doesn't work. He makes the call on the course of action—a slingshot around the moon. (That, incidentally, is classic problem solving. We have three options, two won't work, so we're taking the only one with half a chance.) The engineers start work on sub-plans to meet the many threats, among them that the capsule will run out of power well before reaching Earth.

# The Six-Step Mission-Planning Process

A FLEX plan starts intentionally with what the team leader "intends" the mission to achieve; as you read earlier, this is the leader's intent. The next item states the team's mission objective and the courses of action to achieve it. Together, the leader's intent, the mission objective, and the course of action answer the who, what, when, why and what-ifs of the mission, as well as measure its progress.

FLEX planning is a relatively fast yet considered process. What the team needs to achieve is set by its leader, but the planning itself is done by the whole team, with any outside subject matter experts or facilitators who would add insight. It needs that diversity of thinking to make sure that the plan is as solid as possible. And it needs the people who are about to execute the mission. They know what they can and can't do, how they will do it, and what they will need. And when it comes to the mission itself, they will own it. But without a plan, there is no mission, so we start a mission with mission planning because it lays the foundation for the Six Steps to Mission Planning. The six steps are as follows:

1. **Set a mission objective** that meets the leader's intent. It must be clear, measurable, and achievable. (Where do we need to be, and why?)
2. **Identify any threats**, controllable and not. (What's in the way?) . . . . . . . . . . . . . . . . . . . .

3. **Identify your resources** we can draw on. (What can help us to meet our objective, or deal with and address the threats?)
4. **Identify the lessons learned** from previous debriefs that we can draw on.
5. **Set out a course of action**: who does what and when to reach the objective?
6. **Set out all contingency plans** and the what-ifs. Prepare for the worst. Finally, invite the challenge, get the Red Team to find the holes in the plan, and then plug them.

# The Leader's Intent – Purposeful Planning

There's that word again, INTENT. I can't reinforce this enough: intent isn't your strategy; it's your idea, your story. Intentions are easy, and impact is hard. Purposeful planning helps you shape realistic intentions and deliver impact.

Planning and execution are ultimately human endeavors, so no matter how clearly defined your achievable objective is, there has to be a point to it, a purpose, and when people know the purpose, they're motivated, enthusiastic. It's up to the team leader to make that purpose clear.

Second, intent shapes perception. Just because we have a neat plan on a page, or an action plan covering what we perceive is everything, there is always interpretation, and it's up to the leader to fill in the blanks and eliminate the prospect of differing interpretations. That's where your HDD comes in. Each mission is planned to pursue a strategic objective towards the HDD. It may go exactly as planned, it may go a little off course, or it may be opportunistic—but every mission is pointing in the right direction if it's pointing towards the HDD. Without that clear alignment, good people may be on good missions that may seem worthwhile, but they don't advance the team or the organization toward its goals. They get overwhelmed and busy. The interpretation is wrong. They haven't understood the true purpose or the true intent of the mission.

Mission planning will set a specific, immediate objective, but the leader's intent is the intended effect of that mission. It's what happens in the market when the plan is implemented and the actions are complete. You must be clear and eliminate misinterpretations.

Certain leadership and planning philosophies stand the test of time, whether it's the fifth-gen era or the 1940s. For example, the Tuskegee

Airmen of the U.S. Air Force's 332nd Fighter Group were famous for three reasons. Their P-51 Mustangs were painted with red tails (hence the movie *Red Tails*), they were African Americans (initially facing immense prejudice as the first in the USAF), and they were one of the most effective fighter groups escorting U.S. bombers over Germany during World War II.

Escorting bombers was a dangerous business. The German pilots of the Luftwaffe were battle-hardened aces with years of combat experience. They had tactics and weapons all designed to shoot down the American bombers before they got to their targets. Part of that was penetrating the screen of escorts by shooting them down too.

You would think, then, that the escorts were rated and rewarded for escorting their bombers safely to and from their targets. Not so. Fighter pilots in the U.S. Army Air Forces (as they were known in World War II) were rewarded for one thing only—that is, shooting down enemy fighters. They would paint a swastika on their fighter plane for every downed enemy, and if you shot down five Germans, you were an "Ace," with all the respect and privileges that status brought.

Knowing this, some pilots saw their objective as shooting down German Messerschmitts. Surprisingly enough, that suited the Germans. They saw the weakness of that thinking and made themselves live bait. Sure enough, they were soon drawing the fighter escorts away from the bombers and distracting the American pilots by engaging them in a dogfight. That would leave the bombers protected only by their own guns, which was no real match for a second wave of Messerschmitts, who would then ruthlessly pour their bullets into the defenseless B-17s and B-24s.

Of all the U.S. squadrons, only the Tuskegee airmen decided, as a squadron, not to take the bait. They correctly interpreted the intent of their mission, which was to get American bombers to their targets and get them home safely. Shooting down German Messerschmitts was not what the Allies needed the escorts to do. They needed their bombers to get to their targets and drop bombs. Shooting down an enemy aircraft might have been part of the "how," but it wasn't the objective. Because they stuck to their bombers, they lost bombers on only seven of 179 escort missions, about half the average of other fighter groups. They didn't really care about being aces. The Tuskegee airmen had plenty of combat missions to prove their mettle—proving it the right way.

# Step 1: Set the Mission Objective

Remember, objectives drive action, and when we achieve our objectives, we deliver our HDDs. What are we trying to achieve? Why are we doing this? What's the point? What does "good" look like? It's hard to overstate the value of a good mission objective. It's fundamental to team engagement—without clear objectives, what's the team doing? People have to know what they are trying to do, and why that's worth doing. That's why they've joined your team, your club, your business, your government. If a good, clear mission objective is given to them, you're off to a good start. Here's a challenge for you: ask the next person you see what their life objective is or what they want to achieve by the end of the day; if they have to think about it, they're not FLEX. These objectives drive our daily activities.

This is true of both short-term and long-term objectives. A short-term mission has the advantage of being something that you and I can go out and start executing today. If you don't have clarity around it, however, it will be a long day. A poor objective for a long-term mission means it will be a long year, if not two or three. What a waste. A FLEX mission objective will be clear, measurable, achievable, and aligned to the HDD, and the team will deliver the "how" with their day-to-day actions. Here's an example, for the fictitious "Afterburner Vintage Cellars," a winemaker.

*"NMT (New Market Team) will launch our new Grenache "G-LOC" on 1 November and achieve 10,000 bottles sold within the first six months by targeting premium wine consumers through our established high-end retail and hospitality channels."*

## Make Your Objectives Clear

Mission objectives must be CLEAR. That means everyone briefed to do the job knows exactly what the job is. The mission objective is a sentence, and every word matters, even the order the words are written in. If it's an acronym, does your team know what it stands for? If it's a generic business term (sales, competition, costs), have you given it a precise definition? Define all of the nouns. If it's a technical term used in your company, make sure everyone on the team knows exactly what it means. Push hard on the meaning of every word. You don't want to be arguing about it after the event. No interpretations, no ambiguity. If there's the slightest shadow of a doubt about anything in the objective, you can be sure someone on your team will interpret the word the wrong way. Don't give them that chance.

*"**NMT (New Market Team) will launch our new Grenache "G-LOC"** on 1 November and achieve 10,000 bottles sold within the first six months by targeting premium wine consumers through our established high-end retail and hospitality channels."*

## Measurable

Immediately after a mission, you have to ask yourself one question: "Did we achieve our objective?" There are only two possible answers to that question: "yes" or "no." If you have the words right, then your objective was clear and unambiguous, which means the outcome was measurable—yes or no. You included a specific action or a specific number or a critical time element in the objective that was measurable. Nothing subjective. If there's a number involved, you need to be able to chart it. If there's a checklist involved, you need to be able to tick it off. If the mission is to "launch a product," be clear on the measures that will determine whether the product has, in fact, been launched. In the end, everyone must be able to answer "yes" or "no"—as soon as the mission is complete. Anything else means you didn't frame the objective in a way that made it clear and measurable.

In the same vein, a mission objective must be to achieve something tangible, something objective, not subjective. No matter how desirable it is, it's not measurable to say we want to "increase quality" or "launch a new SKU in Asia as soon as possible." Yes, quality can be measured, but only if you clearly set out what that measure will be. "Our new soap will receive five-star reviews for quality by no less than 90% of the reviewers." Or use due dates. "Our company will develop a new product that will meet 10 percent of the forecast demand of our top four Asia-Pacific customers by 1 December 2017." What have we achieved in that mission objective? In one sentence, we have aligned R&D, logistics, marketing, sales, HR area managers, and executives to what we are going to do— and how we know whether we've done it; that is an objective measure of success. Objectives and opinions don't mix. Get rid of any hint of anything subjective, including opinions, in your statement.

*"NMT (New Market Team) will launch our new Grenache "G-LOC" on **1 November and achieve 10,000 bottles sold within the first six months** by targeting premium wine consumers through our established high-end retail and hospitality channels."*

## Achievable

Mission objectives have to be achievable. Nothing undermines confidence or erodes motivation and energy faster than being asked to do the impossible. Tough missions are OK. They can be challenges that bind a team forever. A mission can be a stretch; it can require a huge effort. But it has to be possible.

Too many movies have tales of heroic actions by soldiers or superheroes who have attempted the impossible to save the day, inevitably at a huge cost, maybe even their lives. Leaders who ask for another's inevitable sacrifice—when an option otherwise exists—immediately lose the respect of their team. Business is not life and death. A team or individual on a road to nowhere will not travel far. For the modern Air Force, the loss of one life means that a mission has failed, no matter the impact.

Fortunately, the FLEX planning process will determine whether an objective is achievable or not, a determination made by the team itself. If it looks impossible, there are options. The team may seek additional resources. More often, the objective can be adjusted. The best adjustment is to shorten the reach of the mission. If the original mission looks impossible yet still valuable, break it down into steps and make the first step achievable. Then build on it—see what's possible from there. The Afterburner Vintage Cellar Team wouldn't publish their mission objective if it wasn't run through the six-step process and red-teamed, so it's safe to say it's achievable!

## Mission Objective Testing

See if these mission objectives pass our four tests.

*"Train the sales staff on the new product."* Nope. No measure of success.

*"Train all client-facing sales staff on the capabilities and design of the new Dynamo 9000."* That's certainly clearer, but is it measurable? In part, it is—we can tell whether training was conducted, and whether all relevant staff attended. Is that important? It could be, particularly if our firm was having trouble setting up classroom training and getting people to come. But it's unlikely to be the effect we're looking for.

*"Conduct classroom training on the new Dynamo 9000 so that all client-facing sales staff know 90 percent or more of the critical product informa-*

*tion by 1 February 2024."* Now we're getting somewhere. But is it where we want to be? We can see that the effect we're looking for is not the training per se but sales staff knowledge. If that's the effect we're looking for, do we really need to direct the team on <u>how</u> to achieve that effect? If this is a mission for the learning and development team, do we need to say <u>how</u> they should get that information into the heads of the sales staff? No. The team will work out the <u>how</u> in their course of action. In the mission objective above, we are thinking more narrowly than we need to. The following mission objective would serve us better—it is direct, yet empowering:

*Ensure that all client-facing sales staff know and can use 90 percent or more of the critical Dynamo 9000 product information by 1 February 2024.*

With the Dynamo 9000 being launched on 1 February, we can be pretty confident that this mission will align with the firm's strategic HDD.

Here's another example, this one starting with an HDD that is similar to an existing global athletic apparel business we helped to become flawless with their many product launches. Let's call them "Nake."

HDD (External): "To share the joy of football with every man, woman, and child on Earth."

HDD (Internal): "Our vision is to become the largest provider of affordable soccer apparel globally by the 2030 World Cup." Supported by beautiful imagery and content of children playing in the streets and Lionel Messi or Beckham as brand ambassadors, wow, we're all set! If I'm an accountant, designer, marketer, or salesperson, and I love soccer, I want to be on this bus! We create gravity to attract not only the team we want but also the team we need!

Company Objective: *"Nake will increase ARR to $157m by the end of 2024."*

Team Objective: *"The Georgia Account Team will increase quarterly sales to $2.8m by the end of Q2."*

Now you may notice there is no "why" in these statements. That's because the company covered that in their HDD. The resulting objectives are clear, measurable, and achievable.

# Step 2: Identify Mission Threats

As a fighter pilot, I know someone is out there wanting to shoot me down, or at least deter me from getting to my target. That gets my attention. That gets the attention of all of us, and whether it's combat or training, we ALWAYS introduce threats. As fighter pilots, we want to know everything about those people and what their jets can do, bar nothing. We want to know how they were trained, what their mindsets are, the capability of their jets, their weapons, their ground radars supporting them. I want to know what they had for breakfast and if they're angry with their wife or kids. You get very serious about gathering information when your life is on the line.

The threats are not deadly in business, but they are just as real, and you don't want them getting in the way of your success. "Be paranoid!" said Intel's first CEO, Andy Grove. In the most constructive of ways, paranoia is healthy. Dig down and really work out what your weaknesses are, what the competition could do to your plans, what could go wrong, what even could go so right that it would distract you from your mission. There will be threats, no matter how seemingly straightforward a mission is.

At this stage of the process, your team needs to identify what your threats are—internal and external—and whether you can control them. Like everything in FLEX and in life, you're aiming at a sweet spot: not too few threats that you miss some, but not so many that they become a list or even demoralizing—and your plans to meet them become chaotic.

Classify your threats. If a threat is controllable, you can plan for that control in your course of action. If it's not, you'll need a contingency plan. But don't leave anything out.

## Internal Threats

"We have met the enemy, and he is us." So said Walt Kelly to introduce his Pogo cartoon in 1953. It's a great line because it points you one way and then brings you back to the place that matters. You and what you can control.

We may want to deny it, but our personal, internal threats are the most common threats to a mission's success. We get distracted; we lose confidence, focus, energy, or the will to lead. These are ever-present threats that we deal with in the execution phase of the FLEX cycle, where we have effective actions to combat them.

Chapter 6: The Six-Step Mission-Planning Process

The internal threats that we're most interested in at this stage are those that exist within your team or the organization itself. Do you have the resources and funding you need? Do you have the senior leadership support that you need? Do you have the skilled personnel? Do you have the technology, tools, or apps? Are there any relationships within the team that might blow up through the mission? Are your communication lines and methods as clear as they need to be? Will you have the information you need to make decisions when you need it?

Pfizer is one of our clients. Years ago, we helped them through a problem with their new product plans. We were going through the FLEX process and, when we got to the threats, the room buzzed with what their competitors were going to do, the tightening of government funding for prescription drugs, and the skyrocketing costs. But in the end, they decided that the biggest threat was internal: a personality and priorities gulf between the medical teams, the compliance teams, and the marketing and sales teams.

In the pharmaceutical industry, there are scientists who work on the next generation of drugs, medical specialists who conduct trials to secure their safe and approved use, marketing teams who gather the information to plan and launch the new product, and sales teams who visit the doctors and hospitals in order to have the medication prescribed. There are also compliance teams that sit in between new medicine and sales because there's a litany of obligations under U.S. law to ensure the "features and benefits" vs. "side effects" are properly conveyed, and the consumer isn't effectively "sold hope." Ideally, they all work together, but in this case, we could see that they did not. The medical guys were properly scientific, cautious, and unwilling to make any product claims until all the evidence was in. The marketing and sales guys were outgoing, looking for action, itching to take great new products to the market. In our case, the medical department wasn't supplying marketing with the trial outcomes, or even the trial timelines. They weren't stonewalling, they were simply operating under the fundamental legal obligations they had to conform to, against which marketing timelines weren't considered important.

Everyone in the building wanted these new game-changing Pfizer products to deliver great patient outcomes and contribute to sales and profits. We helped Pfizer identify this threat, and now, each group appreciates the others' roles and obligations much more clearly. In no small part, this was due to their working on their annual product plans together. Once they got together and talked through the process and burdensome demands of getting the new product to market, collaboration soared, and the plans began to jell.

Communication is a topic unto itself. One of our clients started a health-care company. The two founders were very different, but they worked together well. Their secret? They set aside a half-hour every day to sit down in an anteroom and talk. Just talk.

You can't expect even a like-minded business partner to think and act the way you do. Some partners will communicate the way you do, some won't. Some will make their displeasures known face-to-face, others will smile in apparent agreement in a meeting and then make an unexpected reversal later. That may be gamesmanship, that may be cunning, or it may be that they simply come from cultures where confrontation is avoided.

It's up to you to find out where they really stand and bridge the gap. We see it in NFL coaches' briefs; the players' heads are physically nodding, but the brains are trying to process information that's actually ambiguous or contradictory. True partnerships are hard. Blending background and cultures are hard, whether your partner is from across town or across an ocean. Communication issues are an item on your list of threats.

## CIA – not what you think it is…

The biggest internal threat we see across all of our clients? We call it CIA. These are the deadly triad of **C**omplacency, **I**ndifference, and **A**pathy. They can rear their ugly heads in you, in your team, in your customers, in your boss. These are the people who don't care about your mission nearly as much as you need them to. Your team has become apathetic. They've assumed you and the mission away. And so, too, has the rest of your organization: they've got their own issues to deal with, so don't expect them to save you from yourself. Some may even go so far as to be jealous of your assignment and wish you failure. It happens. So go back to Andy Grove—be paranoid. FLEX uses interim meetings and X-gaps to check up on individual performances in a peer group setting. It roots out members who have lost their way and helps them get re-engaged. We prepare for the worst, so we'll enjoy the best.

## External Threats

You need to be as curious and imaginative as possible when it comes to identifying threats from outside your organization. Consider the horror of 9/11. In light of this unexpected attack from within, the United States military asked the screenwriters and directors in Hollywood to come up with a fresh list of possible attacks using their big screen imagination. We missed one thing, they said; we don't want to miss another. They were curious, as they should be. It was a sort of red-teaming on a national scale. It was much needed.

The external threats to your mission will depend on the nature of your mission and its timeframe. For example, if your mission is a one-day event, you'll need to consider anything that could disrupt it that day. The weather (I use the Windy App to check for storms and crosswinds), for instance, or your IT connectivity, a missed flight (are there two flights between my flight booking and the sound check?), a bad meal (I eat the plainest of foods before an international travel day), who's working remotely and who's in the office (people you need might suddenly not be available), public events in the vicinity, and guests who cancel. If anything involves a car for transportation, check online for updates on roadwork.

One of our Afterburner events was recently disrupted because the President was in town and the airport was closed. If you're holding your event at a large hotel or convention center, you'll expect the hotel or event staff to do the advance work; but what if they have new staff or didn't understand your brief properly? If you're in charge of the location and its preparation, it's up to you.

If you're giving a speech or presentation, you have to consider whether anything would make the content redundant, or worse. A comedian tells the sorry story of telling a string of great gags about a divisive public figure, only to be met by horrified faces. Did he know the figure had died overnight? Should he have checked? Should he have had other material? Make a checklist of the possible and maybe even crazy external threats to your event, and run through it as a habit.

On a larger scale, external threats are unlikely to emerge without some sort of warning. Competitors nearly always announce launch dates of new products in advance. Service companies nearly always announce new features in advance. What will you do about that? Is that on your checklist?

My first business, CTG Global, was contracted to get people into dangerous situations to deliver humanitarian projects in Afghanistan, keep them healthy, get the job done, and get them out again safely. That was my checklist of threats for us: In-Alive–Out-Alive, and it was entirely up to us. There were no travel agents capable of getting our customers safely to the worksite, overcoming disputed visas or transport interruptions, and either corrupt, overzealous, or overly suspicious officials. To recruit people, we paid extra wages, added extra security, gave them insurance, and maintained a fleet of specially secured vehicles; we valued our people and our clients and we got things done. All this was happening in a cash economy, so securing cash became a daily mission of its own. Back in the office, my partner and I spent most of our time keeping the cash flowing and building and keeping relationships.

You might think the biggest threat to CTG's business was a war, terrorist attack, or tribal dispute. No, the biggest threat was the loss of our reputation. If we could not look after our employees and the people we brought in could not do the assigned job, the UN and other relief agencies would no longer contract with us. So, every CTG assignment started with a two-week no-questions-asked probation period. If a client wasn't happy with a worker, or a worker wasn't happy with a client, the worker could go home. No other personnel firm in the Humanitarian sector operated that way, and no other firm grew as fast or as surely as we did. The point is, we focused on identifying and addressing the core threats, not every threat, and used our FLEX tools to manage them.

The threats to your business will be more obvious but equally dangerous. Obvious sources of threats are the actions of your competitors, like a major price reduction, the kind of self-destructive price dumps, counter-promotions, "10% less if you find a better price," disruption to the supply chain, technology obsolescence, factory capacity or re-tooling, demands for promotional support beyond your immediate budget, strikes, bad public press, and so on. No wonder leaders are overwhelmed and burning out!

This is what we mean by situational awareness, the need to understand your operating environment and what's happening in it and to be ahead of everyone else's decision-making. You never know what's going to happen. The true test of your team's FLEX-ability will be how you adapt to it and reframe threats as opportunities.

## Controllable or Uncontrollable Threats

A client in the nutraceutical space left for a national convention only to arrive with news that new, restrictive rules had been placed on the very ingredient his company was hyping. Faced with what was by all means an uncontrollable event, his team successfully pivoted to an alternate SKU with alternate benefits and launched on time; we had planned for this with them. Why? Because there was a risk the TGA would say no, so we had another product that was 70% less effective but still delivered the impact.

There are controllable threats and uncontrollable threats. Controllable means that the planning team can negate, mitigate, or avoid the threat; that is, the team can take some action so the threat does not take place (negate it), or, if it does, it will not affect the mission because its impact is reduced (mitigated), or the entire mission is planned so that it doesn't matter if the threat is realized or not (avoided). If the team can control a material threat, it should do so as an item in its course of action by including an action specific to the threat. If the team can't control the threat, it becomes a contingency, and there will be a trigger point and action if it happens.

The FLEX process asks you to take action on the things you can control, and to prepare for those you cannot. Let's take the weather, for instance. You've got an outdoor event coming up, and it may rain. You can control that threat either by mitigating it (umbrellas and sturdy marquees) or avoiding it (holding it indoors). But a thunderstorm? If you've gone ahead with the outdoor event, a terrible storm is pretty much uncontrollable. You'll need a contingency plan and triggering events to activate an alternate action.

Most of us are price sensitive in our markets. We can hedge some of the price fluctuations that affect us, like energy, interest rates, currency, and commodities, but not everything at all times. Property developers find themselves particularly exposed to fluctuations in interest rates, or unemployment. The slightest move downward in either of these metrics nearly always triggers a downturn in prices. They have to react.

What about the impact of approvals? A project might get so delayed by red tape that it pushes out the build times past the peak of the market, forcing a company to sell off inventory at a discount. You may be able to mitigate risks in an approval process, but perfectly pick the swings in the market? What's the contingency plan when that threat materializes? If you plan ahead, you have an action. During a downturn in the financial markets, one of our clients used its cash buffer to buy out its entire bank loan on a construction project rather than suffer losses by fire-selling inventory at a discount. Another simply halted construction but stayed current on all indebtedness. An airline will send excess jumbos to the boneyard for storage until demand returns. In Saudia Arabia, the Kingdom Tower came to a halt and stayed that way for several years. With new money, construction restarted.

# Step 3: Identify Your Resources

Let's assume you've locked in your mission objective and clearly defined the threats standing in the way. Now it's time to marshal your resources. But before diving in, keep in mind Daniel Kahneman's planning fallacy: people tend to underestimate the time, costs, and risks involved in their plans because they're overly optimistic. This fallacy usually shows up in two ways: overestimating what you can achieve (ambitious objectives) and underestimating what it will take to get there (time, resources, or effort).

Identifying resources isn't just a box to check—it's an intentional effort to explore every avenue you have at your disposal. Use curiosity and imagination here. With the right mindset, you'll realize you've got far more tools and assets than you think.

Start by focusing on the most pressing threats. Match each one to a resource that can blunt or neutralize it. A single threat might need multiple resources—no problem. Look around your organization and your team. Who's got the skills, expertise, or insights you need? Who's got the bandwidth to support? If you don't know what's out there, take the time to find out. Walk the floor. Ask questions. See who's doing what and how they could help. Your goal here is to uncover untapped potential, both in people and in tools.

Next, think about what you personally bring to the table. Most of us have more connections and assets than we realize; they're just hiding in plain sight. Who have you met in your career, at school, or in social circles? Those relationships are resources waiting to be activated. Don't stop there. Think bigger. What financial resources are available? What about spaces, equipment, technology, or materials? Every organization has its hidden gems—you just need the curiosity to find them and the creativity to put them to use.

Adopt an expansive mindset. The more situational awareness you build within your organization, the more opportunities you'll uncover. And don't forget about relationships outside your team: clients, partners, vendors, alliances, or specialists. These connections can unlock unexpected solutions. People generally like being asked to contribute in meaningful ways. It's human nature to want to be part of a win, so don't hesitate to ask for help—within reason—and be willing to reciprocate when they need support.

Build relationships intentionally. Volunteer for cross-functional projects. When you talk to people, listen more than you speak. Don't just ask them what they do; instead, share your mission and ask how you can help them succeed. That will give you insight into what they're doing now and what they might be able to do in the future. You never know when those connections will become resources you can draw on.

Resources aren't just tools and equipment. They include intangible assets like goodwill, favors, or relationship capital. Tangible resources might include money, AI tools, marketing systems, facilities, or materials. Intangibles—like goodwill from past collaborations or informal alliances—can be just as valuable. Don't overthink it now. You'll revisit your resource list when refining your Course of Action in Step 5.

The key is to think creatively, stay curious, and always keep your mission front and center. With the right mindset, you'll find the resources you need to overcome your threats and achieve your objective.

# Step 4: Plan Your Debrief Actions and Evaluate Lessons Learned

You'll learn a little later in this book--you can jump to Chapter 9 now if your attention span is limited--that we learn from debriefing. Debriefs provide us with specific actions to take on the next mission to improve the likelihood of achieving or improving another mission tomorrow. This is where we put those actions into the plan, to make sure they aren't just spoken about; they're planned, briefed, and executed.

Lessons learned are money in the bank. They're the mistakes not made, time not wasted, and improvements from one week to the next. Lessons learned help you grow by 1% each and every mission. Let me explain.

You'll know as well as I do that there's a big difference between data and knowledge, and between knowledge and wisdom. I may know some facts, and I may know how to do things that involve those facts. But am I wise enough to make the right decisions with that knowledge, and remain curious about the things I am yet to learn and understand?

If we view data or information as noise, we begin to understand the value of knowledge and wisdom. On any given day, the average American consumes approximately 34 gigabytes of data and information; that's the same amount of information your great-grandmother consumed in her entire life; you don't need that much information!! Knowledge helps us contextualize information for our own use; it's situational awareness for you. Wisdom is taking that knowledge and passing it on to others to enhance their situational awareness. Lessons learned equip us with the knowledge and wisdom to improve each plan. Wisdom created from the **application** of knowledge, aka doing something/action, is potent. That's why lessons learned are critical to the planning process. We take the lessons learned and the actions we've taken previously to accelerate the planning process by doing the right things again. We accelerate execution success by avoiding the same mistakes made in the past. That's why it is money in the bank; it's knowledge capital to invest in the future, and if you don't document it and capture it in your plans, it'll disappear faster than a teenager's allowance. Never to be seen again.

A fast-moving consumer goods company (FMCG) has likely launched a thousand products over the years. Those launches almost certainly involved hundreds of people, each of whom had experiences, both good and bad. Those collective experiences are the hard-earned, street-wise knowledges gained from real-world activity and are certainly inherent wisdoms the company should add to their databases. But can they access that wisdom? Given the power of today's databases, computing power, and the rapid adoption of machine learning and AI, we are able to store knowledge in greater quantities than ever before, access it in microseconds, and contextualize it in an instant. But that's a nirvana that seems to have eluded all but a few organizations that seem to wallow in information rather than drive impact through insight. It's not that it can't be built, it's that your people don't demand it. People tend to prefer to work things out for themselves and reinvent the wheel. That's natural, and such curiosity and independence are welcome when we're plowing new ground or where time and money aren't important. But that's a huge waste of time and knowledge when we have the data and the wisdom at our fingertips, yet lack the effort to retrieve it.

With FLEX, lessons learned come from the immediate past. With FLEX, every mission is debriefed so that the specific mission experiences can be lessons learned for the next mission. That's an iterative process, one mission improving the next. That also helps expand our standard operating procedures for the next mission and the next. Taken together, we avoid repeating mistakes, we capitalize on the intelligence and wisdom gleaned from a mission, and we put them into our new plan to help make your mission a success.

If time and resources are important to your organization, then ask three questions:

What standards are relevant?

What relevant experiences are there on the team?

What relevant experiences can we tap into from outside the team?

"Relevant" is the key word here, especially for lessons from outside the team. And as we did with resources, the lessons you're after are only those that are associated with actions and that are fact or experience-based. The ultimate goal is to increase your chances of success and/or help you avoid a threat. You're tapping into a team that knows its business and knows its history—it has situational awareness—so allow yourself to tap into its experience and memory.

## A Lesson Learned We Can All Apply

Have you heard of Hofstadter's Law? It nearly always applies to every major program or project. "It always takes longer than you expect, even when you take into account Hofstadter's Law." That's a lesson learned by any and every company or individual who has embarked on any meaningful mission. But that's not the touchstone of this thought.

One of the lessons we almost always find relevant is to deal with the person, not just the facts. Putting a human face to things can move mountains. Well-known across the pharmaceutical and FMCG industries is the Tylenol story. In October 1982, seven people in Chicago died after taking Tylenol capsules, then the leading painkiller in the U.S. Someone had put cyanide in the bottles and placed them back on the supermarket shelves. Johnson & Johnson might have dealt with this behind the scenes and out of sight. Instead, they did everything as openly as possible and with complete transparency. They took 31 million bottles off the shelf and destroyed them all, then replaced them with bottles that had new, tamperproof packaging and tamperproof caplets. They kept the public and authorities fully informed. In other words, they opted for integrity as a company, kept their people visible to the public, and invested in high principles and standards. It's a lesson of responsibility and success that still resonates to this day.

# Step 5: Assign a Course of Action

Here's where Steps 1 to 4 come together into action. A course of action is essentially a simple three-column list that sets out a series of tasks, assigns each task to an individual, and gives it a due date. It is a classic, who-does-what-by-when (see Table 1). Unlike an objective, an action is binary—it is either done or it isn't. Courses of action include decision points that may trigger different tasks or options, or that allow tasks to be skipped.

Note it's a "course of action," not a checklist of tasks. No one gets excited about tasks—FLEX organizations get excited by <u>action</u>. And never include how tasks are to be done, nor state the obvious, nor restate a standard procedure.

Is this when you hope to nail your outcome in one hit? No. Remember, small wins. Each step in the plan suggests a threat or highlights a piece of missing information, which requires an assessment, which demands a response. As each step is identified, you'll think of the resources and lessons learned to make that step a certainty rather than a hope.

Remember also that our way of planning is iterative; planning never stops. In the end, you'll move to contingency planning and red-teaming. Our process is all about testing and re-testing to iterate and improve the plan quickly and efficiently in the available time. At this point of the process, we are planning as if the world were a perfect place; we'll troubleshoot it later at Step 6 once we have the basic plan laid out.

## A List of Actions

The team will need some form of logic to help identify actions that, done together, will reach the strategic objective. In an air mission, we think of the lines of operation and the associated units needed to complete the mission. For example, if the day's mission is to protect a specific area for a specific time, we would assign actions to various combat, logistics, and communication units. But if the mission is to keep a larger area safe, the lines of operation might include counter-insurgency action, humanitarian action, governance capacity, water infrastructure, telecommunications, shipping lanes—a whole host of responsibilities that have a common purpose need to be independently managed. If you think that each of these lines of operation are strategies directed towards an HDD, you'd be right.

**Table 1. Clear Course of Action (Objective: Complete Migration of Legacy CRM to Hubspot by 31 August 2025, HDD: To be a cloud-native organization by 31 Dec 2025)**

| Who | What | When |
|---|---|---|
| Samantha | Define Migration Objective and Scope | Day 3 |
| Samantha | Assemble Internal Data Migration Team | Day 5 |
| Michael, Jamie | Audit and Assess Existing Data | Day 15 |
| David, Alex | Map Data Relationships | Day 18 |
| David | Develop Migration Blueprint | Day 20 |
| Jamie, Vendor Team | Prepare the New System | Day 25 |
| Michael, Jamie | Secure Legacy Data Backup | Day 30 |
| David, Michael | Pilot Data Migration | Day 40 |
| Samantha | Evaluate Pilot Results | Day 45 |
| Sophia | Conduct End-User Training | Day 50 |
| Samantha | Create Communication Plan | Day 55 |
| David | Execute Full Data Migration | Day 70 |
| Sophia, Alex | Validate Data Integrity | Day 80 |
| Samantha | Launch the New System | Day 85 |
| Samantha, All | Final Debrief and Lessons | Day 90 |

Ultimately, a very limited number of courses of action will deliver the objective one level up into the team leader, and one level down into the execution layer. It's engineered to deliver situational awareness: "One up, one down."

## Process for Creating a Course of Action

A course of action is assigned to every threat. It must be stated clearly and as simply as possible. Who-does-what-by-when is the measure of a proper course of action. How do you create a course of action? First, do it collaboratively. Brief the whole team. Review the first four steps—the mission objective, relevant threats, resources, and lessons learned—then start putting down responses.

Everyone has a chance to get involved and contribute; if there's a challenge getting everyone physically in the room, dial them in on a video call. If part of the execution team is missing, make sure they send a representative. A gap in planning will only deliver a bigger execution gap. Plan individually and together; you'll need to drill down into your area of expertise before sharing your plan with the team. By working out the details individually, then coming together to share your plans, you'll get fresh thinking and a range of perspectives. Conversely, you'll avoid the Type A who hogs the airtime and trips the team into passive receive-only mode. You'll avoid "Groupthink" and the risk that everyone gets behind a poor plan because that's where the energy is—and nobody wants to stand in front of a rolling train with an alternative view. You'll avoid the Abilene Paradox of groupthink, where an entire group agrees on a plan that no individual actually wants.

Always come back together at the same time. Have each team member present their plans so that the nature and purpose of each approach is clear. The mindset here is not to select the best plan, but to create a single plan from the best ideas from the team.

The final step is to resolve the various courses of action into a single plan. To do that, choose the easiest, cleanest, most comprehensive plan, and use it as a base on which you will build the final plan. Mark each task as an action (A), a contingency (C), or delete (X). Finally, once consolidated, have a look at the final plan to clean up the steps, and see what gaps or threats remain.

Again, Flawless Execution uses a *process* because winning, successfully achieving the desired outcomes, the HDD—all of these are to a fighter pilot of paramount importance. No one remembers everything, no one has all the answers. Processes help us cover all the bases. Processes fight forgetfulness, ego and brain farts. Processes structure our work product, and we like all of those benefits. This is a tested, structured way to bring differing ideas and opinions together with a clear line of sight to our HDD.

# AI Sidebar: The Abilene Paradox

Say you're all having a long lunch, it's the holiday season, the conversation is flowing, everyone is relaxed and could happily sit there all day. But somehow sitting in one place all day doesn't seem the right thing to do, so someone asks whether they should get up and walk a mile down to the river to sit for a while at another favorite venue. It's a fair suggestion, but intended more as a half-hearted suggestion than an actual one. But everyone's in a good mood, so they decide to go along with the new plan, even though they're really happy where they are. The party breaks up, people walk in pairs, the rowdy sharing of stories stops, prospective couples angle towards each other, and by the time you arrive at the new venue, half of the people are gone. You've gone from everyone being 100 percent happy to half the party being 50 percent happy and the other half being somewhere else. And all without realizing it, you have succumbed to the Abilene Paradox.

# Aviator Sidebar: Air-to-Air Combat

Let's say our four F-35s are flying a mission in a combat zone, and I'll caveat the data below as unclassified and generic in nature. We expect to engage enemy bandits, and so need decision points leading up to the "merge," the moment at which we would intercept the bandits and engage them, if we can't figure out who they are prior. The first decision point is an expected event that comes at over 100 nautical miles (111 kilometers) out from the merge: we will declare the threat hostile and commit our force to the engagement. As long as the ratio of threats to resources is no more than (an unclassified and example only) 3:1 against us, our four Lightnings should win comfortably. We continue. If they split into two groups, we will do the same. The second decision point occurs at 40-miles (74-kilometers)-to-merge: we fly to a higher altitude to maximize our missile capabilities. About 40 seconds later, at 20 miles (37 kilometers) out, we lock our missiles onto different targets and launch them. Inside 20 miles, things get a little hectic, decision-making is compressed to seconds. My controller is telling me about other bandits that are trying to sneak in while I'm committed to the first group. I'm "Winchester," which means I've run out of missiles and I only have the gun, and I have to see the bad guy up close to use that; I'm all in. How close do these new bandits get before I have to deal with them or "pump out," turn away from this fight, buy some time, build in some distance between me and these two groups before "re-attacking"? We are constantly assessing: range, angles, my altitude, the bandits' altitude, whether the radar is working properly. Am I targeted? Is that "spike" (the indication of another jet's radar in the cockpit) from these bandits? Why is it coming from over there?

These decision points might occur 20 to 30 times in a half-hour mission. At each of these points, we need to know what the options are, who will make the decision, what information they need to do so, and who is providing that information. That decision point is an item on the course of action. The team has to be prepared for them, and the plan ensures they will be.

# Step 6: Confirm Contingency Plans

Standard Mindset: "Everyone has a plan until they get punched in the face."

Fighter Pilot Mindset: "Plan to get punched in the face."

By now, the only thing we haven't planned for are the threats that we cannot control. Now it's their turn. Because we know our standard procedures so well, and we've nailed down the plan for the mission, the last 20-25% of the planning process is spent on contingencies. Your team needs to answer every *relevant* what-if they can think of and be ready to respond dynamically. The keyword here is respond, not react. Having thought of responses, you are already ahead of changing conditions. If you have to react to unknowns in real time, you are already behind. Planning responses to the what-ifs creates time and headspace—and time and headspace are exactly what you need when you have to work through unexpected obstacles—and, as we all know, the road to success is laced with obstacles.

The challenge with contingencies is that anything can happen. If you have a Chicken Little Complex, then everything feels like it's going to go wrong; if you're a devil-may-care type, then you're probably wondering what's the point. The key with contingency planning is to try and identify the sort of likely scenarios in the context of the mission.

Really, contingency planning is a process to prepare yourself emotionally for the unexpected, because let's be honest, when things outside of your control happen, it gets your heart racing. Think of the social media campaign that failed to deliver any impressions, the recalled products due to a manufacturing error, the investment you made the day before COVID hit. Contingency planning is preparing for the likely worst-case scenario, ensuring you have a plan. There is always something you can do when things go pear-shaped; the key is to think about it and prepare for it.

## Contingency–Trigger–Action

To be ready for a what-if, Step 6 asks you to <u>clearly define the contingency</u>, <u>the trigger that highlights to you that the threat has become real</u>, and <u>your pre-planned responses.</u> Most threats will have two triggers: a lead indicator that warns you the threat is very likely, and a lag indicator to announce it's arrived. It's not always possible to have a response to a lead indicator, but it's mandatory to have a response to a lag indicator. In our jets, we get tones when an enemy missile site locks us up with their search radars. We initiate preliminary responses. If we get a second tone, we know the enemy has launched those missiles. Now we're actively responding by pumping out expendables, flares, chaff, or a decoy to distract the missile's "eyes" and yanking the jet defensively to defeat it kinetically. Lead indicators (Trending data). Lag indicators (Uh oh, it happened already).

Rain is a potential threat for a sales event. Your lead indicator is a 24-hour forecast that it will pour on your important day. Start putting your alternative plans on standby. Your lag indicator is the rain itself. Now you must take action using your preplanned responses.

Sometimes there is no lead indicator. Consider freight companies. Contingency planning is nothing new for these operators. Trucks have timetables, but timetables are subject to traffic delays, road construction, accidents on the Interstates, and most certainly weather. A freight company knows that a substantial rise in fuel prices can wipe out an entire profit margin, so they have contingency plans in place for that, too. A lead indicator might be the news that national or regional crude inventories are falling, so the company acts by increasing its tier pricing by 0.1% weekly, explaining the reasoning to its customers. However, there is no such lead indicator for an explosion and fire at a critical refinery. Because of that, the price of diesel fuel instantly rises by 25 percent. With only a lag indicator, you have to take instant action. In this case, the company imposes an immediate freight surcharge for non-metropolitan deliveries to help recover the increase in wholesale prices.

## The Red Team

It would be a remarkable achievement for your team to come up with the perfect plan for any mission, much less a complex mission with numerous contingencies, on the first attempt. It's a difficult task, made more difficult by the inherent tendency for teams to rely too much on their own knowledge, myths, and stories, and tend to be a little too optimistic on the outcomes. That's particularly the case when a team really likes a plan, can "see" it happening, and tastes its success. They've bought into it, they've sunk their emotional capital into it—and they will be blind to its threats. That's something we avoid as fighter pilots and part of what business author Daniel Kahneman calls the "inside view" in his book *Thinking, Fast and Slow.*

What we both need is an outside view. Instead of launching the plan and later having mistakes, have a fresh set of external eyes test it out now before you start. We have a saying, best let someone shoot holes in your plan before the bad guys shoot holes in the jet. Let an outside team tear it apart, find the flaws, confirm or refute your assumptions. They'll think of threats you hadn't thought of and test the baseline data and assumptions. Best of all, they will remove the planning fallacy of optimism. Bring in the Red Team.

Before every single mission we fly, we have an experienced aviator, an individual not involved in planning the mission, run their eye over it to identify any obvious mistakes.

## Invite the Challenge

Bringing in a Red Team without offending someone is no small task. That's why we embrace the fighter pilot mindset of iteration; specifically with red-teaming we say, " Invite the Challenge." By inviting the Red Team into the process, we put ourselves in control and, as such, we're emotionally prepared. We are asking for a critical eye; it's not forced on us, and we want our plan to be *better*. We started this; we wanted the insight. By Inviting the Challenge, we automatically shed defensiveness and turn what could be confrontational into a value-added feedback session. That improves everything, particularly our situational awareness. The Red Team should consist of two to five people who are external to the planning team. If you can only find one person, that would be great! Run with them and don't be shy to use your AI platform too. The Red Team needs to know the context and implications of the mission, see experiences in similar operations, and hear the differing perspectives of customers, competitors, vendors, regulators, etc. In our language, they should have situational awareness of the mission and be able to suggest additional threats, resources, and lessons learned. They cannot be participants in the mission, and they must want the mission to succeed. They're particularly useful in challenging your mission objective's "achievable" component.

It's essential that the Red Team session be held in person or over a live video link. (Every time we've weakened that rule or asked people just to "look over a plan," it hasn't worked. If it's done remotely, there are just too many distractions, and the lack of focus makes the effort nearly pointless.) Hold the Red Team session in a room with minimal distraction so that the focus is on the plan and only the plan. Have the planning team leader present the plan visually in charts, dashboards, and writing. The team leader guides the Red Team through it, but is not talking over their reading and thinking.

Have two of your team members take notes. The Red Team knows you want alternative perspectives. They should ask clarifying questions and then offer comments, one after the other, until they have no further comments to offer. Each comment is offered with the phrase, "Have you considered . . . ?" The two scribes work in rotation, so as not to miss anything when the comments flow quickly. This part is not a debate over whether or not the plan is a good one. There is no place to either attack or defend it. Its purpose is to consider additional thoughts on the mission's assumptions, actions, threats, and impact. There is only one thing you say in response to a Red Team critique, and that is "thanks." This is a one-way conversation.

After the Red Team leaves, the team addresses each comment and adjusts the course of action if and as needed. That's it.

The term "Red Team" has taken on many different meanings for organizations and individuals who "specialize" in red-teaming. But in FLEX, its role and commitment are very simple. We're looking for an unbiased, experienced, valued opinion and an external agent to hold us accountable to our plan. No preparation or specialist expertise is needed. Just be there for the Red Team session.

## The Last Rounds of Planning

There is usually a time gap between the formal planning process's end and the brief's start. Don't waste it. Stay alert to any new data, possibilities, or situations that might prompt you to reconsider some element of the plan. The world is ALWAYS in motion; you want to adapt to it, not react to it. In fact, the plan is only finalized in the acts of writing it up, and delivering it is the brief. That is when all the possibilities have been reduced into a single, clear, coherent course of action.

My partner and I kept honing our plans for CTG Global for eighteen months before finally launching into Afghanistan. Were we poor planners and procrastinators, unwilling to take the plunge? No, I hope not! We just knew that working in a country that at best could be described as "in reconstruction" and at worst as the contested territory of rival warlords was not something to take on lightly. And we were working on those plans in the evenings after our day jobs. When we were finally ready to bring our strategy to life, we switched to CTG full-time, finalized and planned, briefed ourselves on the first daily mission, and continued a daily/weekly/monthly/quarterly cycle of plan–brief–execute–debrief for the next four years.

# Tip: The Six Steps for HDD-building

This was the most challenging part of writing this book! Finding a place to explain how to build an HDD! You need to know about HDDs to understand mission planning, and you need to know how to build HDDs, too! It's really simple. Use the same process and methodologies as you use for Mission Planning, except for Step 5. Instead of Courses of Action, you're creating supporting HDDs. If you find your supporting HDDs look more like actions (binary measures), then stop. Your HDD is a mission objective now, so time to build your mission plan.

Remember, HDDs define the future; objectives define action.

# 7 Brief (Putting Your Plan into Action)

For a team to execute flawlessly, the leader must brief the team and each individual in it. That means that every single person who will be on a mission must be in the briefing room for the brief, no exceptions. Everyone must know—beyond a shadow of a doubt—what to do at each decision point, and what to do if something goes wrong. They must be able to visualize their role in the mission before they go out to deliver it, and that means they have to be there.

Let's get this next thing perfectly clear. The person standing at the head of the room briefing the team on the missions is the leader of the team. He or she may not be the most senior person on the team or the most senior person in the company, but right now, they're the leader of the mission and responsible for delivering the objective; they have the collective situational awareness of the team and they address the team with authority, confidence, certainty, conviction, and without equivocation. One person is standing up in front, the rest are seated. This still functions in today's low-authority leadership environments of the modern era; all we're doing is connecting a leader to an outcome vs. old-school hierarchal leaders of people.

When the brief starts, open planning ends. When the brief starts, collaboration is over, the good ideas factory is closed. You never ask for opinions, never say, "What do you think if we do it this way?" You state things with finality, speak with the aura of invincibility, exude certainty about the plan, and exude a winning attitude about the mission. No one leaves the briefing uncertain of the mission or their roles. No one leaves the room confused or worried. The mission is well-planned, and the outcome is a success.

Which brings us to the second part. With FLEX, the leader delivers the brief with the same care and preparation as the mission itself—because the brief is the mission. A room or virtual space is set up for the purpose, and the mission is laid out on whiteboards or online through simple PowerPoint presentations, usually with lots of pictures and images. The leader "snaps in" the team by revisiting the big picture, the "why," then confirms the mission's objectives, reviews the situation, confirms the standards that apply, and lays out simply and clearly who does what, when, and why, and includes the what-ifs. Everything is scripted. Nothing is left to chance. And, most importantly, the leader checks that each individual knows and understands their roles using inquiry-based communication techniques.

# Pilots say, "Brief the plan, and fly the brief."

Ask a businessperson how their mission went, and they'll answer, "Fantastic, so good. It was amazing." When a sportsperson comes off the field and gets trapped by a roaming mike, they mumble something about a tough game, having played hard and having done well. Ask a fighter pilot how their mission went, and all they'll say is, "We executed the brief." That's it. In our minds, the mission is so tightly tied to the brief that executing the brief is a success! In our world, in the FLEX world, we brief the plan and fly the brief. We would no more fly a mission without a brief than go to work naked.

In his poem "The Hollow Men," T.S. Eliot talks of the shadow that falls between conception and creation. You do not want to stay in that shadow. Sadly, too many of our clients do. For too many of them, there's never a brief, only ambiguous meetings out of which come people still questioning whether the plan will work. Rather, coming out of a briefing, people should feel accountable and aligned, certain of the mission and its success, and have zero questions about the leader's expectations and the team's actions. And most of all, ready—even eager—to execute. If not, they've stayed in Eliot's shadow for way too long.

# The Leader's Brief

As Celine Dion said, "It's not about the song; it's about the singer." If you don't think that's true, think about the difference between the song "Poker Face" at after-work karaoke vs. Lady Gaga in concert. Both "live" with the same words, beat, and melody, but the experience is vastly different! The briefing is the same, as are the words, the beat, and the melody. Now is the time for you—as a leader—to perform (don't worry, you don't need a good singing voice to be FLEX; you don't even have to dance, though it'll definitely make an impact if you do).

The leader's brief is a vital step forward. The plan is a good plan, or it wouldn't have made it this far. It's now up to you to deliver it with conviction and certainty. This is not just a ceremony, and it's certainly not just another meeting. It has to be done well for the mission to be done well. It is the only one-way communication that takes place in all of FLEX. You are no longer facilitating or canvassing for ideas or opinions—you are delivering. You have control. It is time to set your style, reinforce the culture and the standards you want for the team, and ensure everyone understands expectations, roles, and responsibilities all the way to the execution rhythm. Nothing is now collaborative. It's your show.

Note also that "leader" refers to the person leading the mission and thus leading the brief. That doesn't mean it's the most senior person in the room or in the company hierarchy. I can't tell you how often I've led a four-ship of jets, and a pilot with me flying #2, #3, or #4 outranks me. That is perfectly OK. I'm leading a team that has specific talents and has come together to deliver very specific, discreet outcomes (objectives). Our rank is immaterial. We're all focused on the higher purpose of winning the mission; egos are checked at the door.

One more thing. As the leader, you're assuming full accountability for the mission objective. You own the failure and share the success. The team respects you for that and fully appreciates the need for a person in command. Any division of authority would, at this point, weaken the team. The briefing marks the moment you are it, and with it comes respect. You are accountable for leading their mission, and the team is accountable for their roles in it. And don't forget that good followership is as critical as good leadership.

At the end of George Clooney's briefing of the heist in *Ocean's Eleven*, a team member asks the obvious question: if we get past security, through the locks, into the cage, down the elevator, past the armed guards, into the vault, invisible to the cameras, and get the cash . . .we just walk out untouched? A pause from Clooney as Ocean, then, "Yeah." "Oh . . . [nod] . . . OK." Respect for Ocean's authority has been expressed, and the team understands the plan.

Another note. Typically, the more dangerous the mission, the more precise the elements in the brief. In hospitals, surgeons and head nurses are becoming more and more meticulous in their pre-operative briefings. In the Agile management approach, we see this as well—it will be a stand-up and likely more pointed and sharper briefing when you're dealing with a Program Increment (PI) rather than a routine change. All this works with FLEX. A FLEX briefing is clean, clear, and precise.

# B-R-I-E-F the Plan

The plan for the mission now becomes the content of the brief, and the tone changes. While during the planning phase you're asking the team for ideas, during the briefing phase you're declaring the results. Alone or with your team, you have now reconciled any disagreements or uncertainties and merged the best into one ironclad mission plan. You now have it, and you will present it to the team. Standards support performance, and the easiest way to perform as a leader is to be prepared and follow a standard briefing format that covers everything you need to do in order to transition into execution. The word "BRIEF" is a mnemonic we use to keep us on track and to remind us that we must present the brief in the proper sequence.

**B**ig picture

**R**estate (mission objective)

**I**dentify (threats/challenges and resources)

**E**xecute (your course of action)

**FLEX**ibility (contingencies)

If that sounds like the steps in your mission planning, you're right. FLEX keeps things simple by repeating the same thought patterns across the plan, the brief, the execution, and the debrief.

So let's break it down.

# Big Picture (Why)

You always start by explaining why a mission even exists. Repeat your organization's High-Definition Destination (HDD) and the strategy, organizational culture, and identity to get there. Having the big picture makes all the difference, particularly because missions are dynamic and team members have the discretion to exercise options based on the real world, and that can be often. They have to know what this mission, if successful, will support. They need to have this "big picture" situational awareness. That way, when decisions have to be made on the fly—and they will—they can be executed with the right impact in mind.

# Restate the Mission Objective (What)

The way your brain focuses its neural energy or "firepower" is using "big to small" theory; we need to understand the big picture or gist of something before we understand the small pieces, or the details.

That's why we start by restating the mission objective: what is the impact we are trying to achieve? It reassures everyone that nothing has changed since the planning phase, or, if it has, what and why. Remember to use words that are clear and unambiguous, and have objectives that are measurable, achievable, and aligned. And don't assume that your people get it right away. Repeat the objectives, then meet their gaze and look them in the eye. That eye contact gets them focused and their brains engaged.

Every mission and action in that strategy will have an impact on the team, on the organization, and on its environment. Think of all of this as one great interconnected system. The team has to know why this mission is important.

# Identify Your Threats and Resources (Who)

This part includes the major threats you've identified and the resources you've attached to deal with each. Start by listing the top threats that the team will have to watch out for, then list the resources that will help them overcome the threats and reach their objective. It's a recap, not a discussion, but it must give your team enough situational awareness to make the right decisions as threats materialize. This section is about transitioning from a thinking mindset to an action mindset.

# Execution—Who Does What by When (How)

This is where three quarters of your briefing time should be spent. This is why the team is in the room. This is when they will reaffirm their assignments from the planning phase. How will we get the mission done? Here you will present the Courses of Action items to the team. Make this a clear, methodical listing of the actions each person is expected to take. When you're done, they must fully understand that the actions given to them are their responsibilities alone. The whole team hears the assignments so they will all know what each other are doing. They all know how those actions will interact with their own, and therefore they can see how they might support each other as wingmen.

The aim here is to make it simple. It's not to tell each team member to fill 9 to 5 with work. Remember, in a fighter squadron, flight leaders don't want their pilots to have to think very hard when they're engaged in combat. We want their minds to be as clear as possible for the actual engagement, to be free to focus on the planes and missiles they're up against, and not trying to remember their next steps in the mission.

# Timelines (When)

The best briefs take the form of a simple decision timeline. For example, say the jets are en route to the target. At five minutes out, we will arm our weapons. At two minutes out, if all looks good, the flight leader will call us to commit and head in. Those are decision points, not yet actions. If the operating conditions are not right, then the flight leader will make the decision to adapt or abort the mission. All this is scripted before takeoff, laid out on the decision timeline, and briefed to us, point by point. We don't know what will happen, but we do know what we will do when it does happen.

Part of the course of action and the brief will be the timing interval for the X-Gap meetings, the regular team check-in for any changes to the plan and the progress against the timeline. As said before, we want to make sure execution stays on its very unique timeline, and put in corrective action if does not.

# FLEXibility—Ready for Contingencies (What-If)

How many plans call for a team member to do something, yet are silent on what happens if things go wrong? The FLEX plan covers threats to the desired course of action—and defines what to do when things go wrong. The FLEX brief covers threats. Controllable threats are listed and mitigated as part of the core plan itself. Uncontrollable threats are identified as contingencies, and for each contingency, a possible action is indicated.

You present this section at the end of the brief. Clearly restate the threats or contingencies, then the triggers that force a decision on that threat, and the actions that flow from those decisions. Your team members can check their plan to know what actions to take, but they have to recognize the trigger when it happens in real-time.

# A Brief's Last Words

A fundamental principle of briefing is that everyone understands the expectations and the plan—that's why we "finish with finesse." We end the brief by covering three things of equal importance: <u>questions from the team</u>, <u>checking that all is known and well</u>, and a <u>positive call to launch the mission</u>. A brief that ends well is the right launchpad for your mission.

<u>There are two simple rules for the questions.</u> Before you answer a question, repeat it for the group. Second, never repeat something negative. If the question has a tinge of doubt to it, confirm it as a positive. Remember Clooney: Are we just going to walk out with $150 million in cash? Yeah!

<u>A brief delivered is one thing. A brief absorbed is another.</u> Be sure your team knows exactly what it has to do. How you discern that is a question of personal style. Some will eyeball each person in the room in search of any lack of conviction. Some will ask questions. As a fighter pilot briefing my team, I call out a question, pause for a response, and then pounce on one person for the answer. "Pose, pause, pounce" shifts my team from passive receivers of information into engaged seekers of knowledge. If this becomes practice, every member of the team is more attentive during the brief, because they know there's a good chance they'll be asked a question at the end.

<u>And what about a closing call to inspire your team?</u> Absolutely. This can be anything from a Bear Bryant-styled inspirational speech or a quiet, confident, matter-of-fact ending. You know your team and what they need to hear better than we ever could. Go soft or go hard, but your last words should be positive.

# Chapter

# 8 Execute (Keeping People, and Yourself, to the Plan)

One reason that so very few plans survive reality is that people are human and they don't always stick to the plan. They lose focus...Distractions lead to a 27% increase in the time it takes to complete a task while causing 2X as many errors, and that's just one person's distractions—extrapolate that across a team! Digital distractions account for most of our execution inefficiencies today, and they have the added effect of depleting our energy and overdosing us with dopamine, which leaves us fatigued, agitated, and deriving little pleasure in the small wins that are so important for success. So, the question we also have to ask is, if I'm being distracted so often, who else am I distracting?!

There are other reasons, some of which are beyond our control. The by-product of a perpetually connected "always-on" culture we live in, is being overwhelmed that there's too much to do and not enough time to do it. The root cause for the majority of execution (in-the-moment) failures is task saturation. There's too much going on, too much interference, too many interruptions, too much information, and there's never enough time for one mortal to manage things and get hard things done.

At the other extreme, inactivity can be the culprit. Plans stall out and accidents happen when there's not much going on at all. There are not enough stimuli to keep the mind active and focused. Either way, you need to protect against this loss of focus and keep people on the plan. We worked with a terrific sales team who supported each other to the hilt. Being Gen X, Y, and Z-heavy, they used text messaging for everything, from sharing new leads and information to giving each other encouragement and congratulations. It was a stream of positive reinforcement and sometimes useful data. Yet, when they sat back and looked at what was happening, they realized the cost of those interactions may have outweighed the positives. Yes, the new information was coming in "live," but was it distracting them from their immediate task? They were responding to each other in real-time, and that's usually good, and they were adjusting their course in real-time, and that could be good, too, but was it? Was it thoughtful, or reactive? Were they in the present, or just a bunch of thumbs flying over a cell phone, texting and texting again? The reality was that this team constantly pulled each other away from their objectives, increasing workload and busy-ness and reducing their impact on the business.

# Why People Lose Focus

Since our last book, there's been significant research on the topic of distraction. We're not the experts on why you get distracted; we do know our stuff, though, when it comes to staying focused and creating that flow state through the concept of a "Mission Bubble."

To help you understand why it's important to schedule focus time (what we call your mission bubble), browse below to gain some insight into what some of the world's top thought leaders have to say about focus and distraction.

## 1. Dopamine and Immediate Rewards (Nir Eyal, author of *Indistractable*)

Hardwired into our evolutionary biology, and more simply to ensure we survive and propagate as a species, our brains are wired to seek out immediate gratification, which distractions offer in abundance. When we receive a notification, a "like" on social media, or an email, it activates the **dopaminergic system**, giving us a brief sense of pleasure. This immediate reward is far more compelling than the delayed gratification of focusing on a long-term task or goal. According to Eyal, digital platforms are designed to exploit this neurological pathway, using **variable rewards** to keep us coming back for more. The unpredictability of these rewards (similar to a slot machine) creates a subconscious feedback loop that actually encourages distraction!

## 2. Cognitive Load and Fatigue (Daniel Goleman, author of *Focus: The Hidden Driver of Excellence*)

Sustained focus requires the **prefrontal cortex**—the area of the brain responsible for decision-making and impulse control. Continuous focus can lead to **cognitive fatigue**, making it harder to maintain self-control and resist distractions. Goleman points out that in modern work environments filled with constant digital interruptions, the brain's capacity for attention is overtaxed. As a result, we gravitate toward distractions that offer a quick mental break. The shift to more enjoyable, low-effort tasks like checking social media or chatting with a colleague is a form of mental rest.

## 3. Default Mode Network (Cal Newport, author of *Deep Work*)

At the risk of oversimplification, the brain runs two networks, effectively on and off. These are called the Task Positive Network (TPN), which activates when you are focused on a task, and the Default Mode Network (DMN), which activates when you are not focused on external tasks. The DMN encourages mind-wandering and daydreaming, providing a mental break from focused work. Newport argues that this mode, while often necessary for creativity, can become a source of distraction when over-engaged by technology. The allure of constantly switching between tasks feeds this neural network, making it harder to engage in the kind of sustained, deep work that leads to high productivity.

## 4. Digital Minimalism (Tristan Harris)

Tristan Harris, a former Google design ethicist and co-founder of the Center for Humane Technology, describes how digital platforms are intentionally designed to distract us. He calls this the **"attention economy,"** where tech companies compete for our limited cognitive resources. Harris explains that algorithms are crafted to exploit psychological weaknesses, making it incredibly difficult to stay focused. He advocates for **digital minimalism**, a practice of intentionally minimizing distractions by controlling technology use.

Basically, you're hardwired to be a distracted mess, which is where FLEX is really useful! It's designed with these, some say human performance "design flaws," we say human nature, to be tamed and managed by ALWAYS starting every conversation, meeting, or stand-up with the desired objective and impact in mind.

# The Sophomore Risk

Sometimes, people who ought to know better just aren't paying enough attention to what's going on. Overconfidence leads to cut corners, false assumptions, or just bad judgments. Research into Air Force accidents reveals a curious statistic. Errors are more likely to be made by pilots with four to seven years of experience than by either the newest pilots or the aging pilots. Why is that? Take a look at Figure 14. The dotted line shows that pilots are constantly building up their skills and experience. Unfortunately, the curved line says their confidence and their lack of focus rise even more steeply. In the beginning, new pilots are fully engaged in the new experience and make good decisions even when facing very new situations. Some call this "rookie smarts." But four years later, they're in a danger zone, they think they're invincible, that they know it all—until they come to their senses and again realize you have to pay attention if you're flying a 45,000-lb. machine with 50,000 lbs. of thrust at 1,200 miles per hour. Maybe they've had a couple of close calls, maybe they learned from a tragedy suffered by a squadron mate.

We see that same cycle at universities. As a first-year freshman, you're a little clueless and therefore cautious. Having survived that, you look down from the heights of the second year. You're confident, cocky even. You're a sophomore—literally a "wise fool" in ancient Greek.

It's the same at work—you come in new and fresh, and your eyes are wide open, looking for opportunities, for traps, and for assurances. As soon as you're comfortable, you start to take things for granted, perhaps a little too often. It only takes a few mistakes to get called back in line, because now, for the first time, your performance doesn't match your potential. But nothing's fatal, we can keep going. We get through the sophomore hubris and move on. And if we do, the wisdom and experience kicks in and we can begin to lead again—we're the old pilot.

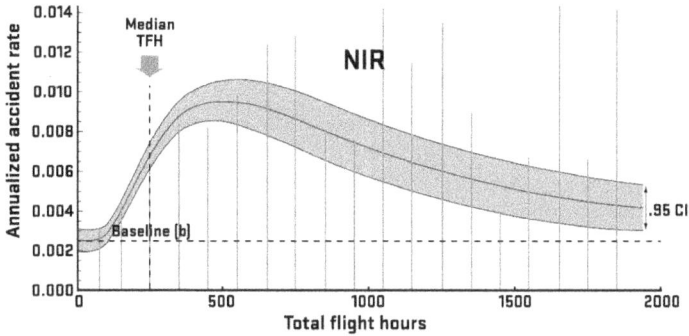

*Figure 14. Aviation accidents vs. pilot experience. FAA*

# Are You Leading a Business or Busyness? The Saturation Risk

"Hey, what's happening here?" Last words spoken by the distracted and task-saturated Captain of Eastern Airlines 401, seconds before crashing into the Florida Everglades, 29 Dec. 1972.

The standout, most significant risk to flawless execution—or any execution—is the silent killer called task saturation. What is task saturation? It's the PERCEPTION that you have too much to do and not enough time nor tools or resources. I deliberately capitalize perception, as your feeling of overwhelm or burn-out is mostly an "own goal." You feel it, usually when it's too late. It overwhelms you, and whether that feeling is real or imagined doesn't matter. You're not thinking straight. You're not performing the way you and your team need you to. You may let someone down, or worse. Most of us are unaware of it when we reach that state of mind, and in our fighter pilot world, far too many task-saturated pilots fly their jets into the ground.

In business, task saturation manifests itself in any number of ways. Very common: far too many people wear the look of overwhelming "busyness" as a perverse badge of honor. You know the ones. They have a to-do list that goes on for two pages. They pull an all-nighter before a killer presentation. They jump on cross-continent flights to chase one more meeting, to make up for a problem that was really someone else's fault. They like to be in three places at one time—two virtual and one physical. Their calendar is booked back-to-back from 7 a.m.-7 p.m. That's one hell of an important person right there. It feels so good to be so valuable, so needed. No matter that their performance is plummeting, errors are climbing, their desk looks like a battalion of ants tracking honey, and their inbox is littered with 1,000s of unread emails.

Task saturation in business is a sugar hit; it's nothing to be proud of. Pilots learn that lesson the hardest way of all, seeing a comrade and mate lose their life for no good reason. Every old fighter pilot has lost a close friend who flew a perfectly good jet into the ground. They were good pilots, and if you asked them how they were five seconds before impact, you'd have got a smiling thumbs up. But they died task-saturated, and never knew it.

The U.S. Air Force has done a lot of work identifying the tells of a task-saturated pilot. Pilots consistently say they feel great when asked what they feel when they feel stressed. Of course they do. When the human body feels as if it has too much to do but nonetheless has to do it all, our chemical survival mechanisms kick in. First, dopamine and those feel-good endorphins hit us, and we feel great, energized, ready to climb that mountain and skip down the other side. It's a wonderful feeling, but it lasts as long as this sentence. Before long, the feel-good endorphins fade out and our bodies' natural ways of dealing with stress become oversaturated. Our hypothalamus triggers a stress response and releases corticotropin-releasing hormone (CRH). CRH stimulates the pituitary gland to release adrenocorticotropic hormone (ACTH), which then prompts the adrenal glands to secrete cortisol into the bloodstream. It's a highly complex biologic reaction; however, the effects on our health and well-being can be devastating. Nervous tension kicks in, we become fatigued, exercise becomes too hard, our immune system is working overtime, we eat energy-producing sugars and carbohydrates, which triggers an insulin response, which makes us even more fatigued, and we spiral down into burn-out, depression, you get the idea.

# Overcoming Task Saturation and Keeping People to the Plan

Whatever the type of task saturation, the results are not good. Missions fail, personal dreams are blunted, careers and even lives are lost. Pilots know task saturation and prepare for it as part of our plan. We use our checklists, focus on our performance indicators, and cross-check those instruments with absolute determination. Thankfully, we have a wingman, and we watch out for each other. Our wingman checks for blind spots and signs of task saturation. We pilots never go anywhere without a wingman. It's all part of our plan.

When you sense it—if you sense it—respond by shedding tasks until you have your head back in the game. First things first. One step forward. Fly the plane and take a deep breath.

# A Dashboard, with Primary (Attitude) Indicator and Cross-Checks

In business, the popularity of data dashboards comes and goes. They're in vogue today, not in vogue tomorrow. Not with us. There are about 350 indicators in the cockpit of a fighter or a commercial jet. Nobody can keep track of 350 indicators. The answer is to be able to always see four or five critical indicators, and if there's anything unexpected showing up, to look at the other relevant instruments. The layout of our cockpit digital "dashboard" (Figure 15) was designed and tested and then improved over billions of flying hours by millions of pilots flying under conditions ranging from hardcore combat to the drumbeat of on-time commercial airline schedules. The dashboard is arranged in a hub-and-spoke layout. The central instrument in the hub is our primary indicator, the attitude indicator or "artificial horizon." This tells us that the aircraft is flying with the sky above and the ground below, and that we're straight and level. If we can do only one thing, we focus on this instrument and adjust our wings to keep the plane level. It's also the only instrument that gives us instantaneous feedback, which is why we spend 80% of our time looking at it. It's the one data point that gives an instant response; we control it, and it's action-oriented.

The secondary indicators form the spokes around the hub; these are all lag indicators, what you may call KPI's or OKR's. These are the all-important indicators of the plane's performance—our speed, altitude, and the direction we're headed, plus our trending instruments. The central instrument tells us we're straight and level; the others tell us how we're doing, our results, and whether these are trending the right way. This cluster of instruments highlights the big picture, and when one of these indicators starts to misbehave, we pull up various menus and subsystems on our display to identify the underlying cause. The hub-and-spoke layout of the cockpit keeps us focused on the right things and gives us a cross-check while at the same time showing us how we're doing against our strategy, all with results on the single page. In practice, we scan the dashboard constantly, and every scan passes over the center hub.

How would you or a business keep an eye on four, five, eight, or twelve indicators at a time? Many businesses use dashboards, but there are three standout features to the cockpit-style dashboard that aren't often seen in business.

First, the primary indicator is the largest image and is at the center: you can't miss it. Yours should be too.

Second, all of the indicators are visual. You don't have to read anything when your eyes are rattling at 1,200 miles per hour. You can quickly scan across the dashboard and see that the indicators are where they should be.

Third, and most importantly, if you're off strategy, your instruments will tell you what to do to adjust, correct, and guide you back on course. For each dial, there is a corresponding action to take to move the needle.

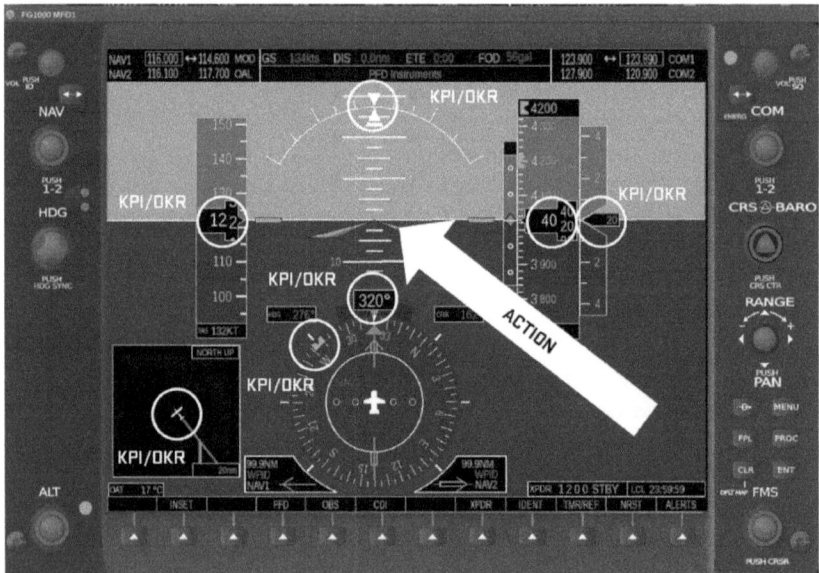

*Figure 15. The Modern digital flightdeck. Speed, height, heading, wings level, position, trending correctly*

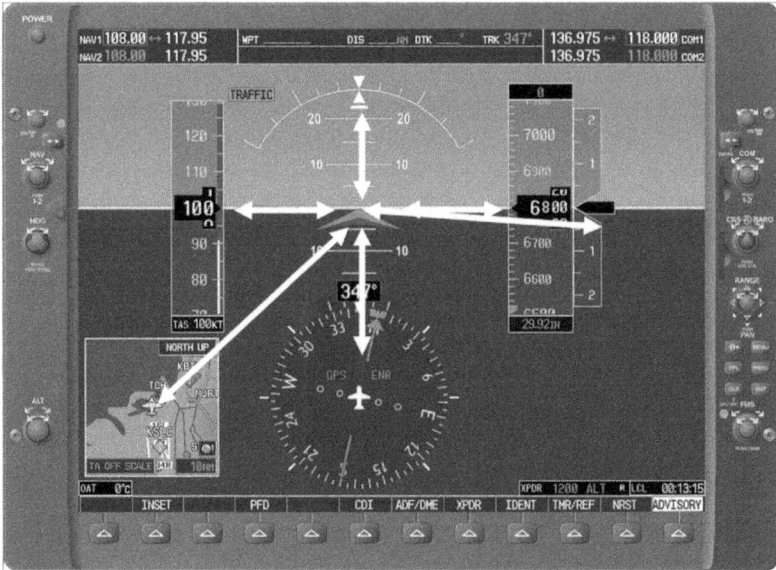

*Figure 16. Cross checks, focused on action, monitoring performance. Analyze, fly, analyze, fly, analyze, fly, analyze, fly, and achieve the mission*

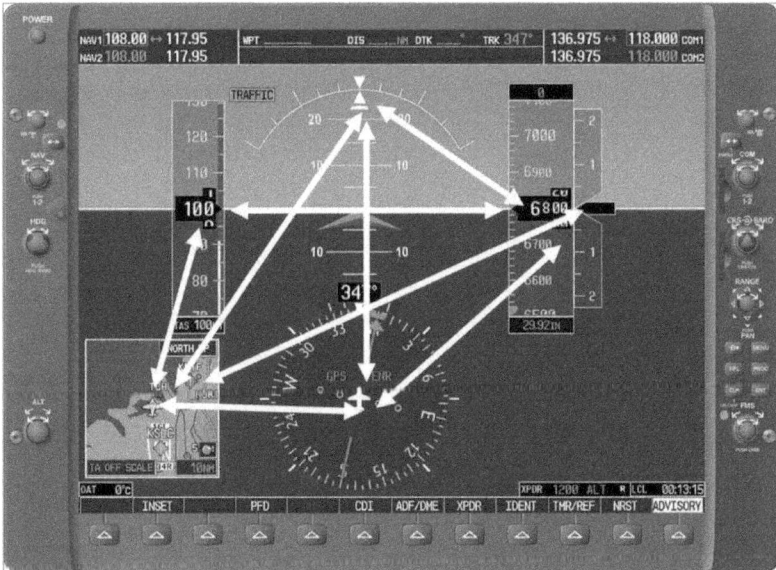

*Figure 17. Business leaders as pilots "chasing the numbers" display, analyze, analyze, analyze, analyze, lose control*

Your business will have its own key performance indicators, and these will make up the company's dashboard. If it's the CEO's dashboard, it will show the CEO's priorities, and in reality, this should be the overarching business dashboard, as the buck stops with the CEO. Some dashboards will have the share price as the large, central instrument; others will have profit, or revenue, or margin, all depending on the company's current strategy and priorities. The main thing is that the instruments must make the status of the business clear to the person using the dashboard at any point in time.

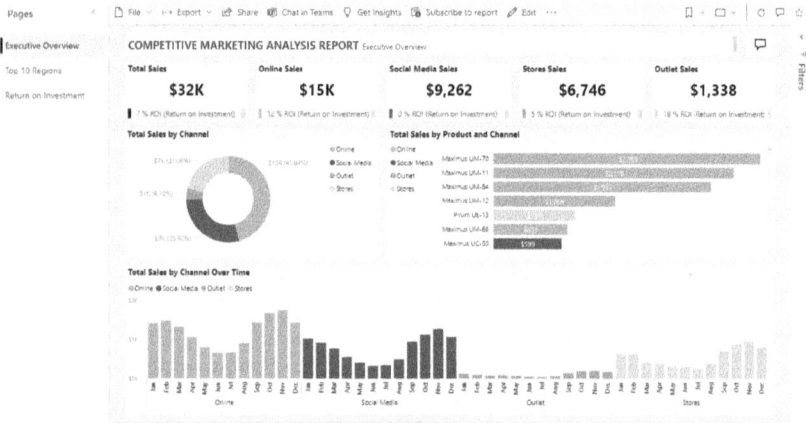

*Figure 18. A Simple Microsoft Power BI Marketing RAG Dashboard*

Should everyone in the company focus on one dashboard and only one? No. People on different layers or within different teams have their own missions, objectives, and dashboard. The indicator that shows them whether their objective is being met should be that team's primary indicator. Other indicators should reveal factors that may contribute to that objective. For example, the CEO's profit indicator may appear as a secondary indicator to be cross-checked, because it may reveal whether unbudgeted resources are available (or not) to help meet your objective.

Many companies want their employees to have one universal dashboard. But that implies everyone in the company has the same priorities as the CEO. That is a deeply flawed strategy; the intention is "One Team, One Vision." However, we need to distill that down to the individual layer so every member of the team knows their number. When they hit their number, they fulfill their part of the contract, which delivers the overall intent. One team means all headed in the same direction, not all doing the same thing. My four-year-old son plays soccer, and I was thinking about this the other day: you don't want to look like a bunch of four-year-olds playing soccer, every player chasing the ball (a singular objective) rather than playing their position (your objective). It's funny to watch, sure, but there's not a lot of ball hitting the back of the net.

# Use Your Wingman!

Remember your task-positive (TPN) and dormant mode networks (DMN)? You can't be on both networks at the same time. You can't think and do simultaneously. Have you tried to fill out a spreadsheet and meditate at the same time? It's impossible. That's an extreme example; however, when we're flying, whether it's in combat, training, or a milk run, taking the jets to a different base, we always have a wingman.

We know that when you're busy flying and leading the mission, it's easy to lose your situational awareness as you focus on engaging a target. That's what our wingman is for; a wingman knows when the lead is busy and keeps tabs on the big picture, and vice versa—the lead keeps the big picture while the wing is busy executing the mission. This leadership dynamic is very FLEXible, the simple rule being that whoever has the best situational awareness at any point in time has the lead.

If it's the wingman, there's a formal handover of the leadership role from the formation leader, who either points ahead if the wingman can see hand signals or calls "press" on the radio; once the formation leader has situational awareness again, the wing hands the lead back again. It's dynamic and ensures our leaders avoid tunnel vision and heading off on tangents that fail to deliver the mission objective.

With two minds and two sets of eyes and ears looking out for each other, we exponentially increase the probability of success of each mission. Call it mutual support, call it a double act, call it whatever you want, but the idea is the same: each pilot keeps an eye out for the other's blind spots. These may be literal, behind the aircraft, or metaphoric, the cognitive biases we all have, that we're unaware of, that lead to flawed decision-making. When two people are in a meeting, you hear more things. When two people go to a meeting, they are far more likely to plan ahead for it, to consider the threats and contingencies. They are likely to role play, challenge each other, negotiate better, follow up with more enthusiasm. In sales, we are often so immersed in the conversational details that we lose the big picture. Having two sales reps in a meeting, one doing the talking (the action brain) and the other observing and keeping an eye on the big picture (the thinking brain), helps you both maintain your situational awareness.

Many executives have enjoyed the benefits of a true working partnership, or a trusted second-in-command, a 2IC, to take over the reins when needed. Co-founders Scott Farquhar and Mike Cannon-Brookes of Atlassian, the teamwork software company, shared the CEO role from the firm's startup days to its 2016 listing on the New York Stock Exchange. They shared the workload and the stress of building a business, yet took the breaks they needed, with one of them always in the office to keep things going. True partnerships can be invaluable, and we fighter pilots take that one step further. We don't go anywhere—anywhere—without a wingman. We don't fly a mission, we don't go out at night, and we don't take on important roles or personal missions without having someone by our side. Your wingman may be a life partner in your family or a formal business partner. It may be someone with whom you share experiences, or someone you work alongside within your company or your community. Wingmen know each other's roles and objectives, know the threats to those objectives, and know how and when they can support each other.

This mutual support is less an action item and more a fighter pilot mindset that people on the teams share. It starts with situational awareness. Yes, there is that mission awareness, but there's also an awareness about the person you're supporting: their fears and motivations, critical tasks, and what will make or break them. Without that people awareness, you're a passive observer rather than an active wingman.

Despite what you see in the movies, wingmen are not always physically close. Sometimes the wingman is back in the home office. Truck drivers, couriers, and cabbies typically work solo, and that can be as frustrating and as tiring as their days are long. Groendyke Transport and Sears Home Services are two American organizations that saw the problem and, as well, a solution. Their drivers needed wingmen, and the most natural wingmen for their drivers were their dispatch operators. These experts knew what the drivers were doing at all times (or should be doing), had the personal skills to check in with them every now and then with well-needed banter, and had the technology at hand to follow their progress. All the dispatchers needed was a little extra time to help out. In the end, by making a small investment of extra time in support of this system, Groendyke gave the dispatchers the time they needed to support their drivers, which quickly paid off with more reliable deliveries, happier drivers, and fewer accidents.

It's one thing to be aware of something, another again to say something. The U.S. Coast Guard has studied the causes of 389 marine casualties in 1998–99. In 68 percent of cases, it wasn't that the critical information wasn't available or known. It was that either the people who had the information didn't recognize its importance and the need to share it with others, or they assumed that the others already had the information. Some call this the "common knowledge effect," knowledge so common that everyone assumes everyone else knows it, but most are wrong. Overcoming this issue is part of the FLEX mindset: don't be shy about speaking up if you see something that may be a problem.

You might have noticed by now that "defensiveness" has no place in a FLEX mindset. If you think speaking up in a team room or partnership is hard, try it in surgery. That's where the line holds firmest; we've trained surgeons to be comfortable saying: "Make sure you all let me know if you see me do anything dumb, different, or dangerous." "See something, say something," you might say. This is what leading in the moment is all about.

# Task Shed – Stop Doing Things that Aren't Delivering an Impact

It takes self-discipline to stay focused through our daily cacophony of personal and work meetings, calls, and emails. It's even harder now with our glued-to-hand smartphone and its world of alerts, distractions, and temptations. It has become ever more critical now to be able to cut through a task list and shed whatever you don't really have to do.

With FLEX, you have a wingman to help keep you focused, to help shed tasks, and to do the tasks you can't. If you need to, work with your wingman and problem-solve how to shed tasks and how to tap into other resources. On a daily basis, focus on your objectives, then look at what you have to do and what you can shed. Consider the following:

- Turn off your phone or put it in another room
- Close your laptop
- Write down your objective on a piece of paper, away from a digital distraction (or download the mission planning worksheet from the Afterburner website!)
- Write down three actions you can do right now to inch closer
  - Action 1: Must Do – Things that the law, your boss, your standards, or an emergency require you to do. You may not like them, you may

rather do other things, but there's no avoiding these, so best do or delegate them as quickly and as clearly as possible.

- Action 2: Should Do – Your core job. The missions you're on, that take planning and diligence, and that your performance will be judged on—by you, your family, your boss, or your partners. Plan your days and weeks around these.
- Action 3: Nice to Do – These would definitely be worthwhile in the perfect world, but not at the expense of your core job. Things that contribute to the plans of others, to your learning, to your relationships. Do them by all means, but in gaps that emerge in your core program. The "nice to do's" are a real trap because on their own they seem worthwhile, but together they're a procrastinator's Christmas. Use them to keep your activity menu fresh, not as the whole menu.

Compare these priorities with your own time management approach and see what approach would suit you best.

# Checklists – Simplify Your Execution

Most people hate checklists. They can be painstaking. They're not much fun. It somehow feels beneath us to use a checklist, as if we can't think on our own! It's an embarrassment. It runs counter to deeply held beliefs that the truly great among us—those whom we aspire to be—can handle complexity and high-stakes situations. The truly great are daring. They improvise. They do not have protocols and checklists. So why do we need them?!

Maybe our idea of heroism needs updating. Of all the things you'll read about in this book, debriefs and checklists stand out as two bedrock fundamentals in the fighter pilot community—but they are as rare as hen's teeth in our personal and business lives. Of the two, the checklist is like the poor cousin at the ball. Everyone gets excited about a nameless, rankless debrief, with all the impact on learning and culture it can carry, but very, very few people get excited about a checklist.

So, why do we love checklists? Using a checklist means we're getting ready to fly. Working through a pre-flight checklist calms our nerves and puts us on the same frequency as our crew, our team, and our commander. It standardizes the mundane and the routine, so we avoid silly and preventable errors, and it also calms our nerves and emotions when we have to think quickly in an emergency situation. Picking up an emergency checklist gives us time to think through what-ifs and how we will respond. By using our checklist, we know that all the basics are in order, which gives us the headspace to drill down on the complexities of our mission and the creativity we'll need to solve its problems. Think of it this way: checklists shed tasks while keeping you on task with the mission. Far from being a poor cousin, our checklists are our wise elders.

If I wrote another book, it would be *Checklists Are Not for Dummies*. Three examples come to mind. In his 30-year Air Force career, one of our pilots twice flew without his checklist. Both times, nothing went wrong, there were no emergencies, no accidents. There was no cause for him to find his checklist, and if there had been, he probably would have known what it said, anyway. But he couldn't do what he was sent out to do. He totally missed the mission's objective. Why? Not having his checklists threw him off. His patterns were disrupted and so too was he. He couldn't get his head in the game. It derailed his thinking. He felt task-saturated during the whole flight, hobbled by the nagging perception that something was not in order. Nothing went wrong, except he didn't achieve the mission. Is that how you measure success in your business? Is the goal "well, nothing went wrong" or "we must hit this production target"? Without checklists, you'll likely achieve the former, you'll struggle to hit the latter.

In 2008, Harvard Public Health Professor Atul Gawande and his team researched a hypothesis that said that checklists in the OR would help reduce avoidable deaths and complications. After excluding other factors, they found that deaths occurred in 1.5 percent of the operations that didn't use a checklist, but in only 0.8 percent of the operations that did—a 47 percent reduction. Literally hundreds of lives were being saved. They also found that serious complications fell from 11 percent to 7 percent of all operations—a 37 percent improvement. Nobody expected that sort of magnitude. Professor Gawande was so astounded he wrote a book, not on public health, but called *The Checklist Manifesto*. Needless to say, checklists are now mandatory for surgery in those hospitals and in many others.

In our world, they came about earlier. Checklists have been a standard for pilots flying airplanes since 1935 when a prototype Boeing B-17 Flying Fortress crashed at Ohio's Wright Field due to a stunningly simple pilot error. After takeoff, the plane's nose just kept angling up—it didn't level off at all—and eventually the plane was almost vertical, stalled, and dropped back to Earth. The Air Force's best test pilots had forgotten to unlock the plane's elevator controls, they couldn't move the nose up or down—one simple step in a hundred steps. The Air Force finally realized that, when confronted by the forest of procedures and the many instruments needed to fly a modern aircraft, even their best people would make mistakes. Checklists have been mandatory ever since. With them, young and inexperienced people can operate expensive machinery in complex situations. Without them, mistakes are certain.

Finally, let's go back to the movies. *Apollo 13* captured the life-saving utility of checklists when aviator Jim Lovell found himself in command of a spacecraft 200,000 miles (321,800 kilometers) from Earth with barely enough battery power to light a flashlight. NASA was facing what could have been one of its greatest disasters and possibly the end of its space program less than a year after the 1969 moon landing. Flight director Gene Kranz, he of "failure is not an option" fame, helped keep Lovell and his crew calm, while trying to solve the problem. Ken Mattingly, the astronaut originally slated to fly the mission, was put to work in a simulator to figure out how to fire up Apollo 13 on a AAA battery. He worked for hours in a race against time, trying sequence after sequence, failing again and again. Finally, with everything in the simulator powered down or turned off, and with next to no time left, he finally found a solution. The sequence was transcribed into a simple, step-by-step checklist, and sent to Lovell. It saved Lovell and his crew, the mission, and the NASA space program. The Apollo 13 story proved once again that a checklist beats task saturation, simplicity beats complexity. The checklist got them home.

# Rules for All Checklists

Failures in offshore drilling have received a lot of warranted publicity in the last decade. Failures on land are even more common, if less damaging. One international energy company tested the blowout preventers on its active drill pipes every two weeks—until one of the company's best drill operators accidentally sheared the pipe during a test. On investigation, the company found the operator had survived 38 close calls in fewer than a hundred previous tests. The tests were routine, but also dangerous. The operators just didn't focus and didn't learn from the near misses. After implementing checklists, their focus returned, and there have been no incidents or close calls since.

There are two critical rules for a checklist: keep it simple, and use it. The best way to ensure a checklist is simple and used is for the people who use it to be the ones who write it. Say you've got a team who has done more than their share of product launches and launch events, but there have been a few simple errors of late and you want them to consider a checklist. Or perhaps you've got teams of experienced, frontline operators working on shale oil fracking, offshore wells, coal mine draglines, geoseismic testing. If you walk up to any of these teams with a nice sheet of laminated paper and say, "Hey guys, could you follow this checklist from now on?" would they take notice? Rather, it would be much better if you explained that checklists were proven to save lives, time, and money, and that it was up to them to create the checklists that work for them. That's how the best checklists are created and how they get used. Get specialist help by all means, but don't just deliver the end result.

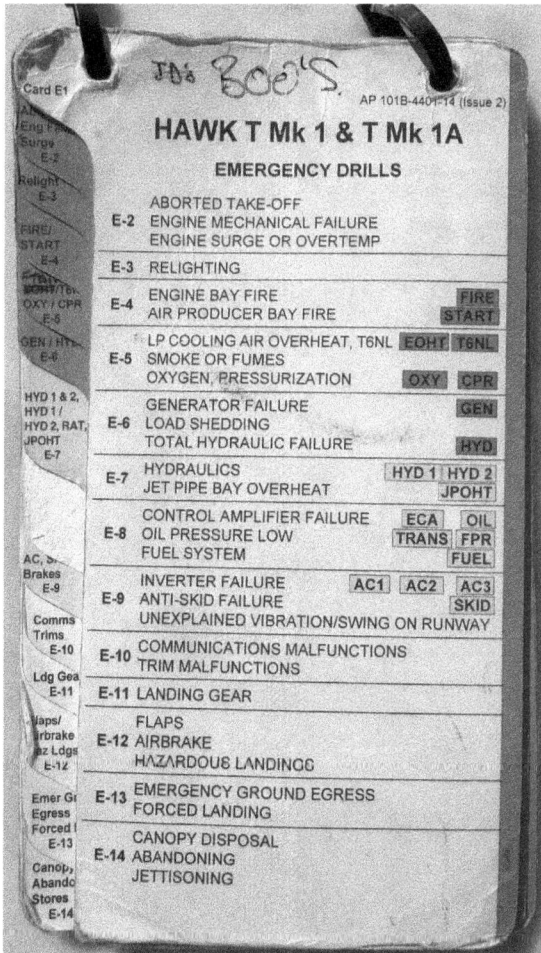

*Figure 19. My Trusty Pilot's Checklist, thumbed and used over 100s of flights*

# Rules for Checklists

There are some basic rules for creating an effective checklist. Here they are:

- Keep it simple.

- Define the trigger points for actions.

- Fit it all on one page. These are memory-joggers, not phone books.

- Utilize nine steps or less, including cross-checks. The rest are SOPs. There's no need for "breathing steps," as in "Remember to breathe," that state the obvious.

- Use clear, concise language. Really push the meaning-to-ink ratio. If you don't need a word, cut it. If it's not clear to the operator what it means, replace it. Only include what has meaning, and no more.

- No distractions. Use basic fonts, no borders, no decorations, no emojis, no arrows to large words saying, "This is important. Please read." No large words anywhere.

- Test it with other operators. Not only the team that developed the checklist, but others. They're the ones who will use them, and who will know if they'll work or if it's missing something.

- Keep it with the operation. If it's a checkout checklist, keep it at the checkout. If it's a pipe-testing checklist, keep it with the pipe. If it's a perforation gun, keep it with the gun.

- Read them aloud. The checklists are designed for an operator and wingman, whatever the task. Steps, cross-checks, and confirmations are always verbal, and if possible, also visual.

# AI Sidebar: Our Task-Saturated World

Think you're never task-saturated? Think again. A UC Irvine study found that the typical office worker gets interrupted every 11 minutes. The chart summarizes a survey by Udemy and Toula that sheds some insights into our task-saturated world. Here's some statistics they offer:

- On average, 84.4% of workers are distracted at work.

- 98% of workers experience at least three to four interruptions per day.

- 80% of workers say they are less distracted working from home.

- 70% of workers say they are distracted away from work by in-company digital messaging platforms.

- 66% of people admit to being distracted by nomophobia, the feeling of not knowing where your phone is.

- Distractions cost workers an estimated 2.1 hours per day.

- It takes workers 24 minutes and 15 seconds to refocus after being distracted.

- The average worker wastes 60 hours every month due to workplace distractions.

- Distractions in the workplace cost American businesses as much as $650 billion annually. 55% of work productivity is lost due to the distraction of cellphones.

- Social media distractions cost businesses $4,500 per employee per year.

- 24% of workers miss deadlines due to distractions.

- Distractions can lead to employees making 2X as many errors as usual.

- Americans check their phones 144 times per day.

- But workers who turn off their phone notifications have 50% improved productivity.

- 47% of people say they feel a sense of panic or anxiety when their cellphone battery goes below 20%.

- On average, people take nine and a half minutes to get back into a productive workflow after switching between digital apps.

- 45% of people say context-switching makes them less productive. 43% of people say switching between tasks causes fatigue.

– art –

*Figure 20. We are distracted at work. Australian HR Institute*

Chapter 8: Execute (Keeping People, and Yourself, to the Plan)

# The Debrief

**"The debrief is more important than the mission itself."** Every Fighter Pilot

Debriefing is the head, heart, and soul of iteration, a foundation of fighter pilot mindset. Author Jim Collins believes that truth within an organization is essential for a successful organization, and that some form of debrief is essential for that truth. "When you conduct autopsies without blame, you go a long way toward creating a climate where the truth is heard." It's such a climate in which learning, leadership, openness, and honesty can thrive and meld a tight team. If your team is full of highly skilled and motivated rockstar professionals, you may find little need for pep talks to get things going, but even so, after the mission, you need a clean debrief. On the other hand, if your team is just starting out, is a bit nervous, or is made up of average Janes and Joes (note: there is nothing wrong with average by the way, I made a very successful career being very average at everything), then a debrief offers a philosophy and cognitive framework for essential psychological safety and learning support for them to get on top of their game quickly. The debrief gives the team closure on its accomplishment, closes the loop on individual and collective experience, and breaks through the biases, beliefs, behaviors, and myths that foment inside any organization. Whatever has happened, there may be feelings they don't want to carry over to the next mission. There may be too much pride in the accomplishment or some annoyances or frustrations between team members for gaps. Good, right on target, or bad, the debrief gets them out of the way. Recognize the mission for what it was, acknowledge it, and move on with a new way of executing something, or a removal of outdated or ineffective practices.

Second, acknowledging a mission's quick wins is critical. Debriefing reinforces that there have been wins and that acknowledgment helps gain momentum and confidence. Teams understand that it's not a lucky streak and that they are building their ability to lead, change, and get things done—even on a long, complex, and uncertain mission. A team that has had a month of short-term wins and learned from each one in a debrief is feeling pretty good about itself and the changes it's made.

So, too, is each individual on that team. There is a need, as John Kotter calls it, to generate short-term wins.

Third, win or lose, the debrief reinforces the team's ownership of the result—that we did it together as the squadron, no matter the result. It is not about individual performance, but team performance. Just as there is no blame being cast, the debrief is not a claim for personal credit, either. As we'll see, the focus is on what happened, not who is responsible. Each person gets to understand and respect the challenges and successes that their colleagues have met and achieved. Each person gets to appreciate the honesty with which their team talks about what they might have done better. Each person takes on the responsibility to learn from what they hear.

Finally, the debrief builds the credible, high-trust leadership needed for a tight team. Just like every other part of FLEX, we believe sound principles and the opportunities to practice them develop impactful leaders. Debriefs are one of those opportunities. Via the debrief, leadership is developed, practiced, displayed, and observed. In a debrief, everyone works through the same pattern, starting with the team leader: examining what happened and what they could do better individually, and how to capture that learning for next time. Junior executives have the opportunity to follow the modeling of their mentors. The next wave of corporate or family leaders are being formed.

Let's take a look at how the New York Giants first started their FLEX debriefs in 2011, and how debriefs became common practice for the eleven conference-leading teams in the 2015 season. Through the debriefs, the Giants learned from themselves what they had to do if they were going to make the Super Bowl again. They began to take responsibility for their own performance, as individuals and as a team. They got better each week, they enjoyed the benefits of the fighter pilots' "Accelerated

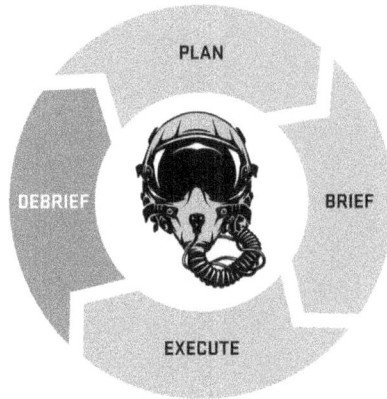

*Figure 21. The debrief starts after the mission is executed.
The lessons learned and actions identified to close the
execution gap are transferred into the plan.*

Learning Curve." The debriefs built in them energy and purpose. Each player identified what they had to do better and what help they needed from others to do that. Eli Manning picked out 30 plays and ran the film for the team. Anyone who saw something that he felt he could've done better was supposed to speak up. If a player didn't own up to an error, one of his teammates could point it out. Only that never happened, said receiver Michael Clayton: "When a Brandon Jacobs run came on the screen, the running back almost immediately said, 'I should've hit that hole harder.' On a pass play, a lineman said, 'I need to knock that end's hands down so you've got a clearer path to throw, Eli.' Receivers said they needed to catch balls and block safeties better. Tight end/fullback Bear Pascoe said only a couple times did Manning maybe add a point or two." What you see in this example is that the Giants were changing themselves as much as they were changing their culture. Positive culture (mindset and intention) and continuous learning (through action) are the two big payoffs of doing debriefs often and well. As you know, it kinda works–the Giants went on to win the Super Bowl.

In helping countless companies with debriefs, time and again, we see that internal communication is usually a missing link. If things were being said, others hadn't heard it—and that's a learning issue. If things weren't being said because people weren't comfortable saying it—that's a culture issue. People are holding things in. What causes this could be low self-esteem, confusion, or embarrassment. Principally, it is a survival instinct, it is fear-driven. Fear of judgment. Fear of failure. Fear of being cut from a team. Debriefing provides a framework for psychologically safe conversations because the focus is on what's right, not who's right.

In 2012, the Group for Organizational Effectiveness in Albany, New York, reviewed 46 studies on the impact of debriefing in business, medicine, aviation, and similar settings. They drew some very favorable conclusions. They found that, on average, "properly conducted" debriefs improved team and individual performance by 20 to 25 percent. More structured and disciplined debriefs improved performance by a higher 35 to 40 percent, on average. Finally, and importantly, the authors found that debriefs required little time and very few material resources.

The debrief we run has the elements that the Group for Organizational Effectiveness identifies as essential for an effective debrief. We call it the ORCA debrief, an acronym that stands for the rules of the debrief. You're **O**bjective. You look at **R**esults. You identify **C**auses of underperformance. You conclude with a recommended **A**ction. ORCA.

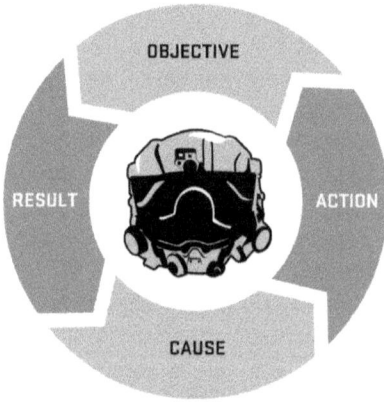

*Figure 22. The ORCA Debrief Method*

Did you know that orcas, its marine mammal namesake, are considered to be one of the most intelligent mammals in the animal kingdom? Did you know that they are rapid social learners and use debrief techniques to modify their behavior? Back in July 2020, Orcas started to randomly attack small sailing vessels off the coast of Spain and Portugal, and no one knew why. Researchers identified 52 attacks in that year; two years later, it was 200 attacks. Uniquely, the orcas seemed to be specifically attacking the rudders of vessels near them, trying to break them and presumably leaving the vessels to run adrift. Andrew Trites, professor and director of Marine Mammal Research at the University of British Columbia, says there are two main theories behind this. One is that it's play. If it's playing, the orcas enjoy the cause and effect of ramming the boats, like wayward teenagers bored on a Friday night. The second theory is that it's revenge. But for what? Perhaps it was revenge for the multiple boating accidents where the Iberian killer whales, unique to the North Atlantic, had been rammed or injured by the heavy keels silently gliding through the water on sailing vessels. Either way, scientists say the behavior is extraordinary and that these whale pods have seemingly learned to scale up their attacks from merely damaging a boat to immobilizing a boat and, more recently, sinking three vessels. ORCA is a thought-out, intelligent process used to debrief a mission. Through the debrief, we accelerate our learning curve, accelerate our personal growth, accelerate innovation, and, most importantly, accelerate the achievement of our most audacious goals.

## It's What's Right, Not Who's Right

In the context of debriefing, the principle "It's what's right, not who's right" emphasizes focusing on the issues and solutions rather than assigning blame to individuals. This approach creates an environment where team members focus on the planned objectives and the factual data at hand after the execution of the mission. By concentrating on objective analysis and collective learning, the team can identify the root causes of problems and develop effective strategies for future missions. There's no scope for personal opinion in a debrief, informed opinions are encouraged, and the pursuit of fact is sacrosanct.

## Nameless and Rankless

The Air Force practice of debriefing was conceived and developed during the Vietnam War. Before that, through World War II and the Korean War, the Air Force debriefed in the same way that other forces did it: at the bar, with very minimal note-taking. But the United States was losing far more planes and pilots than their technological advantage should have allowed. The response to that was a formal post-mission debrief. This debrief became a place where everyone who was part of the mission could hash out what went right, what went wrong, what that meant, and what could be done about it the next time. It became open and honest, the nameless, rankless forum that searches for root causes, irrespective of who was involved.

Frank and sometimes frankly intense, the debrief became a place where everyone, aces and novices, could learn how to survive and complete their mission. And it did just that. Strategies were changed, tactics improved. Some 900 aircraft were lost in Operation Rolling Thunder, which was before the rollout of debriefs, and just 131 in Operation Linebacker, after.

# AI Sidebar: Ray Dalio's Principle of Radical Transparency

Ray Dalio, the founder of Bridgewater Associates and author of *Principles*, advocates for a management concept called **radical transparency**. This principle is based on the idea that openness, honesty, and transparency should be embedded in an organization's culture, enabling better decision-making, stronger trust, and continuous improvement.

## Key Elements of Radical Transparency

1. **Open Communication**: At the core of radical transparency is the belief that all employees, regardless of rank or position, should be open to sharing their honest opinions, critiques, and feedback. This creates an environment where truth is prioritized over hierarchy, and people feel empowered to contribute their ideas and concerns without fear of retribution.

2. **Data-Driven Feedback**: Dalio advocates for the use of data and systems to capture honest feedback, allowing employees to analyze and improve their performance. Bridgewater famously uses a tool called the **"Dot Collector,"** which allows employees to rate each other's decision-making and input during meetings in real time. This provides a continuous flow of feedback that is open to all within the organization.

3. **Meritocracy of Ideas**: Radical transparency fosters a culture where the **best ideas win**, rather than those from the highest-ranking people. Dalio believes that decision-making should be based on objective reasoning and merit, not personal biases or power dynamics. By exposing ideas to scrutiny, it ensures that only the strongest ideas prevail.

4. **Open Access to Information**: In line with transparency, Dalio ensures that employees have access to vast amounts of information, including meeting recordings, memos, and other critical internal documents. This eliminates the typical "need-to-know" barriers that exist in many organizations, encouraging informed decision-making across all levels.

## Benefits of Radical Transparency

- **Improved Decision-Making**: By removing blind spots and biases, radical transparency allows organizations to make better-informed decisions. It encourages rigorous debate and input from all angles, minimizing groupthink and overconfidence.

- **Fostering Trust**: An open environment fosters trust, as employees know they are receiving honest feedback and that no information is hidden. Transparency builds credibility among colleagues and leaders.

- **Continuous Improvement**: Constant feedback and openness help individuals and teams improve. When everyone is encouraged to reflect on mistakes or inefficiencies openly, it creates an environment of continuous learning and growth.

Dalio is a galvanizing figure, accused of bringing employees to tears in his pursuit of the truth, excellence and results. We don't advocate for that style of leadership. However, his dogged pursuit of truth and transparency is one of the core principles he attributes to successfully building the world's largest hedge fund.

# Learning and Culture

"Wise leaders are always engaged in and by the world; they are open to 'reflective backtalk,' they can admit errors and learn from their mistakes." Noel Tichy and Warren Bennis, *Judgment*

If you think there is too much hierarchy in your organization for a debrief, try the Air Force. If you think there's no time for a debrief, try combat. If you think a debrief won't work in sport or business or even at home, consider the NY Giants and the other examples in this book. Better yet, give it a go with your team. We believe the debrief is the single most powerful tool for you and your ambitions. The only reason you don't have time to debrief is because you're not debriefing. You're making the same mistakes, trying to achieve better results with the same behaviors, and attempting to prioritize the reactive hot mess that is a modern tech-powered business.

Primary among the secrets of an effective debrief is the tone—something we call nameless and rankless. Before we start a debrief, we pilots figuratively (and sometimes literally) take off our name and rank insignia before we enter the debrief room. In the debrief room, hierarchies and egos don't matter; leadership, standards, communication, and knowledge do.

# Agility: Fast Learning and Action

From an early age, many of us are encouraged to "learn by doing." Yet we don't automatically realize what we should learn from each event, and do not have perfect recall of those lessons when we require them. If you debrief your every action and learn and understand what happened, then your learning curve accelerates. But it's not just you and the lessons learned from your own fun and adventures; the concept here is to learn from everyone on your team. As you will see, one of the points of the debrief is to flush out what the team learned from the mission. The other point is to capture those lessons learned, share them, and, most critically, put them into action. These lessons are used immediately by the team on their next mission. They are also codified into standards and shared with others in the organization. These become the lessons that teams consider every time they plan. Either way, they are not filed away to go stale; they live and breathe through each stage of the FLEX cycle.

We saw this accelerated learning curve in action when debriefs were introduced at Manheim Car Auctions. Manheim was founded in Atlanta in 1945, when there were quite a few excess military vehicles to deal with. Today, more cars are sold per day at Manheim than anywhere else on Earth. At their Hayward site in California, Manheim sells 2,300 cars each day, each morning, each and every week. When their machine is at full throttle, a dozen stands are selling one car every 60 seconds. How did they reach that sort of efficiency? Until we came in, the boss shared some data and his thoughts for a half-hour or so at 8 p.m., which was at the end of the day and seemed a little late to us. So, we set a FLEX debrief for 6 p.m. the next day. It wasn't perfect. The sales team got there at 6:25 p.m. and we started the ORCA process. Instead of the boss's view, the team got the whole team's view. We did this every night. We debriefed and a couple of ideas were captured to improve the run for the next day. People talked, people listened, people took notes. Change didn't come about after the first debrief, but it started to be noticeable after the fifth, the eighth, the tenth. By the end of two weeks, the debriefs had generated enough lessons learned for the selling day to finish at 6 p.m. Mannheim was doing a full day's work in two hours less time. They were preparing and moving cars even faster, in the right order, with fewer mistakes and with less reworking. That was quite a change—for the team and their families.

If that sort of learning is possible at one facility, what would happen if the lessons were shared across a company? Medtronic is one of the world's largest medical technology and services companies. It was founded in 1949 in Minneapolis and is now headquartered in Dublin, Ireland, with over 85,000 employees globally. It works on non-pharmaceutical solutions for cardiac and vascular diseases, neurological and spinal disorders, diabetes, orthopedics, and other common, life-threatening conditions. Its solutions are innovative, so they have to be tried within a trusted doctor-patient relationship if they are to be adopted. If a doctor will trial a therapy, there is a statistically excellent prospect that the patient will have the desired outcome. The hard part is getting that trial.

At Medtronic, we worked with the national sales division responsible for one set of medical solutions. Its sales president had nine teams with nine VPs reporting to him. The issue was that the nine VPs saw themselves more in competition than as a team acting together. They saw themselves working in regional silos without sharing what they were learning. The sales president had a weekly call with each VP to review how things were going. The VPs felt good about the call if they were ahead of their targets, which, like every business, was often but not always the case. Moreover, they wanted to get out and meet those targets rather than talk about them. So, the sales president took a different tack. Instead of nine calls, he made one. Instead of reviewing individual results, he reviewed what the teams were doing. He structured the calls as a debrief and pushed for cause and effect—the results were noted. In the first week, the Washington VP shared how his team had started a new conversation with a medical center. The Florida VP followed that lead and shared how her team had worked around a problem a doctor had with another device. The ideas started flowing. Each and every week they debriefed in the same objective way, full of curiosity rather than fear. Within four months, the division had sold out of its product. The VPs couldn't get enough of these calls. They were learning almost too fast, and today they call their product process "Flawless Product Execution."

# Tight Culture

It's both hard and often dangerous to try and describe the culture that you want on your team. A small dictionary of adjectives has been used—you want your team culture to be purposeful, engaging, open, performance-based, excellent, trusting, reliable, disciplined, and so on and so on. If there's one word we'd use, it would be "tight." A team that is tight will be there for each other. It will perform purposefully and efficiently in a way that honesty and humanity allow. Its people will fit together snugly, irrespective of their cultural backgrounds and personalities; they will be crystal clear both in their roles and responsibilities to bring the richest skillset and awareness to the team and its job. They will trust and respect each other. Their leader will have uncontested responsibilities. It's a tight team, and they put the person next to them first.

The debrief is a must for a tight team.

# When to Debrief

Here's the secret: We debrief every mission—big or small; win, lose, or draw—immediately after we've finished executing it. That means we debrief daily, sometimes two or three times a day. It's a hard discipline to accept, but it's the only way to capture the benefits of the debrief. No matter how small or quick the mission, debrief it. Even if we don't fly, debrief the planning process. Whatever the result of the mission, no matter how tired you are, no matter how urgent the next thing is, do a debrief. Your mission isn't over until you do a debrief. Just like the FLEX engine says: you plan–brief–execute–debrief. If you have a task, think of it as a mission, and after each task, debrief it, even if only five minutes. It's good to do it by yourself, it's great to do it with your wingman, it's next level to do it each day with your team.

# Win, Lose, or Draw

Many people resist a debrief because they misunderstand what it is. They fear it's to go over the coals of failure and assign blame and punishment. It's the opposite. It's identifying the actions to move forward, solve a problem, or recover from a failure. Whether we acknowledge them or not, failures, bad decisions, and mistakes are always there, and we are aware of them, so let's deal with them! That misunderstanding that debriefing is punitive rather than supportive disappears through the habit of debriefing everything. Whatever the result of the mission, debrief it. Success, failure, near misses, close calls—all of them are outcomes.

The Children's Hospital of Minneapolis had the idea of using "good catch logs" for nurses to anonymously log when they discovered something not quite right with a patient's treatment. These logs were studied independently by others not directly connected with the patient's treatment. The learning took time, and, because it was an anonymous process, it lacked personal accountability, but it was an effective step toward improving the safety record of the hospital. View it as a partial debrief.

Near misses or close calls are those times when the mission met its objective, but it was perhaps lucky to do so. These are particularly valuable to debrief, as they take place free from the consequences of failure. There is clean air to work in and a good opportunity for learning. People can talk about what went off track and how the team recovered from that.

For similar reasons, wins are a must to debrief. The idea is to tease out what was good planning and execution, and what was plain good luck. It's also the moment to review and rebuild situational awareness to consider whether the same actions would deliver the same results in the future. Jim Collins had to conduct his own debrief after many of the companies lauded as business stars in his book *Good to Great* became financial black holes. One of them was Circuit City, then the number two electronics retailer in the U.S. in 1998, bankrupt in 2008.

Another was Fannie Mae, a giant mortgage lender at the center of the 2007 financial crisis. Collins studied these and other black holes to consider how their cultures may have held clues to their downfalls. In *How the Mighty Fall*, he concluded that the first stage of that fall was that those companies had silenced the truth within. They believed their own press. They never questioned their own actions. They never debriefed their success to consider why they were winning, and if those root causes were sustainable. In the end, they were not. Hubris. We work with Fannie Mae today, helping their leaders implement some of the world's most complex banking technology, and they embrace a nameless, rankless culture.

# The Debrief Is Part of the Mission. Debrief the Moment After You Execute.

The debrief is an integral part of the mission itself, not simply something that happens afterward. Factor in the time. Treat the debrief seriously.

Fighter pilots get out of their jets, drop off their helmets and flight gear, and go directly to the debrief room, every time. The Blue Angels debrief with the same routine, over 250 times a year, and they still discover new things and keep the CIA at bay. Debrief the same day your execution phase ends, or the next business day, but not the next week. At the end of every team mission or project, there's a heap of housekeeping to do: filing receipts, completing logs and reports, celebrating the result, reporting back to stakeholders, handing forms over to the ops team. All of that takes longer than a debrief. Remember, the debrief can be as short as five minutes and never more than an hour. Start your debrief and stick with it however long it takes to identify two or three lessons learned, and turn those into two or three actions. The mission is just one part of your FLEX executional cycle. The mission isn't over until the debrief is over. The level of learning is immediate and continuous.

# Practicing ORCA

A FLEX debrief is not an open session to shell peas and pistachios, ponder one's navel or the team's fortunes. Just like a FLEX plan or briefing session, there is a discipline to running a debrief. Here goes:

When. As noted, debrief as soon as possible. At the end of the day, after a deliverable has been completed/missed, or when you have a head-scratching problem. Set specific times for the start and end points, but no more than one hour. This is a time to listen and learn, not to dwell. One root cause is all you need, three if you have that many and have the time. That's it. Finish on time, to the minute, or even better, finish early. That demonstrates effective leadership and builds your credibility. If you can't finish a simple debrief on time, how are you going to go with complex project deadlines? Be ready to debrief when you feel there is a dangerous emotional response to a situation at work. Angry, frustrated, or ecstatic! A significant emotional event can be a barrier, and when identified, schedule a debrief.

Nameless and rankless. This is not a gimmick. Fighter pilots literally and figuratively lose their name, rank, even our personality, when we walk into the debriefing room. We refer to ourselves based on the role we played in the mission rather than using names or call signs. We might be called "formation leader" or "number two" or "three" or "four," as in "Number four was wide and missed their drop point." Nothing personal. Nameless. Rankless. Facts. Do everything you can do to remove your ego from the room, and become a detached, objective analyst of the mission. The point about "nameless, rankless" is that everyone on the team is just an actor in the mission's play. It's not something you ask everyone else to do. It's something you do yourself, and everyone follows. Easier said than done, and that's the point; it helps you turn over the rocks to find the hidden issues.

Where. Anywhere! But it needs to be a literal or virtual sanctuary where the team feels psychologically safe. It could be at the back of a tailgate, in your home office, on Zoom or Teams call, or in a boardroom. Ensure the room is clean: no dirty whiteboards, lunchtime scraps, or coffee cup stains, close the other browser windows and apps on your PC, and focus. The key is to set the tone, "Ok folks, this is the debrief," and from there, establish the right mindset.

Who. This is team business. If you weren't on the team, you're not in the debrief. This is for the mission team itself and only the mission team, and it must include them all. Unlike a planning session, there is no need for external experts, and certainly no room for other teams or people up or down the hierarchy. No one is a fly on the wall. Others will get your lessons learned and the actions you took, but not now; you're just an uncontextualized distraction.

Here's where a team's diversity pays off. Different people are sensitive to different things; their situational awareness makes them alert to different risks. By themselves, they can hold and describe different parts of the mission "elephant." Only when they share their perspective can the team see the whole elephant—a richer appreciation of just what went on in the mission. Only when surgical teams hear the views of everyone in the room—surgeons, anesthetists, scrub techs, circulating techs, nurses— do they get a clear and objective view of what was going on. Just as mission planning benefits from your diverse skills and perspectives, the debrief will draw out different interpretations of the same event.

Make sure the team covers certain roles. The mission leader (who may not be the most senior person from a people leadership perspective) leads the debrief. Assign a timekeeper, a scribe, and someone who will disseminate any data or lessons learned from the debrief.

What. Have available at the debrief any data you need to review performance against objectives. This includes what we call "debrief focus points," that is, notes that the team has taken throughout the mission. Maybe it was recorded on a digital platform—the point is to bring anything that may be useful to debrief. If something bad has happened, or there's been a near miss, or an unusually good achievement—all should be noted and included in the debrief, as these are the things likely to lead to lessons learned and important actions moving forward.

If it was a complex mission, present a timeline of the mission, the mission plan and objective, the actions, the results, the successes and errors, their causes and lessons learned, and the traditional "parking lot" of ideas that might need to be actioned later.

How. What does it take for everyone on the team to feel absolutely comfortable about discussing their role in the mission's success or failure? Getting the tone right from the start is at the core of its value. People need to feel safe and respected. The debrief is the true marker of the team's culture, and the strongest tool for making and keeping it tight. Getting it right is a massive achievement for teams, and it doesn't come by accident.

To that end, the team leader's role is critical. You need an open and honest mind, and the willingness to admit mistakes. You have to set both the ground rules and become the example for others, as follows:

An open mind for open listening. It is not at all rare for two people to be in the same conversation and "hear" different things. What happens is that one person is expecting to hear something, and so hears it regardless of whether it is actually said or not. Scientists call it "predictive perceptual signaling." More often than not, it's a very useful human trait for filling gaps in what we see or hear. But we make mistakes. We think we know what's coming, or we think we know the answer, so our minds literally stop listening and move on to their own conclusions. It takes a conscious effort to stop listening for what you expect to hear. The debrief is the perfect place to practice.

Leader owns up first. Nothing will encourage the team more than for you to call out what you could have done better. A leader who starts with that truthful self-criticism is demonstrating the courage and integrity they want in their team. Even if your performance was really pretty good, find something that you could have done better. Then open the discussion to others: "Did anyone else see me do anything dumb, different, or dangerous?" Demonstrate that the debrief has nothing to do with blame or discipline, but only about finding out what happened and why. Expose yourself for the team to be stronger. "It's not a weakness to make mistakes; it's a weakness to hide them," says an old adage. But people need to feel safe. When it comes to the crunch of finding out what happened (C=Cause), mistakes will be uncovered. Owning up to one's mistake puts one in a better position than someone else pointing it out, and far better than not even being aware of it.

A closed circle. What is said in the debrief stays in the debrief. The debrief discusses those things specifically relevant to a mission's specific performance. That discussion has no relevance to anyone outside the room. Only with that certainty that nothing leaves the room will the debrief underpin the sanctity of performance and the team's eagerness to learn. The team itself will decide what lessons learned and what tacit knowledge will leave the debrief room.

# ORCA

There are four parts to an effective debrief, four simple areas to cover that will build a habit that will transform your life and smash your goals. They may not take long to go over or include much ceremony, but they have to be there, and you can't miss a step!

**Objective**. What was your objective?

**Results**. What is the current result?

**Cause**. What is the root cause for this result? Take accountability.

**Action**. What action will we take tomorrow?

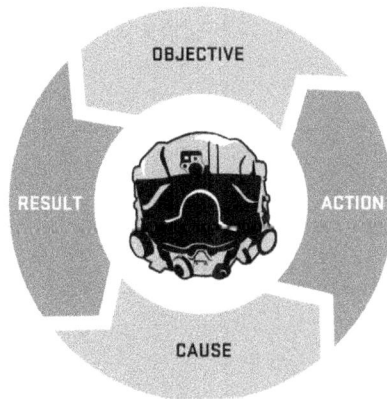

*Figure 23. ORCA*

# O – Objective

At Afterburner, we've facilitated tens of thousands of debriefs across every industry imaginable. From billion-dollar strategies for Nike to tailgate talks for the construction industry.

If you've been working with FLEX to this point, though, restating the objective is perhaps the most straightforward part of the debrief. What was the objective and the course of action to get there? You had a mission objective that was measurable. Did the team reach it: yes or no? What were the hits and misses? What were the debrief focus points?

Then it comes to courses of action. Was each step completed: yes or no? Go through them one step at a time, just as they were laid out in the plan. Step through them one step at a time. Build up a picture of what happened and why. Don't assume you know why things have happened the way they happened. Let the process take its course, and let your team share their perspectives. Don't start assuming what others have done; everyone brings their personal objectives and actions to the conversation. These are the results of the mission, in black and white.

# R – Results

Say the team met their objectives. Say you executed your courses of action all but flawlessly. Did those actions have the effect that the leader and the organization intended? Was it a brilliantly executed mission that achieved next to no valuable impact? Or was it perfect? That's what the team needs to consider.

These days, from the moment you enter a workplace to the minute you leave, virtually everything is measured. If you have a stream of data and KPIs, you have results. You may think you're doing OK, and maybe you are. But if your results aren't in the context of an associated objective, they're just noise—even worse, they are the tail wagging the dog, and your reaction to them, without context, will likely became a serious handbrake to your execution.

The key here is to link your result directly to your objective with zero ambiguity.

# C – Cause

C is also for "curiosity." This step takes us from knowing what happened to knowing how and why it happened. The team takes each result and asks, "How did this happen?" Then, for each answer, they look for the "why." Consider both successes and misses. What let you down if the mission met its objective but had a different impact than you intended? Was it the planning, the communication, your situational awareness through the mission, did you just make a dumb mistake (no such thing as dumb mistakes by the way, just human error), or was it the strategy itself? If you made it through a near miss, what got you through it? Should the plan have foreseen that event? Is the lesson learned to plan for that situation, or is it to keep the plan FLEXible and rely on experience?

The answers may or may not be obvious. Keep drilling down: why, why, why. You will ultimately get to a root cause, the first action or inaction that led to what happened. You must identify it. What began the cascading string of errors or led to the final success? What was the chain of events? Any link that would have changed the course of events? The root cause is the first event in that chain. It may not have been the sweetest action or the worst mistake, but it was the first, and it's an action owned by a person and it's important to get to it.

Make the whole process visual and you'll discover another benefit. At each debrief, put the four headings below on a flipchart or screen, and capture the root causes that led to mistakes or to surprising successes. Then, line up those mission debriefs and see what elements are common to both. If a communication or an alignment issue comes up repeatedly— teams pushing hard but in a different direction from what the leader intended—then you've identified the need for new standards in those areas.

To guide the analysis, go back to the FLEX framework for action to help isolate the different factors that may have contributed to the end results. Table 2 sets out those possible factors. It's a useful checklist to run an eye over to make sure you get to the causes.

Working through the results, you'll have a fair idea of what happened and why. It will be apparent what was done well, and what was done not so well. This is the moment to take individual ownership for that performance, starting with the team leader. This is where the team leader steps up and says, "I made these mistakes, I fess up, and I'm going to fix them. I'm glad to be here!" That's how the flight leaders for the U.S. Navy's Blue Angels start off. It releases tension for the team and demonstrates that It's OK to make a mistake, so long as you learn from it. And that's the whole point of the debrief. We've listed below the common root causes we've observed over tens of thousands of debriefs.

#### Table 2. Common Root Causes

| Culture | Communication | Planning | Execution |
|---|---|---|---|
| Leadership | Ambiguity | Unidentified Threats | Priorities |
| Knowledge | Mis-understanding | Resourcing | Standards and Procedures |
| Organizational Processes | Didn't Hear or Receive Information | Clear Objective | Situational Awareness |
| Strategic Planning | Didn't Have Logins | Program/Project Planning | Checklists |
| Experience | No Reception | Decision Making | Tools |
| Contract/SLA Scope | No Images/ Graphics | Data Quality | Personal Error/ Omission |
| Remuneration | | Roles/ Responsibilities | Lack of Focus/ Distracted |
| Disengaged | | Contingency | Poor Discipline |
| Lack of Training | | Project Methodology | Distracted |
| Well-being | | Metrics | Task-saturated |
| | | Additional Scope | |

# A – Action

This step is what the debrief is all about and drives the fighter pilot mind-set. Intentions fueled by action, and if we don't get it right the first time, we'll try something different tomorrow! We don't want to wallow in the mistakes we made—we're all human, they're going to happen! We want to be invigorated by the actions we need to take tomorrow to do a better job. If you're moderately self-aware and a little bit curious, it's pretty hard to think of a single action you take that doesn't offer a lesson learned. The longer we live and stay open-minded, the more these lessons mount up. Yet the debrief isn't the place to volunteer every personal break-through. What we're looking for is something prominent, a root cause or pattern that will reoccur, and then we identify an action to mitigate that in the future, something that can be replicated by others, safely and reliably. If it applies, we make that action a standard for our organization. For example, my squadron reviewed the three-dimensional distances our jets could be incoming towards each other before they had to veer off to avoid a collision at a closing speed of 2,500 mph. The margins were fine, far enough apart to be safe, yet close enough to be in a position to outmaneuver the other aircraft. We learned some valuable things and passed them on and they became SOP. That's FLEX. The lessons learned need to be explicit and actionable, effective in improving speed, quality, or safety the next time someone tries a similar mission.

Don't be surprised if there are no lessons learned in your debrief. For many of our pilots and facilitators, drawing out actionable lessons learned from a debrief is the hardest part of FLEX. That makes sense: lessons are valuable, so they don't come easy. Keep pushing, though. One single lesson learned is better than none.

## How Do You Transfer the Lessons?

I could answer this question with a single sentence. Transfer your lessons learned and actions into your AI platform. Better yet, upload your entire FLEX cycle, ready for your next execution window. I'll try and explain more deeply. How do you get a lesson into the minds of those who need it most? It will vary based on the severity of the lessons learned and your company's communication channels. Sometimes it's an urgent call to a team already in action. Sometimes it amounts to adding an item to a checklist that captures the new standard operating procedure. Anything in between might use the organization's formal communication and knowledge structures. That means ensuring your lesson is in the right and searchable system, or prompted correctly before uploading into your learning platform. But don't wait for your knowledge management or internal communications team to make a fuss about the news. Share the lesson with anyone you think might appreciate the thought or appreciate that you are keeping in touch with them. If the lesson is important enough to change your standard operating procedures, it's important, period. Let your people know right away! Speed of turning lessons into action is key here, small changes that drive the evolution of your team and business. Use four criteria to make the call:

Who needs this information?

How fast do they need it?

How will we get it to them?

Does this become our new BAU (Business As Usual)?

# The Bathtub

Whatever happened during the mission, whatever happened in the debrief, start and finish on a positive note. Think of it like a bathtub: start on a high, dive down into the debrief, and finish back on a high note. Here's a great way to start: "Here were our three objectives for today. We achieved our primary and secondary objectives. Well done team!"

From there, dive down into the bathtub: "We didn't quite nail objective number three; let's drill down there and focus on that for today's debrief." Run through your ORCA debrief and clearly define your actions moving forward.

Once we have our individual actions, we're back up on the other side of the bathtub finishing on a high note. "Well team, we fell short on this week's sales target; however, I think Anne's action there to tweak our pricing model will really set us up for a big week next week. Great debrief!"

Remember, just doing the debrief is time well spent. The team has committed itself to learn from its actions, and to share those lessons with those who should know. That's no small feat in most organizations. Sometimes, the effort to complete a mission will leave people exhausted and flat. But when there's no debrief, teams seem to simply dissolve and move onto the next job, without ceremony or acknowledgement. That will never happen with a FLEX debrief. The end of the brief will always be more positive than the end of the mission itself. There will always be positives to draw out of the mission. Single one out to finish the formal debrief process and give out your personal thanks for the effort your team put into the mission, and the honesty you all put into the debrief. Don't go back and summarize the results, or anything at all. The team has all it needs now. End it well.

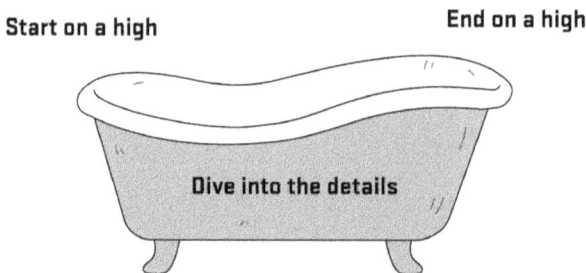

Start on a high          End on a high

Dive into the details

*Figure 24. The bathtub, start on a high, drill down into the detail, end on a high note*

# Just Debrief

One of our previous clients has a pretty famous catchphrase, and it works for debriefing: "Just do it."

We've heard every excuse in the book for not running a debrief. Time is the big one. In most organizations, we're told, "There is simply no time to spare for this type of navel-gazing. We have to get on to the next thing, and we're already a week behind. We don't get the team together even to celebrate a win, let alone trawl through the ashes of a failure." Yet why are you already a week behind? I've said it once, and I'll say it again: 99% of the time, it's because you're not making time to debrief!

Every organization that has made debriefing part of its culture has had the same experience. The lessons and cultural shifts gained from them far outweigh the modest time spent. You will rarely get a better return on an investment.

The second barrier is fear and ego. A debrief calls on a team to be honest with each other, and it calls on a leader to acknowledge their mistakes. Depending on the individuals and the culture, that may not be easy.

Working patiently through a debrief's clear, simple, proven structure is the best way to overcome these barriers. The first time may well be awkward, like all first times. You're new to this and so is your team. But stick to your guns and see it through. We guarantee it will be worth it. Before long, the phrase "Let's debrief" will be much appreciated and uttered with relief that someone has identified an issue and wants to fix it.

# AI Sidebar – ORCA-Powered AI

By effectively combining the Afterburner ORCA methodology (Objective, Result, Cause, Action) with AI tools, you can enhance both strategic thinking and execution through real-time data analysis, feedback loops, and automation. Here's how each stage of the ORCA process can be strengthened by AI:

# 1. Objective: Defining the Mission

The first step in the ORCA framework is to establish a clear and measurable objective. AI can support this by analyzing extensive data sets, identifying market opportunities, customer demands, or internal inefficiencies.

- AI Application: Tools such as natural language processing (NLP) and data analytics can sift through customer feedback, industry reports, and competitor data to help fine-tune your objectives. AI can also monitor external factors (like economic trends or competitor moves) to align your objectives with evolving market conditions.

# 2. Result: What You Want to Achieve

In this phase, the focus is on defining the desired outcome and specific results. AI can simulate possible outcomes and predict success metrics by analyzing historical data, competitor strategies, and market conditions.

- AI Application: Predictive analytics tools can forecast outcomes based on different strategies and guide teams toward the highest potential results. By identifying the most likely successful paths, AI can help reduce uncertainty, ensuring that your desired results are well-grounded in data.

# 3. Cause: Understanding the Root Cause of Challenges

This phase involves diagnosing the underlying causes of obstacles or problems preventing your team from reaching its goals. AI-powered insights can help here by uncovering hidden patterns, inefficiencies, and potential risks that might not be immediately visible to human analysis.

- AI Application: Machine learning algorithms can analyze operational data to identify causes of inefficiencies. For example, AI diagnostic tools can reveal bottlenecks in supply chains, poor team performance, or even customer behavioral trends, allowing you to address root causes before they escalate.

## 4. Action: Creating and Executing Solutions

Once you have identified the objective, results, and causes, AI can assist in formulating and executing actions. AI tools can automate routine tasks, enhance decision-making, and track the progress of your actions in real time.

- AI Application: AI-driven project management tools help with task allocation, resource management, and tracking performance metrics. Additionally, Robotic Process Automation (RPA) can handle repetitive tasks, enabling human teams to focus on higher-value work. AI can also monitor execution and provide real-time feedback, adjusting strategies as necessary based on evolving data.

# Example of Integration

In a medical device company like Stryker, implementing ORCA with AI could work as follows:

- Objective: AI-driven market analysis defines the goal of expanding a product line.

- Result: Predictive analytics simulate this expansion's potential financial and operational outcomes.

- Cause: Machine learning tools identify the root causes of potential manufacturing delays or bottlenecks.

- Action: AI automates aspects of the production process and monitors real-time performance, ensuring swift adjustments based on performance metrics.

# 4 Adapting to Modern Complexities

In **Adapting to Modern Complexities**, *The Afterburner Advantage* addresses how leaders and teams can navigate today's unpredictable and complex environments using advanced concepts like VUCA (Volatility, Uncertainty, Complexity, Ambiguity), AI integration, and iterative thinking. Boo emphasizes the importance of continuous adaptation to shifting conditions, leveraging AI to enhance decision-making, and using iterative frameworks to close execution gaps. By applying these tools, organizations can stay agile, improve team dynamics, and strategically exploit opportunities while maintaining focus on long-term goals.

# The FLEX Team—Beyond Personal Performance

It's hard to imagine a serious endeavor not taken on by a team. Nearly everyone who does something special quickly recognizes the team behind them. When Paralympic champion Kurt Fearnley took on the infamous Kokoda Track in Papua New Guinea without his wheelchair—literally crawling over the trail—he had a team behind him. The entrepreneurial celebrities of our times—Steve Jobs, Mark Zuckerberg, Elon Musk, Oprah, Richard Branson, Bill Gates, Jeff Bezos, Lucy Peng, John Mackey, Anita Roddick, Herb Kelleher, Diane von Furstenberg, Muhammad Yunus, Howard Schultz, Arianna Huffington, Larry Page, Sergey Brin, Fred Smith—all acknowledge that their greatest achievement was the team they put in place to realize their dreams.

Good teams don't happen by accident. A series of decisions must be made about the team's makeup, culture, and how it makes decisions and gets things done. FLEX teams have to have a good leader, but equally, they have to have good followers who share the same purpose and vision and who can step into the leader's shoes at any point, which at some point they will.

# Meet AI – The Newest Member of the FLEX Team

As a professional in the event and conference speaking space, there is no bigger star than the "AI" expert. You'll be booked solid if you know AI and deliver an interesting speech on it. People love it and hate it. AI is in equal measure feared and revered. From taking over the world aka Skynet and the Terminator, to curing cancer. But either way, AI is an incredible resource for a FLEX team.

Rather than me tell you why AI is a useful team member, I thought I'd ask Copilot (pretty cool name right?), Microsoft's AI companion: "Why is AI a good team member for high-performing teams?" Here's what it said:

"High-performing teams benefit significantly from integrating artificial intelligence (AI) as a team member. Let's explore how AI contributes to their success:

Administrative Effectiveness:

AI automates repetitive administrative tasks with precision and speed, revolutionizing HR and other functions. It handles activities like résumé screening, scheduling coordination, and personnel record management. By freeing up human experts from mundane tasks, AI allows them to focus on more strategic and value-driven projects.

Enhanced Productivity:

AI assists teams by providing task-oriented support, especially in challenging environmental circumstances. It improves team-related processes, performance, and outcomes. When teams effectively use technology, their productivity significantly boosts the organization's overall health."

In summary, AI acts as a catalyst for efficiency, intelligence, and creativity within high-performing teams, enabling them to achieve remarkable results. What it didn't say was how useful AI can be in helping us with the debrief by helping us find the various root causes for our shortfalls in performance. At the very least, it gives us a starting point for meaningful, objective, and focused conversations, without someone's human biases. It's also prone to mistakes, so the old adage holds true, bullshit in equals bullshit out, so your keepers of knowledge in your organization need to continually monitor and purge your database.

# Your Hand-Picked Team

Startup companies now define the characteristics of a classic team. Small, nimble, focused—and hand-picked by the company's founders—they have to succeed to get paid and they can't rely on a corporate machine to generate bonuses.

Technology startups can amaze us with the speed by which they take hold of an idea and spread it through our digital lives.

Equally impressive are new companies that enter traditional markets for physical goods and everyday services. Think Harry's Shaving and Grooming, UNTUCKit, or Farmer's Dog.

# Teams that Make Up Organizations

One of the most valuable aspects of FLEX is that it is designed to be used both in small teams and in very large organizations. Think the 307,000 people in the U.S. Air Force, for example, or the 5,000 crew members on an aircraft carrier, almost all of them between 19 and 24 years old. With respect to those aircraft carriers, it's all the more notable that every three years, every aspect of that carrier is renewed, including its crew. On a 36-month rotation, the entire boat gets refitted for another ten-month mission, and 90 percent of its crew will be entirely new. And yet the mission gets executed all but flawlessly because every person on that ship has a clear understanding of how they will work together. That's FLEX in action.

FLEX in business is the same thing. People no longer stay at one company for their entire working careers. Gen Z changes jobs every 1.6 years; Millennials change careers every five years, and change jobs every two-and-a-quarter years. The rest of us are changing jobs every 4.5-5 years. People come and go, and if it's your company, you need a simple approach for the people who join your organization to become one of your team. That's not necessarily easy. But try FLEX; it defines your culture no matter your turnover.

# FLEX Teams in Organizations

Teams are those groups of people who share a common mission objective and who are impact-focused. They are big enough to have the skills and diversity the mission needs, and small enough for each team member to know, rely on, and care about each other. Selection, training, and shared experience allow team members to appreciate the culture, standards, and processes that enable the team to work. They are different people, with different personalities, perspectives, and life values, but they share a common purpose, will execute a common mission, and they will have the desire to achieve that mission.

The teams we'll meet in this book share those team attributes, but are extremely diverse in makeup. They can be small, independent teams, or one of many similar "teams of teams" in a large organization. Surgical teams have been using FLEX with incredible results, dramatically improving their hospital's average performance on some key metrics. Sports teams can involve entire operations, like the New York Giants or the Denver Broncos, or separate units within the team: the offense, defense, and special teams. Sales, marketing, and event people each run a different function in a business; however, the overall success of the business depends on all three operating in synchronicity.

## Creating a FLEX Team

Almost any group of people can become a FLEX team. How? FLEX is all about creating a common intention and objective (this you can define as "purpose"), creating desire and confidence, and setting the foundations for trust. It's all about the roles people play in that team—be it as a team leader, as an essential follower, or in a mobile adaptive workplace, likely both. It's all about creating a team that is impact-focused, performing its mission consistently and reliably.

That's not easy. That's a challenge. There are many components to a team, and many things that can go wrong, but, over more than 28 years, we've turned and twisted the FLEX team concept a million different ways and still find that a successful team boils down to three things: a team's mindset, its skillset, and the processes that bring those together. When you define these three things, you define your team, and new members are quickly assimilated.

## The Respectful Truth of a FLEX Team

FLEX teams care for and respect each other. They share a common culture and purpose. FLEX teams do not gloss over or avoid difficulty just to be polite or avoid conflict. But they do manage these situations respectfully because they have a process to deal with it. "Respectful truth over manufactured harmony" is a common phrase that rings true here. And the leader sets that tone showing their team respect and a caring attitude from the start.

## Leaders, People Who Care

As we will see, respectful transparency and honesty are called for in debriefing a situation that has not gone well, when the temptations are greatest to point blame, make excuses, and undermine people. The debrief focuses on the actions taken and their causes, not blame. That's why there's a very real distinction between an accidental error, which is human and readily forgettable, and a deliberate breach of a mission plan or standards, which is a violation of trust. People own up to their own mistakes because they feel the responsibility to be honest to each other. They care. People feel vulnerable, and it is up to the leader to set that tone, to put him or herself in a vulnerable position first, by being the first to own up to their mistakes. It starts with the leaders, because it's the leader who has to care the most.

## How Do You Make that Care Genuine, Rather than Just a Word?

Where we see the true value of "caring" is the dreaded "reduced headcount" conversation. FLEX leaders approach reduced headcount in a people-centric way vs. a financially-motivated one. A case in point was the German government's policy of phasing out coal mining and energy reliance. The target was zero coal by 2038. This created a major headcount reduction in the coal mining industry and fomented serious protests and civil unrest. The government's solution? To retrain every single coal worker and support them until they were employed in other industries. Everyone was a winner. Was it messy? Was there conflict? Were various closures delayed? Yes, but overall, the strategy is now eight years ahead of schedule with the last coal-powered power plant due to close in 2030. Best of all, unless you chose to retire, the process retrained anyone who wanted to start a new career.

That's the type of care that FLEX creates. Leaders who pull out all the stops to mark occasions that need marking, who don't just place a phone call to order a turkey for the folks working on Christmas Day, but who cook and carve it for them. They go out on a limb and take risks for their team because they care. Perhaps it's because fighter pilots are taught from the outset that they're the most valuable thing in the air, no matter what their jet cost. The jet can be replaced, they cannot. That assurance carries over to the way they treat each other. Despite the forceful personalities in it, a squadron is not the bear pit of egos you see in a *Top Gun* movie, fun though it is to imagine. We care, and through that, we create cohesion.

# When to Lead. When to Follow. When to Collaborate.

The energy and confidence one has in a new leader can become unstuck when that leader is unsure when to make a leader's call, and when to be just one of the team. With FLEX, leaders and followers have a clear understanding of their very different roles. We implicitly understand that during a mission, leadership is fluid, and that a team leader may not always have the best situational awareness. Consider four jets moving across unfamiliar terrain ringed by mountains. My view as a wingman may be better than the leader's view. In that moment, I will step in and assume the lead. We help each other make the right calls.

In the planning stage, there is full engagement and collaboration. Through the agreed and defined process, all points of view are equally considered and respected. Then, when the team next gets together, it's time for the brief. This is the leader's time. It is the time to connect what we want in the future to what we do today. The leader has melded all of the team's input and situational awareness and is saying: "Thanks for all the input, this is now the final plan." The team understands that and goes with it, and the leader is responsible for ensuring the team understands it. It's a purposeful transition between the future (the plan) and today (execution).

In the execution phase, the leader is just another team member with a defined role to play. Everyone knows what they have to do and are no longer looking to the leader for permission or direction. Everyone has a clear understanding of what they're trying to achieve, and everyone is providing their support to reach the objective. This support goes both ways: your wingman is supporting you; you are supporting your wingman. Everyone is now mutually supportive.

When it's all over and the team gathers for the debrief, it's participation and intentional collaboration time again. The leader sets the tone by stating, "I made a mistake. I fess up, and I'll fix it."

# Aviator Sidebar: FLEX in Large Organizations – From Idea to Reality

"Genius is one percent inspiration and ninety-nine percent perspiration." Thomas Edison

Everyone has an idea. An annual strategy is itself an idea. An idea is in reality a best guess as to what the future looks like. Let's consider FLEX from the perspective of a large organization with hundreds, if not thousands, of people—a "Herding Cats" perspective, as we fighter pilots put it. FLEX is designed to be a scalable and repeatable approach to thought and action, which is why its principles are used so extensively in the fighter pilot community and in high growth, highly effective businesses, both. It is designed to be used independently or in unison by multiple teams at any level of an organization. When used in unison, when its teams and objectives are aligned to their ultimate objective, their execution rhythms are in sync, and FLEX will generate enormous energy and impact within your organization. But in the context of a larger organization, can a company use FLEX to execute its *entire* corporate strategy? We know it can, because we've seen it happen time after time again in organizations such as Air Jordan, VMWare, and our very first client, Home Depot.

In such cases, there are three things to consider:

The organizational objective. A larger organization will have its corporate mission or strategy more complex than a team mission's clear, single objective. FLEX can work on an organizational objective, even with many facets. In such cases, each facet must be clear, measurable, and achievable. We will still have well-written High-Definition Destinations (HDDs), and plan on how FLEX can get you there. Like the plan for a single mission, the plan remains purposeful and simple for an organization. When it's done well, it becomes the rallying cry for your people and it shapes the hard decisions when the inevitable tough times hit.

Long-term missions. In large corporations, achieving a corporate strategy or an HDD doesn't happen overnight. We can create multiple, aligned, and sequenced long-term HDDs that cascade from the board room to the manufacturing floor and guide our mission objectives and plans.

Missions to change your system. More often than not, the whole point of an organizational strategy is to change something about the system in which it operates. That takes extra thinking, but in reality, it's only a slight extension of FLEX planning. FLEX enables you to fine-tune your BAU, Business as Usual, to remove those repetitive errors and inconsistencies, and streamline decision-making and action.

Don't get me wrong. At Afterburner, we know how complex organizational strategy can be: we've seen it in action countless times, and FLEX isn't perfect. However, to deal with that, we also need to adopt a fighter pilot mindset, a growth mindset; that is, change is the game, the constant, so we need to start thinking about how we can drive it.

# 11 Closing Execution Gaps with X-Gaps

"However beautiful the strategy, you should occasionally look at the results." Sir Winston Churchill

We recently worked with a U.S. bank to help them execute the implementation of a new Customer Relationship Management system. The CRM project had a six-month timeframe and a lot of moving parts. We had the bank's IT team, an outside software vendor, an independent IT consultant, and the project leaders. As you can imagine, out of the gate, the mood was positive, and everyone was understandably confident they'd get the job done; it was just what you'd expect when a major project gets the greenlight and everybody is at the peak of their Hype Cycles.

But then reality set in. The first check-in point was set for a month into the schedule. The teams went away to execute their missions, but when we regathered, nothing substantial had been accomplished. It didn't take a genius to see that the executional rhythm was all wrong. Likewise, it didn't take a genius to see that the first milestone meeting should have been scheduled earlier. Had they done so, they would have seen that team members were lagging behind or veering off schedule, and they would have taken action right away.

Have you heard of Parkinson's Law? The more time people are given to complete a task, the more time they will take, regardless of the task's complexity? Coined by British historian Cyril Northcote Parkinson in 1955, the thesis is that the work required will expand to fill the time allotted.

If you allocate two weeks for a task that could realistically take only two days, it's likely that the task will stretch to consume the entire two weeks. This happens because:

- People subconsciously adjust their pace to match the time available.

- Extra time creates room for overthinking, over-polishing, or adding unnecessary complexity.

- Perceived Complexity. The time allocated often influences the perceived complexity of a task. If given ample time, individuals may mentally inflate the difficulty, leading to procrastination, unnecessary planning, or overengineering.

Long deadlines foster inefficiency and distraction as there's no sense of urgency. When deadlines loom, the pressure forces focus and productivity. This explains why people often produce more in shorter time frames under stress.

You'll remember the pilot's mantra: "Brief the plan, fly the brief." The brief is the mission; the mission is the brief. We pilots want our missions to turn out like a well-scripted, well-rehearsed play, no surprises. We want great timing from every actor, stagehand, and musician, no missed lines, and if anything goes awry, we want a quick recovery. On top of that, we want everyone to project irresistible energy. That's a great play and a good mission, and if at the end of a good mission we can say, "Everything went according to plan," it would be a very happy day. But it would also be a very rare day because plans rarely survive reality.

# Commit. Adapt. Abort.

Until the last box is checked and the mission is accomplished, we all know that internal and external factors will affect our execution rhythm—good and bad. Consider some real-world possibilities. In the case of this bank, let's imagine that a CRM far more advanced than theirs was launched by a new company. Do they switch gears? What if they had a corporate crisis and resources have to be moved off their project? Rewrite the plan? Let's assume some members take new jobs, what then? Or, assume the software vendor has an update that smooths things out and accelerates the timetable, or, more likely, snags will complicate matters beyond anything in the contingency plans. The world changes, wars in Ukraine and the Middle East, inflation, recessions, elections, and exuberance.

Changes in regulations may demand more or less compliance. On and on it goes, all of which means the plan needs to adapt and evolve.

FLEX not only accepts that reality, but anticipates it. However fast or good a plan is, it's only perfect in the moment it's made. In the next nano-second, there will be a blizzard of circumstances that interfere. As the economist John Maynard Keynes famously said, "When my information changes, I change my mind. What do you do?" Well, we do, too. The facts and circumstances will change as you progress down the execution timeline, which means you will invariably tweak your plans. That's expected. We're not building flawless plans. We're building flawless missions. The FLEX planning process handles that via numerous team check-in points and regular reviews to identify gaps between the timeline in the plan and where you are in the execution phase, to identify gaps between what you want and what you have, between the desired objective and the current status. The need here is to communicate information, up-dates, and progress reports. We do that through a process called an Execution Gap Meeting, or an X-Gap meeting. X-Gap meetings review the team's progress to make sure your execution is aligned to the ob-jective and aligned to the timetable, no matter what the world throws at you. It identifies any gaps and asks the team what to do. In that respect, every X-Gap has a three-part decision matrix associated with it. Do you Commit, Adapt, or Abort? Green light, yellow, or red? The X-Gap meeting is where you identify the gaps between your planned objectives and the reality of today's results, work out why a gap exists, then decide what to do about them, and commit to the next plan.

## X-Gap Meetings Are Powerful

Importantly the mindset we bring to the X-Gap is one that is biased to action; we discuss what you need to do next week and the support you need. It is not updating everyone on your job. It's quick—we believe X-Gaps should be no longer than 15 minutes (it takes about 6 weeks to get that ability), and it requires a dashboard for situational awareness. Keeping on top of things is the driving reason for your X-Gap meetings, but it's not the only one. People are more likely to do things when they're doing it with another person. That's one of the hidden benefits of teams and of teamwork. People don't like facing people when they haven't met their commitments. That's the antithesis of teamwork. There is simply no better way to hold people accountable than a supportive peer group, and X-Gap brings that to the table in five important ways:

X-Gap meetings underscore the leader's intent. Planning and execution are ultimately human endeavors. Just because we thought out the plan to the ninth degree doesn't mean there won't be subjective interpretations, so it's up to the leader to fill in the blanks and bring out those interpretations. No matter how clearly defined your objective is, there has to be a point to it, a purpose. The plan will set forth the specific, immediate objectives, but the leader's intent is the intended effect of the mission. What is the desired impact? What are we trying to achieve as a collective? What's the point? What does good look like? The leader owns the intent. The team itself will take ownership of the objective and the plan to meet it. The X-Gap is where we reinforce the message, the intent. There's a point to a mission, and the team must know it. Purpose is a powerful motivator. It's up to the team leader to make that purpose clear.

X-Gap meetings reinforce culture. The meetings must bring people together. What you emphasize and the mood you set shapes the team's culture and drives behavior. Performance and success are driven by what we believe. What we do is a result of that drive. Your ultimate goal is to create a culture in which people consistently make an impact and surpass expectations.

Responsibility of leadership. By virtue of these meetings, you are restating your personal responsibility for the plan and its delivery. You have to arrive at your meeting totally prepared. Teams follow accountable, engaged leaders. Use the meeting to show your commitment. What you want is what they will want. You drive every aspect of FLEX.

Momentum has momentum. X-Gaps must be frequent and consistent. Fighter pilot missions are briefed and flown on the same day. That's our execution rhythm. Business missions take longer, so don't wait for reality to interfere or to force your hand. Don't let reality set your rhythm. You set the rhythm. Have X-Gap meetings scheduled on your timeline, and use the meeting to maintain or accelerate the momentum. Make momentum a marker of your personality. Infused with a sense of urgency and a sense of responsibility, teams leave the meeting infused with renewed energy and momentum. Momentum creates momentum.

In sum, the Plan articulates who does what and when, and X-Gap meetings review the progress. You'll be able to head off minor problems before they snowball and become big ones. You'll also know if there's an internal threat that might have to be managed now. Nobody can hide if something's not done. Whether it's an honest oversight or a shirked responsibility, the plan will be affected. Working through these human issues builds teamwork, and mutual respect follows.

# The Format for Successful X-Gap Meetings

Just as a brief is not your typical kick-off meeting, the X-Gap is not your typical weekly check-up. Some liken them to a fast-paced fitness session with your trainer: short, focused, and intense. We use ORCA, keep it simple, and then identify where we need to focus the planning and debriefing efforts. Think of an X-Gap as a situational awareness tool that drives accountability and visibility and prioritizes the team effort until the next X-Gap.

The first X-Gap meeting is the moment of truth. Is your team getting the job done? What culture is emerging? It makes sense to hold that first X-Gap meeting early in the mission. Not only does that show leadership and commitment, but it also creates the expectation that the plan should be on track out of the gate—and stay on track at each milestone. Set a date for the first meeting in your first brief and follow this format.

1.  Regular intervals. X-Gaps should be held at regular intervals. Dan Ariely, the behavioral economist, studies why people aren't always economically "rational"; that is, why they don't always act in their own financial self-interest. For instance, letting mistakes linger is not in your self-interest. How does Ariely say we can correct this? Deadlines, he says. Like X-Gap meetings. A series of regular, firm deadlines, he writes, generates better results than either self-chosen or end-of-project deadlines. Again, a predictable tempo helps create a habit of expectations and accountability throughout the project. Over a long mission, the tempo of X-gaps may change, but the changes should be as minimal as possible. Do you have a deliverable this week? X-Gap daily. This month? X-Gap weekly. This quarter? You get the idea, be consistent.

2.  Brief and to the point. Everyone hates a long, drifting meeting. Far from being long and drifting, X-Gaps are short and to the point. 15 minutes is the aim.

3.  Formal and serious. And focused only on the plan.

4.  Setting. The setting should be the same room you used to brief the team, a room clearly set up as a mission room, not the local café. It can be a Zoom call, too, so long as you know the tools and how to make the dashboard accessible to all team members—with video on.

5. <u>Preparation.</u> Preparation is everything. The leader prepares for an X-Gap just as they would the initial briefing. At a minimum, you have an updated action plan that reinforces the mission's objective, desired outcomes, and the overall tone and culture. On their part, team members must prepare for the X-Gap with an honest and accurate statement on the status of their tasks. They must rank each one on one of these three metrics:

**Green**: Completed, or on track and on time.

**Yellow**: There are issues that may block the successful completion of the objective; however, they can be resolved within the team.

**Red**: There are critical issues that will prevent the successful conclusion of the mission without more resourcing and/or a major change that is approved at the top.

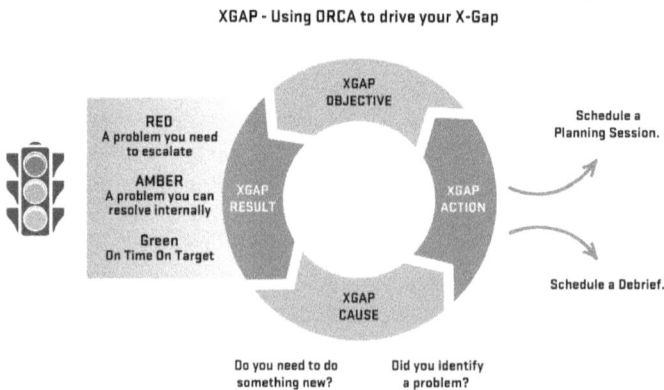

*Figure 25. X-Gap Off Ramps XX*

6. <u>Two x Two x Two.</u> Discuss each task quickly; allow no more than two minutes at the top, two minutes per task review, and two minutes at the end. If a task review goes over two minutes, hold it over to the end, and then continue in an offline meeting, if needed.

- Opening Statement: Two minutes
- Tasks: Two minutes per task
- Closing statement: Two minutes

Chapter 11: Closing Execution Gaps with X-Gaps

7. <u>Avoid social banter.</u> If the team needs a get-together to celebrate a birthday or talk about the football game, do that apart from the X-Gap.

8. Don't allow the X-Gap to become a planning session or a debrief.

9. <u>Some will find irresistible rabbit holes</u> or a technical issue that's really interesting and worth at least a three-hour bar detour. Take it outside. Not here.

A $2 fine jar can work wonders to keep you on task.

We want to keep an X-Gap simple, so we use a modified form of ORCA:

# Objective

What is the objective of the execution gap meeting? Restate the objective of the mission and extrapolate or identify where the team should be right now. It could be as simple as "50% complete." It may be binary, that is, complete or incomplete. Bring your data dashboard to the X-Gap. It is the single source of truth for the team. Ideally, your dashboard is integrated with your data analytics, so they should be live and accurate. Don't have a dashboard? Put your objectives into a single spreadsheet; it doesn't need to be more complex than that.

# Results

What are your results? List the tasks and go over the color codes. Are they red or yellow? That's all we want to know. In an X-Gap we're not talking about green, or any of those results that are on the mark. They're a given, there is no execution gap, so there's no place for this discussion in the X-Gap. Looking for recognition for a job well done? Take time after the X-Gap to celebrate the wins; use the bathtub method here, too.

# Cause

Do your homework and link a cause to the X-Gap. It's usually a human factor issue. The cause of a gap is usually an individual who needs to catch up. The person may be on the team or outside the team. Identify what they need from you and what you need from them. Include the actions they need to take in order to help the team get back on track.

If you don't know what's causing your execution gap, that's OK too. Use the combined intellectual firepower of the people in the room to work that out. Jump on an AI tool. Use phrases like "What are some common reasons XYZ is delayed, or fails?" In any event, it may result in an offline planning session if it's a big issue. The good news is, we know what it is, we know it's a big deal, and we can focus our efforts and lean into it, or make an intentional decision to let it go, or defer to another sprint or execution window.

# Action

Just like the debrief, the X-Gap is all about defining an action at the individual or team level that is aligned to the organization's HDD or your mission objective. List the actions that you need to take or that you need the team to take to close the gap. If you have a problem that needs a team to solve it, schedule a debrief time then and there. If you discover something new and unexpected, run a quick planning session AFTER the X-Gap.

Finally, end with a classic summation. Who does what by when and how do we measure it?

# Example

Here's a very simple example of a task that's gone off the rails and how the format deals with it. Let's say Anne is responsible for managing the technical side of a market research survey. She's supposed to upload the questions to a designated social site, download the answers, and deliver the results back to the team. Jim, on the other hand, is supposed to write the questions. The overall objective is to use the survey data to improve the functionality of a widget.

Anne reports and has a problem. She needs to go live next Monday, and she's behind. At the team's weekly X-Gap, which is scheduled at 3:30 p.m. every Wednesday for 20 minutes, Anne says:

- (Objective) I want the survey questions published and live next Monday. To do that, I need to upload and test them by the close of business today.

- (**R**esult) Yellow. I can't meet that timeline at the moment, but it's fixable internally.

- (**C**ause) I don't have Jim's questions yet. Jim, I know you're busy, but I'm waiting for your questions.

- (**A**ction) I need them by noon tomorrow at the latest. Even a day late, I can tweak my own plans and still be able to go live on schedule, which means the rest of the tasks will remain on schedule.

Now Jim, like the rest of us, is likely distracted, busy, and balancing 50 other things. However, coming out of this meeting, he has clarity—he understands the task and he has an updated timeline. On her part, Anne has delivered a Flawless X-Gap update. She followed ORCA and finished with who does what by when and how do we measure it.

Jim (who) must generate the questions (what) by noon tomorrow (when). How do we measure? It's binary: Anne has them, or she doesn't.

The ideal X-Gap should only require yes/no answers from the team leader and ultimately help the team prioritize actions and promote mutual support. Ann has done her homework in this X-Gap and has come into the meeting prepared. She shows good situational awareness. She mapped out an action plan that connected Jim's gap with her task and her task to the team's objective. The conversation took all of 30 seconds.

# 12 Strategy

Strategy is the future you desire. Action is how you get there. HDDs define our future, and objective guiding action is what delivers it. Remember, Intention + Action = Impact, or more FLEX-specific, HDDs define objectives that guide action to deliver impact.

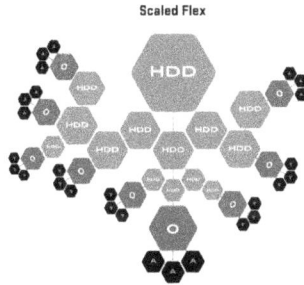

*Figure 26. HDDs Objectives and Action XX*

If our HDD is our clear, measurable, and achievable destination, or what you used to call goals and now call objectives, and the FLEX method is the engine that drives us to that destination, the engine doesn't get you there without a driver or a map. That's you and your strategy. No map, wrong map, or spill coffee on your map—your strategy is now ambiguous, and you'll be driving in circles, or by gut, and it's going to take you a long time to get to your destination, and your team will look more like a herd of dairy cows ruminating in a field than a team of performance-driven superstars.

Your strategy is the story that holds everything together. It's the amalgamation of your HDDs, executed with the right people all pulling in the same direction, all headed to the same destination. When we first wrote *On Time On Target*, there was time to contemplate strategy. You had hierarchies, and those hierarchies operated at the "strategic layer," the "operational layer," and the "tactical level." The strategy was focused on the alignment of tasks and work. Today, strategy requires a different lens, a lens that starts with the impact of your strategy (when our strategy is implemented, what happens for our customers/clients/consumers?) vs. the creation of a linear to-do list for your 48,000 employees.

# Finding Critical Leverage Points

Critical leverage points are important for defining effective strategies. In business, the critical leverage points can be within your company, or they can be external. Sometimes they are the system itself. The computer industry was so focused on itself that it missed the PC. Microsoft and Apple flourished because the system—and the big companies—were too wed to mainframes. No longer.

Sometimes, the leverage points are regulatory. In the early years of the airline industry, passenger airlines carried cargo as a way to stay afloat. In fact, they lobbied Congress so hard that it became the law that cargo had to be shipped on airplanes with passengers. Fred Smith, a Marine Corps veteran, saw it otherwise. He lobbied Congress to allow cargo to be shipped on little jets that would only carry cargo. They agreed. Then he lobbied Congress to allow cargo to be shipped on his bigger jets, cargo-only jets. Today, his company is called FedEx.

Launching satellites into space was a system so rigid and hidebound that it literally invited disruption. No one would sell Elon Musk the boosters he needed to put a satellite into orbit, so he decided to design and manufacture a booster himself—every single part of it. The industry giants laughed and thought he would go away. Instead, the Falcon 9 today is the centerpiece of SpaceX, a rocket company with $13 billion in revenue and a market cap of $214 billion.

A strategy can be opportunistic. A *brilliant* opportunistic strategy can transcend even the immediate opportunity and become universally effective. Papua New Guinea is not the easiest place in the world to do business, but it's in Australia's sphere of influence, so I follow what goes on there. Some years ago, ExxonMobil announced a $19-billion natural gas project there, and the news raced through the country's economy. Builders rushed in to put up housing for the workers and contractors who would invariably arrive. A construction boom ensued. Because of that boom, everything was suddenly terribly expensive. Fuel, materials, labor, expertise—anything you needed cost too much. To make matters worse, much of everything had to be imported, which drove costs even higher. In a matter of no time, the economics of construction were terrible.

But therein lay a leverage point, and we formed a company to exploit it. The weakness in the system was blindly following the it-was-always-done-this-way construction process, even as inflationary data said that it made no sense. Our strategy was to build as much as possible overseas, ship prefab units that were 80 percent complete to Port Moresby as modules, and then finish it all on-site. By doing it this way, we would use less of the very expensive local labor and fewer of the very expensive local materials while tapping into the economics of China and Australia, where prices were reasonable. Our company was pioneering a whole new way of construction, and the numbers worked. Modular was the strategy.

Unfortunately, Exxon abruptly pulled the rug out from under us, deciding living behind barbed wire and guards was a better solution, and the project was shelved. However, we had identified a systemic weakness in the construction world and the core strategy was unaffected—shipping modules of nearly completed construction units and finishing them onsite. So, why limit ourselves to Papua New Guinea; why not anywhere in the world with any sort of construction project that could benefit from our modular strategy? And so we did. It was a small, 14-story hotel project in downtown Perth, Australia, that proved our strategy. It was running up costs to the point where the project was unviable. To make the project a financial success, the construction model had to change—change to our modular process. The project was completely redesigned, built in record time, and is now the tallest modular hotel in the world at 17 stories. Stop by and see it. It is Rydges Perth King Square Hotel. It would not have existed without identifying the critical leverage points within the construction system. We could not have built it without using the FLEX process to adapt the plan to real-world changes and execute the course of action. We would not have built it without Papua New Guinea. Did we deliver our mission in PNG? No. Did we deliver our HDD to build something with modular construction? You bet we did.

*Figure 27. Peppers King Square Hotel*

# Laser-Focused Strategy

Whatever business you're in, you're operating in a system and you need to understand it. A system is something that makes your life easier, is simple, and delivers outcomes with minimal effort. A road, rail, and air system helps you get around easier. The operating system on your PC or phone makes it easier to use. The education system equipped you with the skills to read this book, the ignition system is how you started your car this morning. We rarely think about it; however, your life depends on the effective operation of systems. Try living without a pulmonary or central nervous system. Systems are largely organic. They want to survive as is. They resist change, they fail to evolve without a catalyst. Thousands of people are vested in preserving the system the way it is, and the laws of the jungle apply here; that is, the more powerful the systems, the larger the organizations in it, the stronger it is, and the greater the resistance to change.

But there is a flip side to this. Critical leverage points are those places in a system where you find a single point of exploitation or are a nexus point where multiple other critical points come together. These are the big levers, the ones that when pulled, create the biggest impact. If the system won't work without them, that's your focus, the objective of your mission, and the HDD of your FLEX process. Apply pressure at the right places to change the system from what it is, to what you want it to be. That directed pressure is called **strategy**. The one thing all of the companies in this chapter have in common is a good strategy, and that is fundamental to achieving your goals, your desired outcomes, your HDD. Good strategies well executed will trump everything.

For your system to constantly evolve, it requires constant tweaks and adjustments. Every move you make tweaks the system; however, make a small move, and the bonds give a little, then ease back to where they were. But apply the big force at the right place and the right time, and those big moves will break the bonds like a network of Amazon distribution centers at the center of a transport node near a large city. Clear, believable, simple strategies break bonds and disrupt systems to ensure you evolve and remain relevant. Identify the leverage points, identify the strategy to impact it, pour that strategy into the FLEX process, and watch your people and your business grow. Execute the mission, and your system becomes the new system.

Jeff Bezos is a man with a natural "fighter pilot mindset." He was taking something from today and thinking about how to do it better tomorrow. He was on his knees, shipping yet another order of books, when the results from a survey he was conducting came in. The survey asked his customers a very simple question: "What else would you like to buy from us?" The answers weren't exactly what he expected. "A television," said one respondent. "Sporting goods," said another. "A new computer," said a third. "It was everything," said Bezos in a talk with students. "They wanted to buy everything from us."

And therein lay a problem. Bezos had a nice little business selling books. His competition included a few national book chains and a lot of sleepy mom-and-pop booksellers. He was competing well as an online retailer and, truth be told, his young company was doing just fine. The future looked good. There wasn't much to worry about.

The survey data, however, told another story. His customers wanted him to retail more than just books. "Sell everything," they said, but if he acted on that, his nice little operation would come up against the big box retailers and the hundreds of thousands of local stores with their loyal, local customers. How do you compete with that? Who's going to buy a pair of trousers or a skirt without trying them on first? The retail ecosystem for brick-and-mortar shopping was well-developed and entrenched in the social fabric of America, evidenced by the rapid expansion (and today the rapid decay) of shopping malls. The big players in the market had deep-pocketed corporations with vested interests to keep it that way. In a word, the mall was a ubiquitous destination for men and women, teens and grandparents. Why bother?

For one, it was also a multi-hundred-billion-dollar business. If one could find a weakness, a leverage point, it held out the prospect for untold riches. So, Bezos started mapping out the system, looking for weaknesses, looking for leverage points.

Simple models are some of the hardest to break, and retailing was built on an utterly simple model. Group a cluster of stores together and you have created a shopping destination. Have plenty of parking spaces and make sure the malls are within 3 to 5 miles of 95% of the United States population. Add a food court. Maybe add a travel agency. In one stop, a customer could shop 50 stores at once, have lunch with their friends, and maybe plan a trip to France, all at the same time.

There were, however, some obvious weaknesses. Shopping can be fun, but it can also be a pain. You have to get in the car and drive and spend a little money on gas. Some days are too hot to go out; some days are too cold, and some days bring torrential rainfall. Some days, the parking lots are full, and the stores are jammed. Plus, it can be unpredictable. Some days the store you like is sold out of the shirt you wanted, or the size wasn't available.

Bezos saw those weak points, and in 1998, four years after founding the business, he decided to turn the system upside down. Instead of hundreds of malls and thousands of people driving from their houses to go shopping, why not build hundreds of distribution centers and have millions of packages delivered to those houses? Take away the pain points, offer competitive prices, and deliver their packages within two days. Bezos' HDD was a chain of 100 or more distribution centers out by the Interstates and 100 more fulfillment centers in vacant buildings inside the cities, all poised to deliver any product you wanted in two days. It would be online, so there would be an infinite assortment of products, all without the frustration of an item that was out of stock. If it didn't fit? And consistency? Well, that's a Jeff Bezos hallmark. Do the simple things well and be consistent!

From here, we all know what happened. Stay home. Shop. Save money. Your package is there in two days—and often the same day—with free returns. Those benefits became the backbone of a multi-hundred-billion-dollar retailing empire called Amazon. Bezos mapped out a system, identified weak points, and strategically targeted them to build a new business. You can too.

On August 2, 1990, Iraq invaded Kuwait. In response, President Bush ordered his commanders to liberate Kuwait and neutralize the Iraqi military to ensure such an event wouldn't reoccur. A very thoughtful commander, Colonel John Warden, often considered "one of the most creative airmen of the 21st century," was in charge of the air offensive. He had hundreds of American fighter jets and bombers at his disposal, including the newest stealth aircraft. He had even more jets and bombers from dozens of coalition nations. An air war campaign seemed very doable—until his campaign planners came back with a list of some 300,000 potential military, power, communication, and transportation targets, which was way too many for an aerial campaign. But Warden was undaunted. He began mapping out the Iraqi system. He was looking for leverage points that, if attacked, would minimize casualties on the ground but give him his end results without hitting 300,000 other targets. What were the critical leverage points that he found? The power plants, certainly. But they were heavily defended and would take weeks of determined effort to overcome. What else? The power grid itself could be neutralized, but electricity could always find a new path through the grid, and power wires could be quickly restored. However, spaced within the grid itself were a limited number of "step-up transformers," points where power from the generating plants was aggregated and then redistributed into the grid. Knock out the transformers, and you knock out the grid, or so said the planners. Warden took a closer look. They weren't heavily defended nor easily repaired. There wasn't an alternate mechanism or a back-up system, which meant they were the critical leverage points he was looking for. The aerial bombing campaign written by Colonel John Warden would become the devastating centerpiece of Operation Desert Storm and the 1991 Gulf War. He put the lights out in Iraq in a single night. He didn't even use bombs to destroy the Transformers. The U.S. Air Force invented a unique method of dropping carbon fiber, which deployed spools of fine metal filaments, often referred to as "metal foil," tripping the transformers offline, a little like the circuit breakers in your house! That's high-impact strategy!

Since COVID-19, McKinsey and Co. have observed that corporate strategy has significantly shifted towards faster decision-making and more agile organizational structures. Companies that embraced agile frameworks pre-pandemic have adapted quickly, reducing bureaucracy, empowering cross-functional teams, and fostering innovation. This transformation has been reinforced by hybrid work models and digital tools, allowing businesses to remain flexible and resilient.

Harvard Business School emphasizes balancing short-term flexibility with a long-term focus, using frequent assessments like 30- or 60-day KPIs. A key strategy is agile leadership, with collaborative problem-solving methods and swift issue resolution through "swarming sessions," a process that Agile uses to focus the energy of a team on one issue until it is resolved. Jeff Bezos, Amazon's founder, famously said: "Speed matters in business. Many decisions and actions are reversible and do not need extensive study. We value calculated risk-taking"—highlighting the importance of fast decision-making in today's dynamic environment. How do we adjust our strategy on the fly? How do we prioritize our actions day to day? Who makes the decisions? What if a leader gets sick? Our strategy is how we connect where we want to go with how we do it, and, in this digital age, FLEX is the simplest, most dynamic system there is to build and execute strategy.

# What Bad Strategy Looks Like

Business strategies often fail. This is well-known by now: According to studies, some 60–90% of strategic plans never fully launch. The causes of derailment vary widely, but execution consistently bears the blame.

# Boeing's Strategic Failure: How a Loss of Focus on the HDD and Core Values Led to Collapse

There's a saying amongst pilots: "If it ain't Boeing, I ain't going." Or should I say, there's an *old* saying….

For much of the 20th century, Boeing was an undisputed leader in the aerospace industry, long admired for its technological innovation, engineering prowess, and commitment to safety. However, since the turn of the century, a shift in strategy has led to a dramatic and very public fall from grace. It started with a series of very high-profile disasters, most notably the Lion Air and Ethiopian Airlines 737 MAX crashes. It was followed by strategic blunders, like a loss of focus on core values, poor strategic direction, and a corrosive corporate culture that prioritized short-term profits over long-term stability and excellence. In stark contrast, Airbus, Boeing's chief rival, pursued a more disciplined and forward-thinking strategy, leading to its rise as the dominant player in global aviation.

## The Shift from Aerospace Engineering to Financial Engineering

Many say Boeing's problems can be traced back to the late 1990s, when the company merged with McDonnell Douglas. Analysts viewed this as the moment, the root cause of today's malaise when Boeing shifted its focus from engineering excellence to financial engineering. Historically, McDonnell Douglas's hull losses (crashed aircraft) were statistically higher than Boeing's, perhaps a harbinger of the future. McDonnell Douglas had a more corporate-driven, cost-cutting culture, and its executives began to take key leadership roles at Boeing. The result of the merger, some say, was a gradual erosion of Boeing's engineering-led culture in favor of a shareholder-first mentality.

The clearest manifestation of that was the handling of the 737 MAX program. Instead of designing a new aircraft from scratch, Boeing opted for a cost-saving measure by updating the aging 737 to compete with Airbus's A320neo, which was more fuel-efficient and technologically more advanced. In developing the 737 MAX, analysts argue that Boeing cut corners, particularly with the Maneuvering Characteristics Augmentation System (MCAS), which would later prove fatal according to NTSB investigators. The 737 MAX crashes involved the MCAS and brought to light Boeing's failure to prioritize and find the balance between safety and innovation.

In contrast, Airbus steadily focused on delivering cutting-edge, fuel-efficient planes. The A320neo, with its revolutionary engines and technology, proved to be a game-changer. Airbus's commitment to innovation and long-term planning enabled it to capture significant market share, while Boeing scrambled to mitigate the fallout from its strategic missteps.

# The 737 MAX Scandal: A Symptom of a Bigger Problem

The 737 MAX scandal is emblematic of Boeing's larger issues. The decision to modify the old 737 rather than develop a new model was driven by financial pressures and a desire to match Airbus's success with the A320neo. Boeing's management made this decision despite internal concerns from engineers. The company's once-stellar reputation was damaged by prioritizing speed to market and minimizing costs.

Boeing's handling of the aftermath was just as troubling and a far cry from the Tylenol case study we reviewed in an earlier chapter. The company initially downplayed the severity of the problem, withholding critical information from pilots and regulators and operating with a general lack of transparency and accountability. That only deepened the crisis, resulting in the worldwide grounding of the 737 MAX. Boeing suffered billions of dollars in losses, and the airlines that lost lift capacity and thus had fewer paying passengers lost billions more.

Airbus, on the other hand, took a more measured approach to innovation. While Airbus faced its own challenges, such as delays with the A380 program, it never compromised on safety or engineering rigor. Airbus's commitment to this long-term strategy, even at the expense of short-term profits, stands in sharp contrast to Boeing's. Clearly, in every X-Gap meeting, the teams never lost sight of their organizational HDD.

## Corporate Culture: Boeing's Fall from Integrity

Boeing's corporate culture was a key factor in its decline. The company's focus on shareholder value and quarterly profits overshadowed its commitment to employees, customers, and the business's long-term health. A once proud engineering company with a clear HDD became driven by cost-cutting and outsourcing. Engineers were sidelined, and decision-making became dominated by financial executives with little understanding of the complexities of aerospace design. The HDD was obfuscated.

And it was compounded. The outsourcing of key components and manufacturing processes exacerbated the problem. A related example was Boeing's decision to outsource large portions of the 787 Dreamliner's production. That led to significant delays and quality control issues, and the company's ability to maintain high standards of quality and safety was diminished.

# Look at How Complicated Life has Become for Boeing 737 Max

After its return to service in November 2020, airlines operating the 737 MAX have filed over 1,800 service difficulty reports, covering a wide range of issues such as engine stalls, flight control problems, and anti-icing system failures. The FAA has also issued numerous airworthiness directives related to the 737 MAX, including directives addressing wiring and grounding issues, further damaging its reputation.

In addition, the FAA grounded 171 737 MAX aircraft in 2024 due to production quality issues, further emphasizing the systemic problems Boeing has faced with this model.

While approved for flight again, the Boeing airliner continues to be closely monitored for potential safety risks.

Meanwhile, Airbus kept much of its production in-house, preserving tighter control over quality and ensuring that its products met the highest safety standards. This decision strengthened their competitive position as Boeing floundered.

Let's have a look at Airbus's current performance:

In 2023, Airbus delivered 735 aircraft, compared to Boeing's 528 units, marking the fifth consecutive year Airbus outpaced Boeing. Airbus's success is largely attributed to the A320 family and the A350, where it has outperformed Boeing in orders and deliveries.

New aircraft are on track. Airbus A321XLR—the long-range variant of the A320 family—entered into service in 2024, with demand continuing to grow due to its extended range and operational flexibility. It will be a key player in the single-aisle long-haul market, a segment where Boeing has no direct competitor after postponing its own mid-market airplane (Boeing 797).

A220 Program – The A220 has also performed well. Airbus has steadily increased production, helping it meet the rising demand for smaller, fuel-efficient jets.

A350 – Airbus continues to expand its market share in the widebody segment with the A350, which competes directly with Boeing's 787. The A350 is considered a leader in fuel efficiency and has become a top choice for airlines looking for long-haul aircraft.

# Airbus is dominating Boeing in almost all performance benchmarks:

Order Backlog: Airbus has a larger backlog, with orders equivalent to more than 12 years of production, compared to Boeing, which is still struggling with the fallout from the 737 MAX grounding.

Installed Fleet: Since 2020, Airbus has had more aircraft in service than Boeing, another sign of the shift in market leadership.

New Orders: Airbus secured over 2,094 net new orders in 2023, significantly more than Boeing's 1,314, further solidifying the former's leadership.

# The Financial Impact of the Shift at Boeing

Since the grounding of the 737 MAX in 2019, Boeing has reported substantial financial losses, amounting to approximately $32 billion through 2024. This includes core operating losses of $31.9 billion and net losses of $27 billion, with the company's debt increasing from $13 billion to $48 billion. The company has suffered using the very strategy it thought would improve its financial condition.

On the other hand, Airbus has made over $13.8 billion in profits over the same period. It would have been more, save from a legal issue. That profit includes booking a roughly $4 billion charge for bribery. Airbus may not be the poster child for ethical business, but at least it has stayed focused on building safe aircraft!

## Strategic Missteps and Blurred Vision

Boeing's inability to remain agile in the face of the changing demands of the global aviation market indicates a flawed strategy. As environmental concerns became more pressing, and airlines sought more fuel-efficient and environmentally friendly aircraft, Boeing was slow to respond. Its decision to focus on incremental improvements rather than developing entirely new aircraft left it trailing Airbus in terms of innovation and environmental sustainability. The result was the Frankenstein B 737 Max, whose super-efficient engines threw out all the aerodynamics and resulted in the single point of failure: MCAS. Think of it as a cost-cutting measure where your car manufacturer decides two sets of brakes are just as good as the four you had on your old car, and they consider that it's not important enough to let you know.

Airbus, by comparison, was willing to invest in the future. The development of the A350, a direct competitor to Boeing's 787, was a clear example of Airbus's consistency and adherence to its own HDD. Airbus understood that the future of aviation was in fuel-efficient, long-haul aircraft, with a common cockpit (User Interface in digital speak), and it invested accordingly. The A350's success underscored Airbus's commitment to innovation and customer satisfaction, positioning the company as a leader in sustainable aviation.

## The Impact on the Industry

The consequences of Boeing's missteps have been felt across the aviation industry. Airlines that had invested heavily in the 737 MAX faced operational disruptions and financial losses due to the aircraft's grounding. Boeing's failure to address its internal problems and its continued focus on short-term profits have eroded trust among its customers and stakeholders.

## Conclusion: A Tale of Two Strategies

Boeing's fall from grace is a cautionary tale of what happens when a company loses sight of its core values or blindly follows ill-defined HDDs, despite the warning signs and whistleblowers, and fails to adapt to a changing market. Boeing compromised its long-standing reputation and alienated its customers by prioritizing financial performance over engineering excellence. The 737 MAX crisis is just one symptom of a broader failure to stay true to one's HDD.

# Don't Do a Boeing – Do You Own Your Strategy? Can You Execute Your Strategy?

Any objective, be it corporate or winning a Super Bowl, is successfully reached through strategy. Effective strategy targets a critical leverage point that, when affected, shapes the system the way you want it shaped. FLEX helps you develop strategy in the planning phase and always tests it against the way you're planning on executing it. Many companies have strategy teams, both internal and external. No matter the team and the process, you, and most importantly, your execution team, have to answer the following questions:

- Has your executive team taken the strategy as your leader's intent (the story), and created an HDD (the science), each part of which is clear, measurable, and achievable? Is the HDD the ultimate objective of the strategy?
- Has your executive team identified the threats to achieving that HDD? Has it mapped the system and identified the likely responses from those in the system?
- Has your executive team identified the resources it needs?
- Has your team looked at the lessons learned from previous missions on how to overcome similar threats, weaknesses, or barriers to achieving the HDD?
- Has your executive team identified and prioritized the strategic initiatives such that your team leaders can own the objectives of their individual action plans? Have you nominated the individuals and the timeframe for them to do their part?
- Has an independent, external Red Team stress-tested your course of action?
- Has your executive team built in contingencies?
- Does your execution rhythm include time for regular X-Gap reviews?
- Are there universally agreed-to standards in place—processes, culture, communications—by which the mission and X-Gap reviews will be conducted?

If you can answer "yes" to all these questions, you're ready to put your personal stamp on the strategy and brief the course of action to your executive team. If so, there are two final questions to follow-up on in your first X-Gap:

- Does everyone who is accountable have a clear dashboard to track their performance? Pause, and wait for an affirmative answer.
- Does everyone who is accountable have a wingman to offer mutual support? The same—wait for an affirmative answer.

# 5 The Future of Leadership

In **The Future of Leadership**, *The Afterburner Advantage* connects the core principles of the fighter pilot mindset with the evolving demands of leadership. Boo highlights the importance of **situational awareness**, aligning personal and professional goals, and fostering adaptability. By incorporating the FLEX process and Agile methodologies, leaders can navigate complexity, make informed decisions, and build high-performing teams. This section reinforces that leadership in the future requires a balance of discipline, emotional intelligence, and continuous learning, helping individuals achieve their full potential while guiding organizations toward success.

# 13 The FLEX Cockpit and Our Wings

"The power of one man or one woman doing the right thing for the right reason and at the right time is the greatest influence in our society."
Jack Kemp,
Professional Footballer and Congressman

## The Overall Framework

A jet and its environment are the perfect visual metaphors for FLEX. We get into our jet only after completing the FLEX process. I just want to draw your attention to the middle of the image here, that's you. FLEX starts, runs, and ends with you at the controls. It's not an enterprise tool, an operational tool, or a way of working without you firmly at the controls.

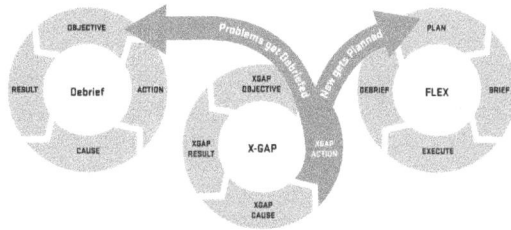

*Figure 28. FLEX drives you forward XX*

## 1. We stay ahead of the moment through Situational Awareness (SA).

Without situational awareness, you cannot lead, make decisions, or get things done. That doesn't mean you're always going to have it; knowing when you do and when you don't is important–because good SA is our ability to make insightful decisions while in action based on the information available around us. SA is the right information at the right time to make the right decision, drive actions, achieve results, and make an impact. During a mission, we need and rely on our situational awareness.

FLEX builds two types of situational awareness. First, it keeps line-of-sight alignment from your actions through to your mission objective to your organizational HDD, and it helps you make decisions now by giving you the right information at the right time. Secondly, it appreciates that you are always working within a complex system or team of teams, and anything you do will have an impact on the teams above and below you, and standing to your left and right. SA gives you an understanding of the impact or consequences of your actions on the people around you. Teams build these SA skills using FLEX, just as they build their execution skills.

## 2. We point our jet toward a High-Definition Destination.

Most leadership models resemble a triangle, the big kahuna at the top, the minions at the bottom, and the impossible mission for middle management squeezed in between. Most program or project management tools are an arrow, or if agile, a circle. FLEX orients the leaders forward, and to evolve continuously, your system needs to be infinite.

The HDD is a detailed image of where your organization is headed with a collection of discreet mission objectives aligned to achieve the overall strategic outcome. The HDD is a vital tool because it inspires and aligns the team toward a common goal. The HDD provides a North Star so leaders and team members who execute the mission can quickly determine if their collective actions are effectively moving the organization in the right direction.

## 3. The heart of our jet is the Plan, Brief, Execute, and Debrief cycle.

The heart of our jet is the FLEX engine, a magnificent all-purpose workhorse that has been tested in every imaginable situation. It is unique in that it propels us forward; however, its components spin in a circle. That's the key to FLEX; despite the fact that we think life, projects, programs, and strategy are an A-to-B exercise, the reality is that they are not. They are all connected, and the iterative thinking that is unique to the fighter pilot mindset unlocks the power of these connections, specifically through the Plan–Brief–Execute–Debrief and Objective-Result-Action cycles.

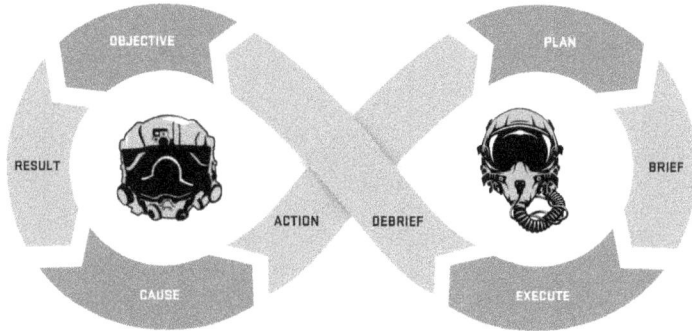

*Figure 29. FLEX is infinite. FLEX defines the future, today, and yesterday and drives you to your HDD with action.*

## 4. We rely on our wings (standards and training) to keep us stable and airborne.

Standards make personal initiative and creativity possible. Imagine how much of a grind each day would be if you started with "How do I tie my shoelaces again?" You can't run a FLEX business without standards, and you can't have standards without your people knowing what they are. Learn your standards and associated skills, use the teach–demo–do process, and repeat it as often as needed, then exercise the discipline to keep standards sharp. The more standardized we are, the more automation we can introduce to our business practices. More automation means more speed, and in today's world, speed is life. Define the standard. Keep lessons and standards at your fingertips, filed and easily searchable, and embrace machine learning and AI, whether as a bespoke internally designed system or off-the-shelf platform.

Training never stops.

Discipline makes you the person others want to work with because they can rely on you. Training is a way of life for high-performing individuals and companies. They embrace it, they want it. New products. New tools. New software. New promotions. New communication standards. If it's "new," it needs training.

## 5. A plane needs a pilot (you), so kick the tires and light the fires.

*Figure 30. You're in control of your cockpit, and your team has mastered theirs*

In the FLEX cockpit, two things happen at the same time. The pilot has to think, and the pilot has to do. The pilot may be a mission commander or a formation leader, a team leader, or a wingman—an empowered follower who may soon be called on to lead. Either way, you have to be aware of the situation, know everything about the mission plan, know everything about your team, and know how it will execute today's specific plan. Surrounded by 300+ instruments and flying at the speed of sound, this is easily one of the most complex mental tasks you can ask of a human being. And it all comes together in the FLEX cockpit.

In a larger organization, the cockpit is also where the individual's thinking—the pilot, so to speak—aligns with the organizational thinking, the collective. Each team member has to have a very sharp idea of the organizational purpose and strategy (HDD) and how their own mission and their role and actions in that mission will fulfill its intention, or collectively, its purpose.

That's an awful lot going on in the cockpit. Fortunately, the FLEX engine of plan–brief–execute–debrief gives us an extremely effective way to manage all of that simultaneous thinking and action. To that end, we use the metaphor of a fighter jet aircraft to depict the layers and how they work together to support us on our missions. That model starts with the wings of the jet.

# The FLEX Wings

"Get the fundamentals down and the level of everything you do will rise."
Michael Jordan

In aviation, you can lose an engine and glide. You can get lost and land. But if you lose a wing, you're in serious trouble. The wings give us lift. The wings provide stability. They allow us to turn and bank. We believe in the wings and take them for granted. They are a given, a mandatory.

In FLEX's philosophy, our "wings" are the combination of rigorous standards, dedicated training, and dynamic systems that define our operations and culture. We see these as crucial investments, for without them, we cannot sustain our business heading and altitude, especially in turbulent times. The essence of the fighter pilot mindset is to lean on established standards and our continuous training to give us the confidence we need to address complex, dynamic challenges head-on, and to adapt them as required to meet the changes of the digital world. Standards are not just support structures; they are lifelines that ensure stability and guide our endeavors within safe operational confines. In a commercial organization, time wasted trying to learn something as fundamental as the Internet—and what it does—is time lost making another sale or refining your production methods. Time spent remembering how I put the landing gear down is needless. It's like breathing to me. It's like tying your shoelaces before a run; it's automatic. We know how to do these things, they are our wings, SOP, and this approach resonates with Albert Einstein's concept of valuing knowledge over memorization, a concept particularly relevant in today's fast-paced, rapidly automated, and data-rich environment. In essence, we aim to eliminate time spent on things that are utterly basic, so we prevent the kind of slowdown that could otherwise occur if we had to recall every detail when we need to have an uncluttered headspace to deal with the what-ifs.

# Standards

The fighter pilot community has a deep commitment to standards. Standards shape every aspect of our work. They provide us with a silent yet potent confidence, equipping us to face the unexpected with preparedness, agility, and an uncluttered headspace. In an unpredictable world, these standards are our rock, allowing us to fall back to basics when confronted with the unexpected, to survive, and to rebuild our situational awareness.

In the world of business, standards are the backbone of operational excellence, streamlining processes and fostering trust within teams. They are the shared language that reduces the time and risk associated with any enterprise. Adhering to standards empowers teams with confidence and readiness to tackle new and unforeseen challenges.

At FLEX, we've integrated standards into every facet of our operations, drawing parallels from the precision and discipline of the Air Force. As fighter pilots, we depend on universal protocols for seamless collaboration. We also rely on our standards to work in unison with a diverse range of teams and individuals, even under the most pressing circumstances.

The very real test of standards came on September 11, 2001. One of the original Afterburner team, AB, was delivering a seminar on the East Coast when the attack occurred. He was 4,000 miles from his squadron, but he knew there was a squadron on the East Coast that flew the same jets as his. He got in contact with them, and within a short time, he transitioned from delivering a seminar in civilian clothes to being a fighter pilot in a flight suit flying combat patrol over major cities. That epitomizes the power of standards. Despite being in unfamiliar territory with an unfamiliar crew, the ingrained Air Force protocols allowed him to climb into a jet and perform his duty flawlessly. This incident underscores how deeply rooted standards can sustain us, mobilize us, and adapt under the most unexpected of circumstances.

The value of ingrained standards extends beyond the Air Force and into the corporate sector. Consulting firms like McKinsey & Co. leverage their own standards to ensure that their consultants can commence work immediately, effectively, and cohesively, irrespective of prior acquaintance with the client or each other. This approach to standards breeds a uniformity of excellence that's predictable and reliable.

Our firm, Afterburner, exemplifies this through our consistent planning and debrief sessions, where we adhere to a set protocol regardless of the client or the number of times we've executed it. This standardization has not only streamlined our operations, but it has also instilled a deep-seated confidence in our team, enabling us to focus on delivering quality service rather than getting bogged down by logistical details.

Consider a snack-food company's production team that manages the output of various products. Their daily routine is dictated by organizational standards—practices so well-embedded that they're second nature. Yet when an unexpected scenario arises, like a trial for a new flavor, a breakdown, or the worst-case scenario, a health scare, they can swiftly pivot, drawing on the collective knowledge bank without starting from scratch. This quick access to information and procedures ensures continuity and efficiency.

While important and encouraged, personal habits and techniques must align with these broader collective standards. They provide a personal touch to the established procedures, ensuring that our responses to new challenges are effective and infused with individual expertise.

Taken together, standards are engineered through a layered system of elements:

- Core Organizational Standards: These are the fundamental practices ingrained within our team's memory, ensuring daily activities run smoothly and efficiently.

- Accessible Knowledge: For less frequent, situation-specific issues, we rely on easily retrievable organizational knowledge, avoiding the need for time-consuming relearning. AI is rapidly improving our ability to access knowledge, although it lacks the context to turn that knowledge into wisdom. That's why being a great leader is recession-proof and an insurance policy for you, keeping your job as AI encroaches into everyone's careers.

- Personal Standards: Individual skills and habits support our action readiness and creativity, as long as they align with the overall organizational direction.

- Initiative and Creativity: Personal ingenuity is encouraged within the framework set by these standards, fostering innovation while maintaining coherence.

In sum, standards are the silent pillars of FLEX's philosophy. They are the invisible threads that weave through our decision-making processes, our daily interactions, and our strategic responses to crises. It's how we show up as a team member and a team leader, parking our ego and stepping into the best version of ourselves. Through relentless training and unyielding adherence to these standards, we've created a culture where excellence is the norm, adaptability is inherent, and quality is consistent. Whether it's a routine day at the office or an unprecedented national crisis, our standards stand as our guide and guard, ensuring that we perform optimally in any scenario.

This dedication to standards is what sets successful organizations apart. It's not merely about the procedures but the ethos that permeates through the company's culture, driving performance, ensuring reliability, and fostering an environment where excellence is habitual. For FLEX, standards are not just part of the process; they are the very essence of our identity and the key to our success.

# Training

Training is the lifeblood of a FLEX business. It transforms standards from mere concepts into actionable practices. It's no secret that in the corporate world, training often has a reputation for being a check-the-box exercise, the first cost to be cut, a distraction from the "real work" of profit-making. But at FLEX, we view training as a fundamental activity, akin to a fighter pilot operation, where readiness and improvement are continuous pursuits.

Why train with such intensity? Because the battlefield of business, much like actual combat, doesn't present challenges sequentially or conveniently; the peaks and troughs often come from nowhere and catch us by surprise. Success depends on sustained performance and the ability to adapt at a moment's notice. This is why we subscribe to the wisdom of legendary coaches like John Wooden, who insisted that true preparation happens long before the game begins by creating practice conditions tougher than the games themselves.

Our training strategy is not reactive but proactive. We train so that when we're in the throes of high-stress situations, our reactions are second nature. The objective is to free our minds for strategic thinking and creative solutions, not to be encumbered with basics that should be automatic.

FLEX training follows a robust, four-step progression:

<u>Desired Learning Objectives (DLOs)</u>: Clear, actionable goals set the stage for focused training. Each session has a purpose, whether it's mastering a maneuver or perfecting a sales pitch.

<u>Demonstration and Practice (Demo/Do)</u>: Learning by doing is our mantra. Repeated practice following the demonstration solidifies skills and embeds them in our muscle memory.

<u>Discipline</u>: This is the commitment to adhere to standards and apply what's been learned. It's about making excellence a habit.

<u>Continuous Training</u>: Skills atrophy without use. Ongoing training ensures standards remain fresh and relevant.

In the FLEX system, we don't distinguish between what to memorize and what to look up. Initially, everything is learned to the point of it being an ingrained reflex. Over time, certain information might fade, but the essence remains. Consider the way we train new maneuvers in the jet. A pilot is briefed, the maneuver is demonstrated, and the pilot practices repeatedly and drills it until the maneuver becomes instinctive. This is how we approach business. We don't learn from manuals alone; we engage in hands-on application, discussion, and repetition until the skill is ingrained. In a like manner, discipline is not just about following a set process; it's about consistency and reliability, qualities that make a team member invaluable. It's up to each individual to maintain that edge.

FLEX extends this concept to how we manage knowledge within our organization. Most of our clients give us a vertical head-nod when we ask them how they do it because most have these four elements wired:

- A well-organized digital repository and custom AI solutions

- Clear naming protocols for files

- Regularly uploaded post-debrief lessons learned and actions

- Quick-access search tools for mission planning

These principles ensure that the company's collective intelligence, its wisdom, is always at the fingertips of its employees.

FLEX represents a culture where training is not a one-time event but a career-long endeavor of curiosity. It's a culture that prizes preparation, values skill, and strives for continuous improvement. We are creating a corporate ethos where the question is not whether we have time for training, but whether we can afford not to train. In the FLEX world, we're always ready; we have our standards and training as the wings of a solid foundation that lifts our performance to meet adversity head-on, to adapt rapidly, and to consistently surpass expectations!

FLEX is built on a foundation where individual and collective practices are in harmony, fostering an environment where we are perpetually pre-pared for action. It's a system where we continuously refine our skills. It's a system where—when new situations arise—robust readiness, a blend of learned responses and the freedom to innovate, meet them. That is our formula for triumph in the ever-evolving landscape of business.

# Chapter

# 14 | Building Situational Awareness

**"Knowledge is knowing what to say. Wisdom is knowing when to say it." Edmund Burke**

There's a term fighter pilots use on the radio. It's called "Tumbleweed." When I called out "tumbleweed" on the radio, it meant I had no idea what was going on. The word is derived from the stuff that blows around in the desert, tumbleweed. And like tumbleweed, I'm up here in my jet blowing in the wind, nearly useless.

My first effort to right my ship is a trained response. Take an ordinary hike in the woods. Losing situational awareness is like being lost on a hike. To regain my bearings, I find something big (like a mountaintop), before I look for some smaller things (a creek and your trail). We call that "Big to Small."

If that doesn't do it, in my world, calling out the word "tumbleweed" triggers a very specific series of actions. The overall battle manager, a person in a large airplane sipping coffee, looking at the big picture on a big radar screen, hears my radio call and will slowly "build the picture" for me. They will tell me where I am and where the nearest threat is, direct me to a safe pathway for me to escape, and give me vectors to the rest of my team. From that, I will "snap" my aircraft away from danger, head towards safety and the rest of the team, and quickly rebuild my situational awareness before pitching back into the fight.

If your team wants to operate successfully within a system, it needs to know its place in that system. It needs to have situational awareness, or, in fighter pilot speak, "SA." Situational Awareness is the ability to find the right information at the right time, so you make the right decision. Every action that results from decisions consumes resources, and any investment in resources without a greater return is the pathway to extinction. Information feeds your decisions, your decisions drive actions, and these actions make an impact. You can never escape this "Do-Loop." If your team doesn't know what its threats are, or doesn't know the impact of its actions, it won't survive.

Fighter pilots have a very particular understanding of what situational awareness is. The situation is an area defined as the airspace above, the ground below, as far as our field of vision, which is a pretty large area. To have situational awareness within that field is to know where you are, who is trying to do what, who is moving where, what the squadron is doing, all with a line of sight to your mission objective. In other words, everything. Everything in that area. Everything that you might come into contact with or have to make a decision about in that vast stretch of territory.

Situational awareness includes the dimension of time. You have an appreciation of why things are as they are, and what they may be in the future. Looking back, you understand the operating environment you're in, the mission you're on, and the needs of your client and the team to surpass your client's expectations. Looking around, you understand what everyone is doing in that environment, friend and foe, and the resources they can draw on. Looking forward in time, you understand the impact of your actions, and the challenges that you might face against the successful achievement of your strategic objectives. You are aware of what is and what might be. When you have great situational awareness, you feel like you're ahead of the game, or, as we put it, it feels like you're ahead of the aircraft.

There are thousands of data points per second at play, and it's impossible to stay on top of everything, and unfortunately—you can't simply pull over and catch your breath—but if you have your SA and you bring situational awareness to others, you are a highly valued partner, an indispensable employee, an exceptional leader, and maybe all three. Situational awareness is wisdom, it is clarity, and it's the foundation of every decision you've ever made, good or bad.

In this chapter, we look at the two principal types of situational awareness that FLEX draws on. The first is the line-of-sight alignment to your objectives, that is, understanding the impact of everything you do and the impact it has on your objective. The second is a simple approach to systems thinking, that is, an appreciation that you are always working within a system and, in turn, a system of systems, or SoS, and anything you do will influence nearly everything within that system. Think of a house and a plumber who turns off the water mains. Every faucet in the plumbing system will go dry.

We also discuss how to build situational awareness and how it feels when you've lost it. An emerging leader may become well known for his or her situational awareness, but it is far more important to have it as a team quality. Team thinking matters. Team consciousness matters. This sounds hard, but teams can and do build group SA skills just as they can build their group execution skills. Building situational awareness is simply part of FLEX, and it starts with you.

# Line-of-Sight Alignment

One of the most critical elements of situational awareness is the ability to see the impact of our actions all the way up to our organizational High-Definition Destination (HDD). That means visualizing how our actions lead to our mission objective, how that objective meets our leader's intent, how that intent is part of your organization's strategy and performance, and how that strategy is leading to your HDDs. Visualizing that line in reverse is also how pilots regain situational awareness from a tumbleweed situation.

To do this, we have to have a handle on the impact of our decisions and actions. In the planning stage of FLEX, we have the opportunity to think through in advance the impact we're hoping to make by a planned series of actions. We have to do it on the run when we're on a mission. That's why we spend time planning a mission. We want our actions to be second nature, well-rehearsed, to have the desired impact, and for them to systemically move us forward along the path to our objective.

To some extent, all of us are impact-based thinkers. If you have ever watched a movie late at night and muttered to yourself, "C'mon—it's not that great a movie—gotta get going in the morning—big day," then you're situationally aware of the impact a late night will have on you tomorrow. As we grow in maturity, we think more and more about the impact or consequence of our decisions and the resulting actions. Surprisingly, however, very few individuals or organizations think of the impact their actions will have on the system within which their businesses operate.

We just push ahead with what needs to be done immediately and face the consequences. There are two reasons for this. More often than not, we don't have an ultimate end point in mind. We're not really aiming for anything. We're just getting through the week, or the quarterly reporting period, or to the end of the year doing whatever is in front of us. We're like the hamster on a wheel, and it's taking us nowhere—certainly not to our life's ambitions or some goals or some strategic objective.

Conversely, we do have this week's objective in sight and an ultimate end point in mind, but we haven't thought how to get from one objective to the next. To solve that, we need to have a "virtual" line-of-sight between what we're doing now and where that takes us versus the endpoint in the future. Are your actions taking you closer or further away? Are you building the skills and relationships to get there? Are you building the personal and team culture to get there? We need to be able to visualize the path, create and follow a long-term plan, and maintain our line of sight on a daily basis.

Here's the rub. All of our actions will have a direct impact (immediate things like appointing a person to a position) and an indirect impact (people being disappointed to miss out on that position). All of our actions will have the intended impact (a team has a new leader, team results improve) and an unintended impact (team morale falling, results improving for unforeseen reasons). Those are part of situational awareness. When we ask, "Do you have SA on the issue?" we're asking you, "Are you seeing what's happening or what's about to happen? Do you see the direct and indirect impacts? Do you see the intended and unintended impacts? Do you understand that turning off the water main means no one can take a bath and they're all going to a party in one hour?"

# Building Situational Awareness

Situational awareness is wisdom. It's a perception that's cheap in hindsight but extremely rare and valuable in foresight. Are some people born with situational awareness? Perhaps. More likely they have disciplined themselves to think about things in a structured, three-dimensional way. Experience is certainly a factor—the grey-haired folks who "have been around a long time." But without curiosity and a way to meld past experience with new data, you're likely to be tumbleweed most of the time.

We strongly believe that by building FLEX muscle and by making the FLEX processes habitual, you create the disciplined execution and expansive thinking that builds situational awareness. The FLEX engine of plan–brief–execute–debrief matches how we humans traditionally learn. In *planning*, we consider new things collaboratively and expansively, taking in outside advice, only to process those ideas into a specific, actionable course of action. In the *brief*, we hear the leader's synthesis of the plan and engage through questions that advance our understanding, stressing elements of situational awareness that will make a difference to the mission. In *executing* the mission, we experience the very things that beforehand only existed in concept, in our minds. We add our own perspectives regarding the situation to the lessons learned. In the *debrief*, we review those perspectives, learning from causes and effects, finding out that two people can perceive the very same event quite differently, and how to reconcile those perceptions into future actions.

For some missions, all the situational awareness you need should be in the room or readily accessible within your organization. For others, tap into external experts to help build that awareness. There will be things you don't know about that will have a material impact on the outcome of your missions. If the mission of your team of six in-house IT specialists is to upgrade your data center with new hardware and expanded storage capacity, you will have the expertise you need. If your strategy is to move that data center to a new location, at the same time transitioning to a mix of proprietary hardware and vendor-owned infrastructure accessing both proprietary and public cloud, then you will need to draw on external experts.

Having situational awareness is one thing; using it is quite another. We think of situational awareness as "perception, comprehension, and projection"—see, think, and act. Most people can see or perceive things happening, fewer will understand or comprehend what that means, and fewer still will project into the future to make decisions on what to do about it. When the U.S. Coast Guard cutter *Cuyahoga* approached the Argentinean vessel M/V *Santa Cruz II* on a clear, calm night on the Chesapeake Bay in 1978, both crews saw each other by eye and by radar. When the *Cuyahoga's* captain turned his ship in front of the *Santa Cruz*, all of his crew saw it, and many understood what the change, of course, meant. But everyone assumed he had his reasons and neither warned nor questioned him. "So they just stood there and let it happen"—"it" being the *Cuyahoga* ramming the *Santa Cruz II* with eleven lives lost. If the leaders had a perception on the Cuyahoga Bridge, there was little comprehension and certainly not enough projection.

Situational awareness is the eyes and ears of your mission. It takes in what's around you now, as well as what's in front of you—all the way to your mission objective.

# 15 The FLEX Way of Thinking

"Before you react, think. Before you spend, earn. Before you criticize, wait. Before you quit, try." Ernest Hemingway

The FLEX framework for action is very compelling; the FLEX way of thinking makes it powerful. FLEX balances direction and autonomy, speed and consideration, simplicity and dynamism, reliability and creativity, process and awareness. These clear, simple processes and constructive ways of thinking allow you to take on the following major challenges that can make it hard to achieve a team's goals:

FLEX takes on uncertainty and complexity with disciplined, collaborative processes. All those new ideas are mounting up. Whatever business you're in, you face more disruptive technologies, more regulations, and more competition. No one person can stay on top of all that. You get anxious, curious, distracted, overconfident—and given the speed of change and the complexity of our environment, there are more ideas, possibilities, initiatives, and challenges coming at you all the time. In that environment, some people are better than others at keeping focus. We need to open up our thinking to a new way of processing all of this, a simple, disciplined approach with a focus on the substance.

FLEX takes on the speed of change with a strong bias towards getting things done fast in a short learning cycle. That does not mean you should respond to everything instantly. Rather, you need to act in a considered way, but quickly. FLEX provides the means to do so, and to keep learning from your actions.

<u>FLEX engages people by giving clarity to their roles, ownership of their plans, and accountability for their actions.</u> FLEX organizations are connected to a sense of purpose, and their people to purposeful things each day, not merely work.

These three FLEX qualities work both for your creative strategies and for continually improving your core operations. They appear through every FLEX process. Starting with your FLEX planning—be it for shorter or longer strategies, programs or projects—they carry right through the briefing, execution, and debrief stages of the FLEX cycle, and strengthen the FLEX wings.

# A Fighter Pilot Mindset Only Goes So Far

As pilots, we deeply believe in the disciplines and the level of awareness we learned flying jets as part of a combat squadron. We relied on it then, and we rely upon it now. Our training and disciplines have become second nature in all our endeavors—in the Air Force, in business, and in our personal lives—and the FLEX process has allowed us to achieve our goals.

We've also appreciated how young men and women have been able to join our air forces with little more than some limited life experience and a dream. And yet, through our processes, we have had the ability to turn them into dynastic performing fighter pilots. Still, we have enough experience in business to know that life on the street, in the factory, or in the boardroom is not the Air Force. Which is perhaps a good thing.

The biggest difference between Air Force and civilian life is that in our civilian life, our important personal and business goals are primarily social. Humans are social animals. In anything we do, we must be aware of and deal with the personal motivations and responses of our own family or team, and the people we have to deal with. That's why we stress that FLEX doesn't mean to "act like a fighter pilot"; it's about "thinking like a fighter pilot." In the Air Force, engaging with the enemy is far removed from this social world. By the time our fighter squadrons are called in, we're no longer negotiating with the enemy. We've stepped outside the sphere of human interactions, and into one where we rarely, if ever, even see the faces of our enemies.

When we moved from the Air Force to negotiating business deals with governments, we realized how much we had to learn about human motivations and behavior. As first-class fighter pilots and squadron leaders, we understood how to work with and lead other fighter pilots. But we'd be the first to admit that was a pretty narrow field of experience. Most fighter pilots are Type-A personalities, treating their teammates as they would other Type-A personalities. In life and in business, we're working with Type-A to Type-D personalities, any one of which may be the key to getting to our HDD. As social animals, we've had to learn that building a workable, working, and social relationship with people is critical. That takes a different kind of wisdom and patience than what we mastered in an F-35 cockpit.

Nonetheless, every effort we've made in our personal and business lives confirms the value of the disciplines we learned in the Air Force. The combination of operational disciplines and emotional intelligence is extremely powerful and leads to engagement.

# Engaging People in Their Own Mission – Skill, Will, and Autonomy

For people to perform at anywhere near their best, they need to be "engaged." To engage people, you need to have a great story to tell them, a story that's believable, direct, and empowering. We want people to apply their ability to do something and their desire to do something. It's the old "skill–will" matrix. We want our people to be moving towards the top right box in the following diagram (see Figure 31).

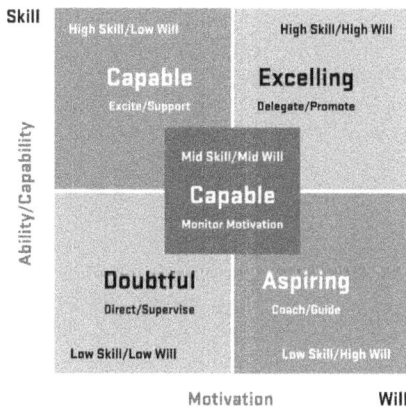

*Figure 31. The Skill–Will Matrix*
*Source: The skill–will matrix is a common management tool, but this version from Dan Spira (©2010) captures it well.*

Take a moment to think where the New York Giants were. Here was a team that had won the Super Bowl four years earlier. They had skill in spades. The will? Sure. But did they have more skill and will than the other 31 teams in the competition? Manning, Cruz, Tuck, and Company tasted victory once and thought they had another shot at it. They wanted it—but it's not enough to just want it. You don't have to look too far to see what might have been missing. With a coaching staff of 18 under Head Coach Tom Coughlin, there's no doubt the players had guidance, support, and excellent plays. What they lacked was a sense of autonomy. You'll never perform to your potential without the autonomy to improvise and act on initiative and instinct. That's part of what we think we accomplished. The FLEX debrief helped them develop the individual autonomy and authority they needed as players and as a team on the field.

If your team has the skill and the will, then it needs its share of autonomy. Whether your team has autonomy or has to achieve it, whether you take autonomy or are given it, doesn't matter. Without it, you'll never perform to your potential. At every stage of the FLEX process, teams take ownership of their mission's outcomes. Sure, they're given the direction and support they need, but they share the autonomy and authority to get the job done.

Being a part of a team that wants and needs autonomy and authority is where you want to be. People need to know that what they're doing matters, and that they have some control over their actions. We went far deeper into this when we discussed FLEX planning, but for now, this quote rings the bell for us and sums it up quite well: As General George S. Patton said, "Don't tell people how to do things. Tell them what to do, and let them surprise you with the results."

# Motivation: Maintaining the Desire to Win

Sometimes even professional athletes find it hard to maintain the desire to win week after week after week. We've all had bad days—a champion golfer who cannot sink a putt for love or money is a familiar, often agonizing sight on the circuit. It's easy to see why so many professionals employ a sports psychologist, someone who can help them refocus on what they have to do.

We've never met a fighter pilot who didn't have buckets of desire when they started. A trainee pilot is up for anything, ready to do anything for the opportunity to fly in their desired squadron. But it can be hard to maintain this will, and they can experience the same low points and setbacks of any career. The FLEX way of thinking helps bring them back on target.

It's the same in business. No matter how much we love our jobs, sometimes getting to Friday can be a herculean task. We've all had those times when we lost all sense of timing during a phone call or a sales pitch. But we don't have the luxury of a sports psychologist. It's usually up to us to turn it around.

FLEX is designed to help you in those moments. It gives you the support you need when you need it; you have your wingmen, standards, and debriefing tools. The FLEX process prioritizes keeping those skills sharp and incentivizes people to develop specialized techniques to do their job better. And FLEX provides clear, reliable, and consistent processes to ensure that those individual skills are applied as a team—a skilled team. Let those skills help you. Tap into them.

The FLEX culture encourages honesty and impartiality when confronting problems. Why are we doing this and why aren't we there yet? Everything about FLEX is geared toward creating a winning culture by generating and maintaining the desire to perform, and that is based on mutual support without shame or judgment. Be it an X-Gap meeting or calling "tumbleweed" on your radio, you have a process built into a FLEX environment that lifts you up when you're off.

# Great Leaders Were Once Great Followers

You can't be a leader without followers, and vice versa. That makes both roles equally important. Being engaged is not one-way traffic. FLEX assumes that each member of the team has a shared leadership role. Team members are taking part in many of the processes that make for good leadership and are learning the ropes. Most importantly, they are supporting their leader in their own learning and practices, and the leaders are supporting them shoulder to shoulder by helping to build respectful truth over manufactured harmony.

Every element of FLEX is designed to fully switch on the people responsible for getting the job done. The four stages of the FLEX engine make sure this happens. Team members think collaboratively and create alignment (Plan), they understand exactly what's expected (Brief), they enjoy mutual support (Execute), and they experience deliberate and intentional review (Debrief). With FLEX, great followers are learning how to be great leaders.

# Beating Complexity with a Clear, Collaborative Process

To solve problems, make decisions, plan, execute, and learn, you need the disciplined, collaborative process of a diverse, aware group, and while FLEX works for individuals, it is designed to get the best out of teams. In truth, one person is rarely enough to eliminate complexity. There are too many traps for an individual to fall into, in both planning and performing. These are the cognitive errors that we mere mortals keep making day after day. We are optimistic by nature and systematically overconfident. Can we build it? Yes, we will say, no matter what the facts say. If we've already invested time and effort, then we'll spend even more to get our job done, ignoring advice to cut our losses. In a complex environment, said Edgar Schein, the father of organizational culture at MIT, "managers as individuals no longer know enough to make decisions and get things done." They need a team.

That's why the so-called "wisdom of crowds" has more going for it than the average bar stool theory. James Surowiecki's book *Wisdom of Crowds* pulls up the classic example of the jar of jellybeans at a school fair. Jack Treynor, a finance professor, ran the experiment with the students at the fair. He displayed a jar of jellybeans and asked each person to write down the number of jellybeans they thought were in the jar. Two people came close to the right answer, but the average of all the guesses was nearly spot on. That's the wisdom of the masses. That's the value of teams. 871 beans was the average guess against 850 in the jar.

Here's another. In his book, *The Difference*, author Scott Page shows how our collective wisdom is greater than the sum of what we know individually.

# Creativity Through a Simple, Repeatable Process

With all that diversity of thought and ideas, expect differing opinions on how to act and how to begin that action. Now merge them. FLEX takes these diverse ideas and fuses them into a common objective. FLEX poses questions that are clear and seeks answers that are clear. The source of those answers doesn't matter, objectivity does. It's like making a strong cable out of thin wires. The process laces the diverse strands of facts and opinions together into one strong plan of action.

It's hard to overstate the power of a disciplined process. In a 2010 study, McKinsey & Company analyzed the tools a company selected in making decisions that affected performance—performance being measured by revenue, profitability, market share, and productivity. There was data (raw company, market, or industry data), data analysis and modeling, and processes. Which of the three had the more significant impact on performance? McKinsey found that performance was overwhelmingly tied to processes. Good data was good data. Data analysis was simply analysis. However, putting decisions through a determined process invariably leads to better corporate results. Just 8 percent of performance was based on the quality of the analysis, while 53 percent was tied to the decision processes. That's right, the decision process has over six times the impact as the analysis it's based on!

Those statistics haven't changed much over the years, except there is now vastly more data to analyze. The research explains why we often suffer from "paralysis by analysis," spending more time than we should on analysis and delaying the decisions we need to make. Perhaps it's because analysis is the easiest thing to do and the one thing that business analysts are trained to do.

Making good decisions consistently is harder still. We're as much of a fan of Jim Collins as anyone. In *Great by Choice*, Collins writes that "the signature of mediocrity is not an unwillingness to change: the signature of mediocrity is chronic inconsistency." That's again where a reliable process comes in—to drive consistent quality in your decisions and actions.

People sometimes misunderstand processes and give them a bad rap. The objections are that they're a straitjacket, that they stifle creativity, that they take the fun out of work. Bad processes can do that. Good processes don't. As Jim Collins calls it: "The great task, rarely achieved, is to blend creative intensity with relentless discipline so as to amplify the creativity rather than destroy it."

# Beating the Speed of Change with a Bias to Action

It's a safe bet to say that the pace of business is not going to slow down any time soon. It's speeding up on whatever measure you choose—product cycles, technology adoption, market volatility, emergence of competition. It took 45 years for telephones to reach 50 percent of the U.S. population, and just five years for cellphones to do the same. The automotive design cycle has tightened from five years to two to three years. But digital services—the smartphones and apps we now rely on to order pizzas, do our banking and monitor our heart rate—make a joke of these cycle times. The speed at which these apps are developed and launched means that a market opportunity must be exploited yesterday, or you're too late.

Hence the belief that it's wiser to act now with an 80 percent plan, than to launch a perfect plan when it's too late. Anne Mulcahy is the former CEO and chairman of Xerox and served on the boards of Citigroup, Johnson & Johnson, and the Washington Post. While at Xerox, Mulcahy learned the cost of being risk-averse and too data-driven. "By the time we would reach a decision that some technology was going to be a home run, it had either already been bought or was so expensive we couldn't afford it." So now she's a believer that "decisiveness is about timeliness. And timeliness trumps perfection. The most damaging decisions are the missed opportunities, the decisions that didn't get made in time." Figure 32 is one interpretation of how value gets crushed by delay; the graph shows how quickly the probability of closing a deal reduces the longer a salesperson takes to respond to an inquiry.

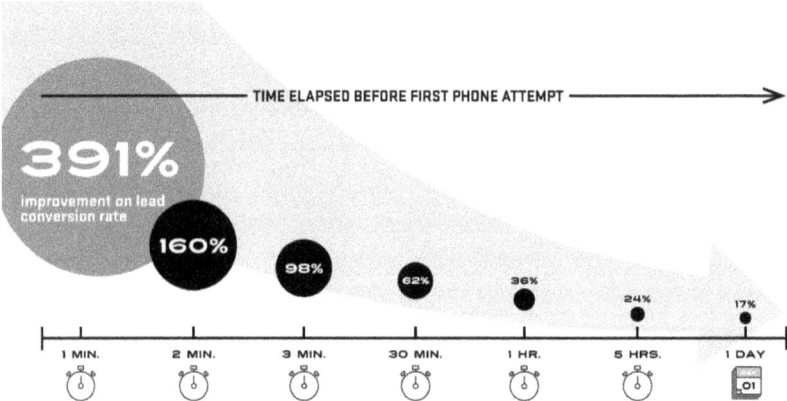

TIME ELAPSED BEFORE FIRST PHONE ATTEMPT

**391%** improvement on lead conversion rate

160%

98%

62%

36%

24%

17%

| 1 MIN. | 2 MIN. | 3 MIN. | 30 MIN. | 1 HR. | 5 HRS. | 1 DAY |

*Figure 32. The time value of action*

So nothing is surer or more clichéd than that we're in a complex, uncertain, fast-moving world. The choice is to sit like a deer in the headlights or to act. FLEX is designed to help you act even when you don't have the answers.

# 16 FLEX and Agile

Many readers will want to compare FLEX with other fast-cycle approaches to performance delivery and improvement, particularly the "Agile" models for software development. To make the book a little thicker, pre-empt the conversation, highlight that we've done our homework, and share our lessons learned from working with hundreds of agile organizations, here's some comparative data to consider.

The term "Agile" stems from the 2001 Agile Manifesto, which was developed by a group that included the creators of Scrum, Extreme Programming (XP), Dynamic Systems Development Method (DSDM), and Crystal. The manifesto sets out four core values for enabling high-performing teams, and FLEX embodies all of these values. Interestingly, these processes were co-developed by a fighter pilot, Jeff Sutherland, who is now also the CEO of Scrum Inc. He graduated from the Top Gun School, flew over 100 missions in Vietnam, and became a doctor at the University of Colorado School of Medicine.

Of these models, FLEX and Scrum stand out as the most streamlined. They have a smaller number of core practices, roles, and artifacts that together form a solid base to build from. Other approaches, SAFe, Rage Less DAD, DSDM, and Crystal Clear, for example, have a large portfolio of possible practices and roles from which you pick and choose.

While FLEX and Scrum are both powerful approaches for getting things done, they can be used together, as they emphasize different aspects of the challenge. Table 3 sets out that comparison. FLEX offers tighter alignment with an organization's ultimate HDD and mission objectives, a greater focus on team culture and development, and more ways to keep a team and each individual in it on track. Scrum and Agile are effective in completing short-term sprints as part of a long-term project.

This matters more and more as firms struggle to align their IT efforts with business outcomes and objectives, particularly where they've invested in myriad methods, frameworks, processes, and services. You need something simple and intuitive to draw these elements together tightly, align them with business objectives, and respond quickly to external threats and opportunities. Something that sits lightly on the organization without displacing its existing processes. Users of FLEX find that it serves this role well.

*Table 3: Comparing Scrum, Kanban, and FLEX*

| Element | Scrum* | Kanban* | FLEX |
|---|---|---|---|
| Purpose | Deliver quality software | Deliver quality manufacturing | Deliver quality, aligned products and services, including software |
| Change philosophy | Only before/after sprint | Any time | Any time, guided by situational awareness |
| Organizational development | Quality, speedy delivery (QSD) | Quality, speedy delivery (QSD) | Quality, speedy, aligned, informed agility |
| Team development | Team accountability | Individual accountability | Team and individual accountability |
| Leader development | Support process | - | Support process and culture |
| Strategic Direction | - | - | HDD |
| Path | Release, Feature, Theme, Epic | Work in Progress | Strategy and operation |
| Major effort | Project (>1 month) | - | Campaign (>2 months) |
| Component effort | Sprint (<1 month) | Continuous flow | Mission (<2 months) |
| Roles | Product owner, scrum master, team | Supervisor, individuals | Champion, team leader ACE, team |
| Owner of effort | Scrum master | - | Team leader |
| Guidance for effort | Backlog ordered by product owner | Work in progress limits | Team leader's intent |
| Objective | Increment in potentially shippable product | Workflow to done state delivering value | Team's mission objective |
| Prioritization | Product owner value rank in backlog information radiators | Product owner value rank in backlog | Champion resolves clashes, finds resources |
| Scoreboard | Velocity, burn downs, burnups, information radiators | Kanban Board | Dashboards |
| Plan | Refinement and sprint planning meeting | Pull work (Team Choice) | Six-step planning |
| Brief | Sprint planning team commits | - | Brief |
| Execute | Daily scrum meeting, sprint review | Build | Wingman, task shedding, checklists |
| Plan revision | Product owner ends sprint, interrupts pattern | Review and measure | X-Gap |
| Review | Demo (aka Scrumming the Scrum, aka Retrospective) | - | Debrief, Lessons learned |

Source: Table data drawn from multiple sources, including www.atlassian.com/agile.

# Chapter

# 17 Becoming Flawless—
The AD/HDD Version
of the Book

We all want to be great leaders, achieve our dreams, and be incredible parents, partners, husbands, and wives. We want to go to work, do meaningful things, and be around awesome people we care about, and who care about us. Can you put your hand on your heart and say that's how life feels for you right now?

In 2020, I was diagnosed with ADHD. My task positive network (TPN) and dormant mode network (DMN) basically stay on at the same time. It's great when I'm hyper-focused, terrible when I need to do things like write a book or do anything mildly academic. According to Edward H. Hallowell, MD, and John J. Ratey, MD, authors of *ADHD 2.0*, a phenomenal book I might add, it's like having a Ferrari brain with bicycle brakes.

So this chapter is for those of you who, like me, just want the details so we can work it out as we go. When you think about your personal and professional goals, are you fearless? Are you flawless? Start by thinking about your top three priorities. What IMPACT are you looking to make? In your life? As a leader, husband, wife, mother, or father? Are you finding it hard to get to where you want to be? For example, You may want to buy your partner a gift partner a gift, that's doing something, or do you want them to feel valued? That's an impact. They are two very different things. Buying something is a nice thing to do. However, there is no guarantee that it will make your partner feel valued. So get curious and find out what their destination is, which is to feel valued by you. Then collaborate and actively work out the actions to deliver that outcome. you may even save a few bucks, as the action was probably something simple like stacking the dishwasher! There may be some personal experience in that story. Are you clear about what "great" looks like in your business, life, and meaningful relationships with people around you? Are you a CEO, an executive, or a frontline leader stressing about hitting your targets or surviving the next big global event? Are you running a charity and overwhelmed by the need you are servicing? Or is it as simple as feeling there's more to life than churning through each day, and you're unsure what or how to get there?

Because FLEX is designed to help people make an impact and get the hard things done, with or without neurodiversity.

In this modern, digitally-powered world, technology and people are fusing closer together, creating a high-speed, information-saturated environment that's unique compared to any other time in human history. Yet, achieving the results you want in a consistent and high-quality manner can feel more complicated than ever. Think about flat "no authority" leadership structures, rapid product lifecycles, and the overall speed of life. We are tethered to a digital device, inundated with messages, and feel exhausted and stressed. Most people are not trained to operate in such an ecosystem—except those in the fast-paced, highly demanding world of fighter pilot aviation. Fighter pilots operate at the very edge of human performance physically and mentally, usually at the same time. We thrive in an environment where, without the proper mindset, skillsets, and toolsets, we would be consistently overwhelmed, an environment where the margins between winning and losing mean more than just a bad day in the office. A fighter pilot's mindset and our fighter pilot methodologies allow us to harness the chaos of a rapidly changing and challenging world. In 1996, we at Afterburner adapted that mindset and those methods to help businesses and organizations like yours push toward excellence, think in new ways, and scale across entire enterprises. Since then, more than 3,500 companies have been trained on our toolset and our processes and have enjoyed consistent, high-quality, repeatable results. Will it work for you? We have an 83% repeat rate with our clients, if that tells you anything.

# An Impactful Mindset: The Fighter Pilot Mindset Is a Growth Mindset for Leaders

There's a lot of noise around mindset out there at the moment. To some, mindset is about being set in your ways. To others, it's about setting your mind to the future and manifesting success. To fighter pilots, it's a little bit of both, and it's how we grow from the person we are today into the person we need to be tomorrow to stay relevant and make an impact. We do this through iteration (feedback loops) that are biased towards action.

# Set Your Future by Starting with the Impact You Desire to Make

Set your intentions with high-definition destinations (HDDs), then design and deliver on your mission objectives with your team.

Success begins with clarity. Setting a clear and committed intention is the foundation of the Fighter Pilot Mindset. When you know precisely what impact you want to achieve, your focus sharpens, and your actions align to create meaningful results.

# Iteration – Results vs. Intentions

The key to evolving your biases, beliefs, and behaviors and ultimately making better decisions, what some call becoming "self-aware," is the habit of intentional reflection or iteration. It's thinking in a circle, where we grow from who we are (today) to who we want to be (tomorrow), getting curious as to the journey so far, and asking the question of why there is a gap between the two (yesterday).

The Fighter Pilot Mindset uses an iterative ORCA approach to refine actions and achieve impactful outcomes. The O in ORCA is Objective, or in fighter pilot speak, a very clear and measurable intention. R is Result, the reality you are in right at this moment. The gap between the two is the execution gap, and we iterate to close it.

# The 3B's. Understand Your Biases and Beliefs Drive Your Behavior

Your biases and beliefs guide your behaviors and decisions. By understanding and aligning these beliefs with your intentions, you create a pathway to evolve your habits and behaviors, forming a foundation for consistent success. If you do it, your team will follow.

The C in ORCA is "Cause" or "Curiosity"; it's an open and honest conversation, usually with yourself or within a peer group, where we discover the cause of the gap between our objectives and results. When we apply the mindset to ourselves, it's usually a bias, belief or behavior. When we apply the mindset across a team, it's likely the same as something with the culture or system you're operating in.

# Bias to Action – Build Your Micro-habits with ORCA

We start with intention and end with action, accountable action. It's these actions, taken daily, that create contextualized micro-habits, or the habits tailored for you, your personality, and your strengths to deliver the impact you've set.

In Chapter 9, we examine debriefing and ORCA in depth. What's important, though, is that you understand that a simple methodology delivers a very useful FLEX mindset. Debriefing asks and answers these questions:

What did we set out to achieve? (objective)

What actually happened? (results)

Why did that happen? (cause)

What will I do about it (action)

# A Simple Method

Our method has four parts: Plan. Brief. Execute. Debrief. It's different from ordinary management processes in that we give your organization tools and techniques to operate like a fighter pilot, to iterate and adapt at speed, and to scale quickly. First, we teach you how to *plan* using a six-step process that fighter pilots use in combat. Next, we show you how to *brief,* creating a shared understanding of the mission objective so your team feels ready and able to "step out to the jet" and perform at their highest level. Then, we equip you with techniques to master the challenge of task saturation and the overwhelm you will face when you *execute* your plan. Finally, we share the fighter pilot's secret to success, the *debrief,* where we quickly identify actionable lessons learned and apply them immediately to the next mission. In the debrief, we teach you to ask: Did we meet expectations today? Why or why not? How can we fix it *now*? This triggers a continuous, iterative cycle that will break you free of repetitive "to-do" loops. Instead, you will streamline your efforts and take your team to new heights.

Flawless Execution isn't perfect execution, it's a way of thinking and a way of working that improves the probability of you delivering your desired outcome no matter how ambitious. It is designed to get you there with less effort. Both in the air and on the ground, our processes have been hardened by decades and decades of experience, and hundreds of thousands of flight hours, They've been proven outside the cockpit with over 2.3 million leaders who've experienced our Afterburner programs. FLEX is a way of thinking and working optimized for high-speed environments, where ambiguity otherwise reigns and where businesses can be otherwise overwhelmed with information.

Can an organization be truly flawless? No. Not even the greatest, most practiced and trained aerial demonstration team, the Navy's Blue Angels, would say that. "In 30 years, we've never had a perfect flight," said one of their pilots. Yet millions of spectators flock to watch their near-perfect performance at air shows all over the world. As Nelson Mandela so elegantly expresses, "I never lose. I either win or learn." At Afterburner, we can't make your organization perfect—but we will drive your organization closer to flawless execution and be a little better every tomorrow.

# The Flawless Execution Model
# The Question is....

You are always working, and yes, you work hard, probably too hard for the results you're delivering. How many meetings have you conducted that only generated more "to-do" lists? There's a good chance you or

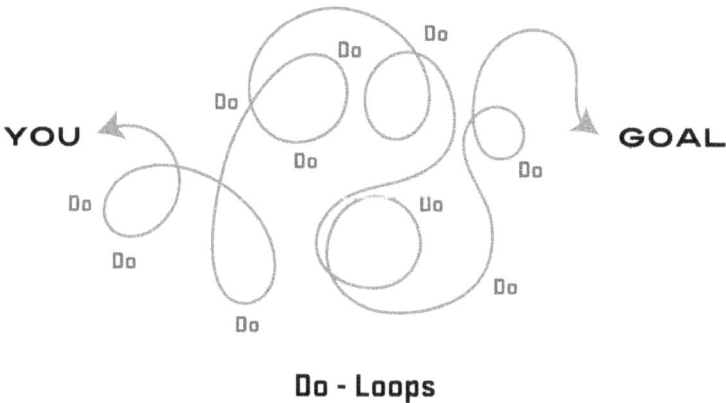

**Do - Loops**

*Figure 33. The Do Loop. You Know You're in a Do Loop if you're busy all the time and getting nowhere.*

your team get sidetracked, follow ideas down a rabbit hole, or get swamped by a never-ending workload, resulting in today's to-do list rolling into tomorrow's bigger to-do list. It's frustrating. But it can be stopped. You're caught in what fighter pilots call the "Do Loop" How do you escape the spiral?

# Here's the Answer

To break free from this continuous "to-do" loop, fighter pilots follow a concise Plan, Brief, Execute, Debrief—and repeat—pattern. This is called FLEX, short for Flawless Execution. The FLEX process connects intention, action, and results in a planned, orderly cycle that delivers desired results. Debriefing is delivered through the ORCA cycle, and when these two cycles come together, we create a system that powers evolution in your business. Say goodbye to change and transformation. There is no one state of being into another; everything is always in motion. Turn it into momentum powered by growth and a bias to action.

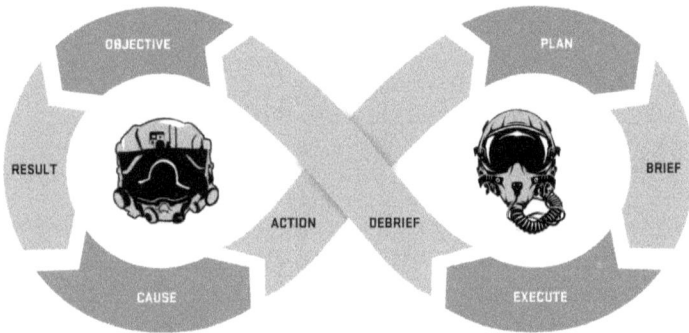

*Figure 34. The FLEX Model PBED + ORCA = Continuous growth and excellence*

Connect your strategic story to granular objectives and then connect actions to these objectives. When the action fails to deliver the objective, debrief it, learn, do it differently and better tomorrow. Until eventually, relentlessly, your strategic story evolves into your reality to your objectives and consistently innovate and grow through debriefing.

At its core, Flawless Execution (FLEX) is about developing flawless leaders and teams, driving a culture where expectations are not just met but surpassed, and where strategies are not just formed but fulfilled. Your successes seem effortless because Flawless execution builds the habits and mindset to drive this success.

This journey starts with the end state in mind. Where do you want your organization to be when it's all said and done? Where do you want *you* to be when it's all said and done?

## The High-Definition Destination (HDD)

The best leaders lay out a road map for their teams to follow. At Afterburner, we call this the High-Definition Destination (HDD). Before you do anything, think about your future, then write it out in clear, simple, yet detailed terms. Do you envision a campus of 3,000 workers developing cutting-edge cellphone apps in San Jose? Do you want to open a restaurant serving fused cuisine on white tablecloths in downtown Manhattan? Write out a high-definition description of the future that you want for you and your organization. Write it out collaboratively, with the team that, with you, will execute the plans to get you there. Think through your goals and objectives together, get the details down together, and when it's done, you have a team that's totally bought into a future you've designed that's believable and achievable. Why is that? Because they wrote it with you.

## Planning

FLEX planning must align desired outcomes to required actions. The HDD maps out your vision for the future. The planning process identifies specific mission objectives you must meet to make the vision a reality. The planning process must also identify required actions to meet those mission objectives. FLEX planning must align desired outcomes to required actions. We must plan fast, small, and often. Fighter pilots get there by using a deliberate, six-step mission planning process.

## The Six Steps to Mission Planning

1. **Objective.** Write a clear, measurable, achievable objective. This is developed by the team, not by the leader. It will likely evolve through the planning process.

2. **Threats – Internal or External.** List the threats to your mission. If controllable, that control becomes part of the plan. If not, park it as a contingency; you'll deal with it later in planning.

3. **Resources.** Every threat needs to be matched by a resource. Who and what, inside and outside your team.

4. **Lessons Learned and Debrief Actions.** Quickly search your memories and databases for things to do or not do in this situation. Bring the actions from yesterday's debrief into today's plan.

5. **Course of Action.** Who (the individual) does what by when? And why? As simple as that. Test the courses of action by inviting in a **Red Team**. These will be people who've been there before, though not involved in the creation of your plan.

6. **Contingencies.** What are the uncontrollable but likely threats, and what are the triggers for actions that you will take to keep you in the game?

# Planning Tips

The more complex a plan, the more likely it will fail. Plan small and plan often. Who. What. When. And the measure of progress/success. A simple rule of thumb: if you're about to expend energy, start with a plan, even if it's five minutes. Define your objective, aka what the point or impact is that you want to achieve today. Fundamentally, a plan is simple. It's an objective (what you want) delivered through action (what you do), and that's it. There can be no ambiguity around small steps.

If you have a complex organization, conceptualize your plan as a series of Lego blocks with each brick representing a single objective, supported by actions. Each brick clicks snuggly together to the next one, building robust teams of teams. You can click as many blocks together as you like into any creation your imagination can conjure!

FLEX planning is fast yet considered. Planning is not the mission. Don't get bogged down. It's far wiser to act now with an 80 percent plan than to launch a perfect plan when it's too late. Any resulting plan is simple yet dynamic—it nails the objective and enables adaptions as required by actual world events. The plan is direct yet empowering—people will have clear accountability and can keep the initiative they need to maintain execution velocity. A FLEX plan calls on your team to be engaged in their mission, not robotic.

FLEX planning embraces open planning. Get the team responsible for executing the mission in the room. Collaborate. Embrace diverse approaches before settling on one or the other.

**Briefing** – It's not what you say, it's what's understood.

The plan is only finalized in the act of writing it and delivering it as the briefing. The leader owns the brief. Take accountability for the mission, set your style, and reinforce the plan's objectives and actions. The briefing is the cut-off point. It's time to stop doubt, uncertainty, and debates and start executing. Brief the plan and fly the brief. This is the team's last chance for clarification.

Here's a simple mnemonic that covers all of the elements of a brief and in the correct order:

**B**ig picture (HDD, situation, intent)

**R**estate (mission objective)

**I**dentify (threats, opportunities, and resources)

**E**xecute (your course of action)

**F**LEXibility (what are the contingencies?)

Check for understanding. If necessary, use "pose, pause, pounce" to switch your team on. Pose questions to the team, pause to allow them to consider a response, and pounce on one of the team members, usually the distracted, unprepared one! This inquiry-based method of communication shifts our team from passive receivers of information into engaged seekers of knowledge. Finish with a positive call to launch the mission.

# Execution - Keeping People to the Plan

In today's hyper-connected, always-on world, distractions are one of the greatest obstacles to successful execution. A single distraction can increase task completion time by 27% and double the number of errors. When scaled across teams, the impact is staggering, leading to inefficiencies, stress, burn-out, and reduced performance. Digital distractions not only consume our attention but also deplete our energy, leaving us fatigued and disengaged. Worse, we often unknowingly distract others, compounding the problem. These distractions are fueled by the allure of immediate gratification—our brains are wired to seek quick dopamine hits, making focus a fleeting luxury rather than a foundational practice.

The Challenge of Task Saturation. At the other extreme is task saturation: the perception of having too much to do and not enough resources to do it. This "silent killer" overwhelms individuals and teams, eroding productivity and clarity. Like overworked pilots flying perfectly working planes into the ground, overwhelmed leaders are often unaware of task saturation's insidious nature, feeling confident right up to the point the wheels fall off; they fail and lose the locker room. This is not just a matter of workload; it's the result of fragmented attention and unmanageable priorities. The cultural glorification of busyness exacerbates the issue, making over-commitment seem like a badge of honor rather than an undiagnosed chronic, and terminal condition.

The Sophomore Risk: Overconfidence and Complacency. Another trap is overconfidence born of experience, a phenomenon observed and measured in Air Force pilots and professionals alike. Inexperienced individuals are often cautious and attentive, but after gaining a little experience, they become overconfident and less focused, leading to mistakes. Known as the "sophomore hubris," this phase highlights the danger of taking previous success and experience for granted. Yet, this overconfidence can be corrected by regular touch points, known as X-gaps, that realign focus, allowing individuals to mature into wise and intentional leaders.

Mission Bubbles and Dashboards. To overcome distractions, task saturation, and overconfidence biases, successful teams rely on tools and systems designed for focus and adaptability. The concept of a "mission bubble" emphasizes scheduling uninterrupted time to prioritize critical objectives, while dashboards—modeled after fighter pilot instrumentation—ensure that teams monitor only the most critical metrics. Like pilots who scan their instruments to stay on course, business leaders must focus on key performance indicators while avoiding unnecessary data that detracts from their mission. By integrating these principles into daily practices, individuals and teams can transform chaos into clarity, aligning actions with objectives to drive impact.

You have a wingman (mutual support). Your second set of eyes and ears; one of you can think while the other is busy doing.

Clear, concise communication. Use standards that everyone knows to keep every interaction sharp and understood. Talk by exception. When you communicate with the team, are you adding situational awareness or contributing to task saturation? What must you do? Should do? Would be nice to do? Do last, if at all?

Checklists. There are two critical rules for a checklist: keep it simple, and use it. The people doing the actions create the checklists. It should be one page with trigger points in nine steps or less. Using checklists calms nerves, aligns actions, and eliminates errors. If possible, two people check it and approve it. "Do–Confirm." Keep emergency and reference checklists where they can be found fast.

Keeping the Plan to Reality. Plans have to adapt because the reality of a situation will invariably throw you curves. Every plan includes team check-in points to review any gaps in progress, which we call execution gaps, or X-Gap for short. We analyze and "close the gap" between the plan (Objectives) and its execution (Results). Each X-Gap is a decision point for the mission: continue, adjust, or abort? Green light, yellow, or red?

Depending on your mission, set meetings on an hourly, daily, or weekly basis as a regular event. These are the markers of your executional rhythm. Allow no more than two minutes at the top, two minutes per task review, and two minutes at the end. Use O-R-C-A, again.

# The Debrief

Debriefing isn't about being the critic. That's easy. It's taking what we learn and putting it into practice because "It's not who's right, it's what's right." We identify "what's right" by continually debriefing the mission through a four-part model that measures mission success called **ORCA**: **Objective**, **Result**, **Cause**, and **Action**. Yes, we may have made errors; just like the Blue Angels, there is never a perfect flight. However, by understanding the root cause of our errors, we can take decisive action and improve the next cycle of performance. Our goal is to close the execution gaps between our objectives and our results.

In a fighter squadron, each debrief follows the same core principles: it is timely, focused, nameless, and rankless. This is not your typical "after-action report"—it is a dynamic conversation about how we can immediately improve execution and get back to the fight. First, debriefs are timely. We debrief within an hour of completing a mission. Have you heard of the memory bias? It means our memories of an event change over time; the further we are from the event in time, the less accurate our recollection. This is why those quarterly reviews are often lengthy and complex; we're always trying to remember what happened rather than fixing it! By debriefing right away, you generate an accelerated learning curve, ensuring you adapt systems and processes to real-world situations, and fix small issues before they become big ones.

Second, we keep the debrief focused and efficient. Did we reach the objectives or not? If not, what were the root causes? What specific actions do we need to take now so we can avoid the problem the next time? You do not need to prolong the debrief looking for multiple root causes for execution gaps. One is enough to get you moving. Do not get bogged down trying to solve complex organizational problems; instead, set up a separate planning session to do the deep work outside the debrief (put it in the parking lot). Your goal is to walk out of the debrief with actionable steps for each team member to take today.

Finally, we ensure our debrief is **"nameless and rankless."** It doesn't matter who you are in the organization or what your role is—from the CEO to the newest hire in the company. In a debrief, everyone has a voice. That doesn't mean we disrespect the position of the people in the group or use the debrief to settle personal scores. We call the process "one up, one down," meaning the leader should start by standing up and facing the team members. The leader establishes authority, then dives into their own mistakes. This opens the door so other team members will admit their mistakes as well. Remember, the debrief is about your team improving performance by shrinking the execution gap: "I made a mistake, I fess up, I fix it, and I'm happy to be here."

Ultimately, the debrief is a learning opportunity for everyone. There is no need to use blame or shame. Focus on process improvement. Motivate your team to take the lessons learned and go try again. Closing the X-Gap moves you closer to Flawless Execution. Remember, for the NY Giants and the Broncos, this is Superbowl-winning stuff!

# ORCA is a mnemonic for the steps you follow in a debrief

**O** - Objective. What were your clear, measurable, achievable objectives?

**R** - Result. What were your results?

**C** - Cause. Be curious. What were the causes for the results, good or bad? Why, why, why? Drill down until you're at the individual level. Debrief the role and the results—it's not personal.

**A** - Action. What action was each team member accountable for? Who did what when? Debrief small actions and objectives. In the fighter pilot world, we debrief the near misses as well as individual habits and behaviors.

The debrief is your secret weapon, both for learning and innovation and for a positive working culture. It gives closure to the mission, bottles momentum for larger efforts, and builds leadership. Keep it "nameless and rankless," hash out what went right and wrong, and leave the politics and egos at the door; in a debrief, everyone wins. Debrief immediately after every mission—win, lose, or draw. It's an integral part of the execution phase.

Remember, debriefing is about closing the execution gap and driving action vs. getting bogged down in the reasons why we're falling short. When you end the debriefing, focus on the positives and over-performance.

## The One Percent?

Every debrief improves you a little before the next and the next and the next. And that improves everything about you and your company's executional rhythms and successes. One percent at a time. In one case, we saw how it accelerated a business by up to 300% and kept them ahead.

## FLEX Builds Great Followers and Flawless Leaders

In the elite wings of the U.S. Air Force, young pilots are responsible for leading missions, squadrons, and units. They are entrusted with taking people and equipment, highly valued in every sense of the word, into hostile and complex environments to fulfill their mission and get everyone home safely. They do so with incredibly high reliability.

It's perhaps cliché to say that great leaders start off as great followers, but they do. By the time these young men and women lead their own missions, they will have been on any number of missions and served under leaders who are as diverse in character and style as they are. Yet the similarities are clear and comforting: following FLEX principles applies equally to leaders and followers, and of course, you need both to execute flawlessly with a fighter pilot mindset.

## The Principles for Flawless Leadership

- Be situationally aware. Are you leading people, outcomes, or moments?

- Respecting truth over manufactured harmony

- Building credibility by admitting your errors and mistakes and taking action to remedy them

- Knowing when to make the decisions—*that* will mark your leadership

- Knowing your team members and making their welfare paramount

- Ensuring a mission serves its aligned purpose and HDD

- Insisting on standard operating procedures, including brief, clear communication

- Ensuring team members understand what to do but are not told how to do it

- Respecting the power of the FLEX framework for action and a way of thinking

## FLEX Builds Great Teams

FLEX teams are highly engaged teams. Why? They understand the purpose behind their actions and they understand the impact their actions will have both inside and outside the organization. FLEX teams should have enough people to have the skills and diversity the mission needs, yet small enough for each team member to know, rely on, and care for each other. One of you will be the team leader and will facilitate the FLEX process on behalf of the others. If your team's a big one, split them up, and share the leadership role within the team as they focus on their discreet objectives. Fighter pilots generally work in teams of two (the flight leader and wingman) or four, by adding a pair together.

Whether your organization is seven- or 700,000-people strong, whether its structure is flat or hierarchical, whether teams are self-forming or designated from on high, whether their work is self-driven or delegated to them as part of a greater effort, a team will come together to get the job done. FLEX empowers teams through these practices:

- By giving teams a shared mental model for thought, action, problem solving, or resolving conflict

- By ensuring teams have the diverse skills and experience needed for the job

- By engaging all members of the team in planning, executing, and debriefing their work

- By tapping into experts with greater experience and situational awareness

- By ensuring that your team's missions are what the organization needs vs. pet projects

- By making members individually accountable for their part of the mission

- By giving teams clear decision-making authority and the means to exercise it

- By giving teams the support they need to stay focused and effective

- By ensuring that teams draw on and contribute to situational awareness and standards that they and other teams rely on

- By giving teams great followers and leaders

# FLEX Builds Dynastic-Performing Companies

FLEX can be used independently or in unison by multiple teams at several levels of an organization. It can be used to set a long-term organizational objective and course of action in the same way as a smaller mission plan. It can be used within the context of a larger mission for which it is an integral component. If there is more than one facet to an organizational objective—the HDD—the missions may be independent. No matter which, FLEX is designed to be repeatable and scalable.

A McKinsey study highlighted a significant reduction in the lifespan of companies listed on the S&P 500 from 61 years in the late 1950s to just 18 years by 2016. For success, a firm needs to get things done and consistently build the capability to do so. It needs to follow a coherent strategy towards an inspiring HDD, both of which keep pace with industry and social change. FLEX navigates to that endpoint.

High-performing companies using FLEX have:

- HDDs that complement a corporate vision or purpose but are more detailed and actionable

- Situational awareness of the connectivity between your networks and systems on the journey to your HDD

- Missions that have clear line-of-sight to the HDDs, either as part of a strategy to deliver something new, or to evolve an existing system, or to perform more effectively within a system

- Performance engines, accountability, and the culture to deliver those missions

- Debriefing to adapt and refine your organization to accelerate ahead of your industry's rate of change and complexity

- Continual refreshing of situational awareness and standards to enhance creativity and improve the rate of innovation

- Highly engaged teams to get all these jobs done

# AI Sidebar: Zoom

Eric Yuan, the mastermind of Saasbee, was born in Tai'An City, Shandong Province, China, and moved to Silicon Valley in 1997 at the age of 27 after eight failed attempts to secure a visa. His Chinese name, 袁征 (Yuán zhēng), includes the character 征 (zhēng), which means "to go on an expedition or journey."

Founded by the then 41-year-old Yuan in 2011, Saasbee started with a simple idea that scaled into a multi-billion-dollar unicorn showcasing the power of vision, timing, and technological excellence.

Yuan, a lead engineer at WebEx, saw the limitations of video conferencing tools available at the time. They were clunky, unreliable, focused on business use cases, overburdened with clunky features, and didn't deliver the seamless user (customer) experience he envisioned as an engineer. Yuan set out to create a product that would make video communication frictionless and accessible to everyone. The goal was straightforward: to develop a video conferencing tool that would "just work." In fighter pilot mindset terms, he took something complex and made it simple!

In 2013, SaasBee re branded and re-launched Zoom Video Communications Inc., better known to you as Zoom, after two years of development. The platform stood out for its ease of use, reliability, and high-quality video, even with poor or spotty internet. Unlike its competitors, Zoom didn't require users to have an account to join a meeting. This ease of access and reliability was combined with a freemium model, quickly earning it a loyal user base. By the end of its first month, Zoom had 400,000 users, and by the end of its first year, it boasted one million users.

The company's focus on customer happiness was evident. Features like simple screen sharing, the ability to handle numerous simultaneous video call participants, and later, artificial intelligence (AI) for background noise reduction and virtual backgrounds, were directly in response to user requests. Zoom's strategy was to make the user experience so superior that it would naturally drive word-of-mouth referrals.

By 2017, Zoom had become a unicorn startup, surpassing a $1 billion valuation. It had also expanded its services to include Zoom Rooms, software-based conference room systems, and Zoom Video Webinars. The platform's FLEXibility and scalability made it an attractive choice for businesses of all sizes, educational institutions, and individuals seeking a reliable communication tool.

Zoom's pivotal moment, however, came in 2020 when the COVID-19 pandemic hit. As governments worldwide imposed lockdowns and people were forced to work and study from home, Zoom became the go-to service for video conferencing after Yuan dropped the time limit for non-account holders.

Its user-friendly interface allowed it to outpace rivals as schools, businesses, families, and friends turned to the platform to stay connected. Daily meeting participants rocketed from 10 million in December 2019 to 300 million in April 2020, reflecting Zoom's explosive growth.

The pandemic also highlighted Zoom's agility as a company. It quickly addressed various security and privacy issues that arose with its sudden popularity, implementing end-to-end encryption and other safety features. This responsiveness helped maintain user trust during a critical period. Zoom's success can be attributed to fighter pilot mindset principles:

Start with the end in mind: From the beginning, Zoom focused on providing a seamless user experience. It started with the end in mind and had a human behavior focus, not a technology/engineering focus. Its intuitive interface required no technical know-how, which was crucial in attracting and retaining non-technical users.

Standardize: Zoom's cloud-native platform allowed it to scale rapidly without significant degradation in service, a critical factor when usage skyrocketed during the pandemic.

Debrief it: The company's willingness to innovate and integrate new features based on consistent user feedback kept it ahead of the competition.

Lead the outcome: Eric Yuan's leadership was a key factor. His focus on customer happiness, company culture, and product reliability set the tone for Zoom's growth; he remained ruthlessly focused, erring towards keeping the platform simple rather than feature-laden.

Win small today: By offering a freemium model, Zoom positioned itself as a solution for both enterprises and individual users, expanding its market reach, allowing it to further capitalize as work and private lives became more integrated.

Don't react, adapt: The company's quick response to security concerns during its rapid growth phase helped it navigate potential setbacks.

As the world looks beyond the pandemic, Zoom's future seems robust. It has become an essential tool for remote work, telehealth, education, virtual events, and even social interactions. The company continues to innovate, venturing into cloud phone services, email, and calendar applications, positioning itself as a comprehensive communication solution.

Zoom's success story is a testament to the importance of user experience, agility, and visionary leadership in the tech industry. Its journey from a startup to a global powerhouse demonstrates what can be achieved when a company remains focused on solving real-world problems with technology that is accessible, reliable, and adaptable to the ever-changing global landscape.

"I'd rather be lucky than good!"

New York Yankees ace pitcher Lefty Gomez is credited with this quote. Pitching the Yankees to six World Series wins, he was a carefree soul who often had teammates offside with his relaxed attitude. His philosophy was simple: Be very good at what you do, remain consistent, and then capitalize on those lucky moments to win.

Lefty understood that it's not just hard work that counts; it's the ability to identify fleeting opportunities or luck and lean into that moment, because it's these infrequent moments in time that make the difference between winning a World Series or not!

In the end, Zoom's story serves as a testament to the idea that, sometimes, the path to exponential growth in business is paved with challenges, uncertainty, and luck. When the world unexpectedly demands innovation and connectivity, adaptable and responsive companies can ride the wave of change to their advantage. Zoom's meteoric rise during the pandemic illustrates that even in the face of adversity, businesses can thrive by embracing change and seizing new opportunities. What was a great misfortune for most of us proved a lucky break for Zoom to become a billion-dollar enterprise.

# Where to Begin Your Flawless Journey

Flawless Execution always starts with the pilot, which, in this case, is you. After that, it doesn't matter where you begin the process. FLEX is iterative after all. Start wherever you find yourself today, in the moment. If a mission is coming up, or you have a specific target you'd like to achieve, schedule a planning session, then do your homework to prepare for it. If you're calling a meeting, run it as a planning session. If the planning is done, run it like a briefing. If it's the midpoint in a mission, run it like an X-Gap. Or if it's the end, run a debrief. To get a grip on your execution and find out what's going on, evolve from "update" meetings to X-Gaps. Wherever you are in the FLEX process, just jump in and get cracking. Here's the process on a page to get you started, or click the QR code to start your learning journey!

The most important thing to remember though?

There's no need to be a fighter pilot to think like one.

## PLAN

The Six Steps to Mission Planning:
1. Determine the Mission Objective
2. Identify Threats
3. Identify Available Resources
4. Incorporate ORCA/Review Lessons Learned
5. Develop Course of Action/Red Team
6. Plan for Contingencies

## BRIEF

**B** – Big Picture Scenario (HDD)
**R** – Restate the Mission Objectives
**I** – Identify Threats and Resources
**E** – Execution = Course of Action
**F** – Flexibility = Contingencies

## EXECUTE

- Establish your Execution Rhythm
- Mitigate Distractions
- Develop Cross Checks (clear areas of focus)
- Seek Mutual Support – who's your wingman?

## DEBRIEF (ORCA)

**O** – Objective = What did we set out to do? Did we meet the objective?
**R** – Result = What were the successes/failures/near-misses/debrief focus points?
**C** – Cause = For each result ask *how* and *why* did this happen?
**A** – Action = Identify accountable actions that reduce failure and improve future execution

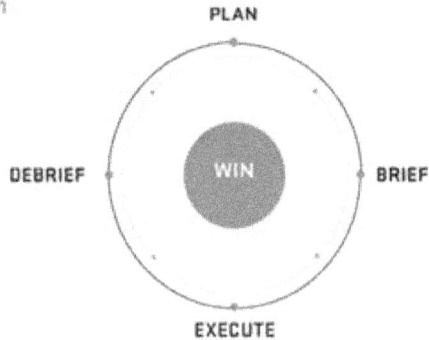

*Figure 35. FLEX on a page*

# Mission Planning – A Quick Look

You don't need to make it difficult; here's a quick plan you can draw up in 10 minutes with your team over a whiskey barrel.

## INTENT

**What do you intend this mission to accomplish and why?**

Old Limestone Mixer for bourbon is the #1 mixer in the largest bourbon-drinking state in the nation. Our corporate mission is to now roll it out to retailers nationwide, and within three years, establish it as the #1 brand by volume for bourbon mixers nationwide.

## OBJECTIVE

**State the objective. Make it clear. Measurable. Achievable.**

During Year 1, launch 12-ounce bottles in high-end liquor stores in 21 targeted states and support with marketing until brand reaches #1 share.

## THREATS

**Identify anything significant that's in the way. Classify them according to the severity.**

-External

Competitive mixers will counter with hefty ad budgets.

Retailers will be reluctant to give us shelf space without financial incentives.

-Internal

We only have $2 million for the launch budget.

Factory output limited and may hinder road to #1 on a volume basis.

-Controllable

**Identify threats you can negate, mitigate, or avoid.**

Factory output capacity limits can be mitigated by contracting with TKK, Inc., a bottler nearby.

-Uncontrollable

**List and rank threats, then address them in contingency plans.**

Competition goes all in with heavy marketing. Counter with 30% shelf allowance.

Retailers hesitant to add SKUs. Counter with 40% sell-in allowance.

-Opportunities (Enticing but distracting opportunities)

**What are the distractions, the rabbit holes that we might fall for but must avoid?**

Retailer will triple order if we do a co-branded label. Decline these offers. Cobranding is not our business and doesn't build our brand.

**RESOURCES**

**Identify the resources you need to help you accomplish the objective. These will be people, assets, technologies, etc.**

Salesforce. All salespersons will prioritize launch during first three months of the year.

Marketing. Strong advertising.

Promotion. Sell-in allowances and shelf talkers.

Cash register coupons on-shelf.

$2 million support budget.

## EVALUATE LESSONS LEARNED

**What did we learn flying similar missions? What relevant experiences can we draw on to make our mission more likely to succeed? Within the team? Outside the team?**

We have brokers in five key states. Last year they failed to make their sales calls on Kroger and Total Wine. Our VP corrected this by traveling with them during sell-in. Be sure to repeat this with new products.

## COURSE OF ACTION

**Review mission objectives, its threats, your resources, and lessons learned, and form clear, easily understood courses of actions. Assign a course of action to individuals. Who does what by when. List priority tasks and decision points.**

Bob: Finalize sell-in plan and retailer incentives. Day 5

Jim: Production manager to build 20-day supply ahead of launch. Day 9

Susan: Prepare battle kits for 120 salespeople/brokers. Day 9

Virginia: Organize national Zoom call. Day 12

Standards: All standards in effect; however, sales force will be allowed to offer 30% off Invoice incentive if needed.

## CONTINGENCY PLANS

**Think of and answer the what-ifs of your mission. What will your response be to each "what-if"?**

Bad weather delays or cancels flight. This is a morning meeting, which is unusual, so will travel a day early and stay overnight in a hotel.

Client's PowerPoint projector turns up broken. One team member will carry our company's mini projector.

Brokers miss meeting. Approved to let territory manager cover meeting.

Order is unexpectedly high. Alert factory manager and President. Permission to tap into 20-day reserve.

Retailers give us narrow delivery dates. Tap into 20-day supply.

## STANDARDS

**Standards are how we operate on an everyday basis and do not need to be included in "what-if" or other planning sections.**

In this case, standards for national account sales calls are:

All team members must have a speaking role that is necessary and authentic. If not, off the team.

All team members have business cards.

Lead presenter preloads final PowerPoint on their computer and onto one backup computer.

Lead presenter aways carries portable battery pack in case laptop runs low.

Sales battle kit includes salesman samples of all items plus select items from rest of line, price sheet, catalogs if printed, sample in-store shelf talkers, etc., mockups of any ads or coop ads, hard copy of presentation.

## RED TEAM ANALYSIS

That's you, why don't you red team the plan and send me your red team boo@afterburner.com

# 2 HDD Planning Sheet

## HDD PLANNING WORKSHEET

Big Picture – High-Definition Destination (HDD):

_____
_____

**1. Your HDD:** Clear, Measurable, Achievable, Aligned to High-Definition Destination (HDD):

| You | What | When | Measure |
|-----|------|------|---------|
|     |      |      |         |

| 2. Threats: (O, O-I, O-U, U) / O, I, U as available | 3. Available Resources: People / Material / Tools / Equip. |
|-----|-----|
|     |     |
|     |     |
|     |     |

**4. Lessons Learned/Debrief Actions:**

_____
_____
_____

Go _____ No Go _____

**5. Supporting HDDs:**

| Who | What | When |
|-----|------|------|
|     |      |      |
|     |      |      |
|     |      |      |
|     |      |      |

Red Team Considerations:

_____
_____

**6. Contingencies**

_____
_____

X-Gap Dates: (same time and place each date) _____
Debrief Date: (w/in 1-7 days of mission completion) _____

©Afterburner, Inc.              AFTERBURNER.COM | 404.835.3500

AFTERBURNER

# 3 Mission Planning Sheet

## PLANNING WORKSHEET

High-Definition Destination (HDD):

_____

_____

**1. Mission Objective:** Clear, Measurable, Achievable, Aligned to High-Definition Destination (HDD):

| Who | What | When | Measure |
|-----|------|------|---------|
|     |      |      |         |

| 2. Threats: (C) Controllable / (U) Uncontrollable | 3. Available Resources: Negate / Mitigate / Avoid / Exploit |
|---------------------------------------------------|-----------------------------------------------------------|
|                                                   |                                                           |
|                                                   |                                                           |
|                                                   |                                                           |

**4. Lessons Learned/Debrief Actions:**

|  |
|--|
|  |
|  |

Go _____   No Go _____

**5. Course of Action:**

| Who | What | When |
|-----|------|------|
|     |      |      |
|     |      |      |
|     |      |      |
|     |      |      |
|     |      |      |
|     |      |      |

Red Team Considerations:

|  |
|--|

**6. Contingencies**

|  |
|--|
|  |
|  |

X-Gap Dates: (same time and place each date) _____
Debrief Date: (w/in 1-7 days of mission completion) _____

©Afterburner, Inc.                AFTERBURNER.COM | 404.835.3500

AFTERBURNER

# 4 ORCA Debrief Planning Sheet

**ORCA DEBRIEF:** Objective, Result, Cause, Action

Debrief Point 1:

| Objective |
|---|
| |
| **Result** |
| |
| **Cause** |
| |
| |
| **Action (I Will Do What by When)** |
| |

Debrief Point 2:

| Objective |
|---|
| |
| **Result** |
| |
| **Cause** |
| |
| |
| **Action (I Will Do What by When)** |
| |

©Afterburner, Inc.     AFTERBURNER.COM | 404.835.3500

## References

### Chapter 1: The Afterburner Advantage, from Flawless Execution to FLEX, 27 Years

1. Buffett, W. (n.d.). *Warren Buffett Quotes*. Brainy Quote. https://www.brainyquote.com/quotes/warren_buffett_108887

2. Wikimedia Foundation. (2024, September 6). *Ooda Loop*. Wikipedia. https://en.wikipedia.org/wiki/OODA_loop

### Chapter 2: The Missing Piece--Debriefing with the New York Giants

3. Giants Super Bowl Postgame Quotes. (2012, February 5). https://www.giants.com/news/giants-super-bowl-postgame-quotes-6911264

4. Kinkhabwala, A. (2011, November 9). *The New York Giants take to practicing military precision - WSJ*. The Wall Street Journal. https://www.wsj.com/articles/SB10001424052970204190704577026582387896436

5. Klippenstein, K., & Boguslaw, D. (2024, April 17). *U.S., Not Israel, Shot Down Most Iran Drones and Missiles*. The Intercept. https://theintercept.com/2024/04/15/iran-attack-israel-drones-missiles/#:~:text=More%20than%20half%20of%20Iran's,was%20a%20U.S.%20military%20triumph

### Chapter 3: The FLEX Process—Software for Your Brain

6. Buddha. (n.d.). *Buddha Quotes*. Brainy Quote.

7. Boucousis, C. (2021, October 6). *The Blue Angels talk debriefing*. YouTube. https://www.youtube.com/watch?v=3wjWmFQJIfA

8. TEDx Talks, & Simon Sinek. (2009, September 29). *Start with why -- how great leaders inspire action*. YouTube. https://www.youtube.com/watch?v=u4ZoJKF_VuA

**Chapter 4: The High-Definition Destination—From Idea to Reality with Flawless Execution**

9. Jobs, Steve. (n.d.). *Steve Jobs Quotes*. Brainy Quote.

10. *VUCA per AI*. ChatGPT. (n.d.). https://chatgpt.com/

11. NPR. (2023, January 16). *Read Martin Luther King Jr.'s "I have a dream" speech in its entirety*. NPR. https://www.npr.org/2010/01/18/122701268/i-have-a-dream-speech-in-its-entirety

12. *The Coca-Cola Company Mission, Vision & Values. Comparably. (n.d.).* https://www.comparably.com/companies/the-coca-cola-company/mission

13. Kotter, J. (n.d.). *Leading Change: A Summary*. Lucidity. https://getlucidity.com/strategy-resources/leading-change-a-summary/

14. *Gartner Hype Cycle Research Methodology*. Gartner. (n.d.). https://www.gartner.com/en/research/methodologies/gartner-hype-cycle

15. McAtee, Dan. (n.d.). *Afterburner Case Study*.

16. *New president and CCO for Harsco*. Stainless Steel World Americas. (2010, November 4). https://ssw-americas.com/new-president-and-cco-for-harsco/

**Chapter 5: FLEX Planning—Plan the Way You Plan**

17. Buffett, Warren. (n.d.). *Warren Buffett Quotes*. Brainy Quote.

18. George, A. (2020, April 8). *How the Crew of the Damaged Apollo 13 Came Home*. Smithsonian Magazine. https://www.smithsonianmag.com/smithsonian-institution/fifty-years-ago-apollo-13-crew-came-home-180974607/

## Chapter 6: The Six-Step Mission-Planning Process

19. Harvey, J. B. (1988). The Abilene Paradox: The Management of Agreement. *Organizational Dynamics*, *17*(1), 17–43. https://doi.org/10.1016/0090-2616(88)90028-9

20. Wikimedia Foundation. (2024b, October 31). *Thinking, Fast and Slow*. Wikipedia. https://en.wikipedia.org/wiki/Thinking,_Fast_and_Slow

## Chapter 7: Brief (Putting Your Plan into Action)

21. Swift, Taylor. (n.d.). *Taylor Swift Quotes*. Brainy Quote.

22. Griffin, T. (n.d.). *Ocean's 11*. The Internet Movie Script Database (IMSDb). https://imsdb.com/scripts/Ocean's-Eleven.html

23. *Book Summary: Indistractable by Nir Eyal*. Sam Thomas Davies. (2024, May 10). https://www.samuelthomasdavies.com/book-summaries/business/indistractable/

24. Talks at Google, & Goleman, D. (2013, December 6). *Focus: The Hidden Driver of Excellence*. YouTube. https://www.youtube.com/watch?v=b9yRmpcXKjY

25. Newport, C. (2015, November 20). *Deep Work: Rules for Focused Success in a Distracted World*. Cal Newport. https://calnewport.com/deep-work-rules-for-focused-success-in-a-distracted-world/

26. Harris, T. (2019, February 5). *CM 125: Cal Newport on Digital Minimalism*. Curious Minds at Work Podcast. https://www.gayleallen.net/tag/tristan-harris/

## Chapter 8: Execute (Keeping People, and Yourself, to the Plan)

27. Vaynerchuck, Gary. (n.d.). *Gary Vaynerchuck Quotes*. Brainy Quote.

28. Gladwell, M. (n.d.). *The Checklist Manifesto*. Atul Gawande. https://atulgawande.com/book/the-checklist-manifesto/

29. *Free Procrastination Tutorial - Kill Your Distraction - Be Crazy Energies - Procrastination*. Udemy. (n.d.). https://www.udemy.com/course/kill-your-distraction-goconquer/

30. About gOE - The Group for Organizational Effectiveness. Group OE - OD Tools and Consulting. (n.d.). https://www.groupoe.com/

31. Dalio, R. (n.d.). *Trust in Radical Truth and Radical Transparency.* Principles by Ray Dalio. https://www.principles.com/principles/f6412dca-b3f9-4dd0-bb65-274869dd21ed

**Chapter 9: The Debrief**

32. Collins, J. (2001, October). *Good to Great.* Jim Collins. https://www.jimcollins.com/article_topics/articles/good-to-great.html

33. *The Orca Debrief Method - The Key to High Performing Teams.* Afterburner. (n.d.). https://www.afterburner.com/the-orca-debrief-method-the-key-to-high-performing-teams/

**Chapter 10: The FLEX Team – Beyond Personal Performance**

34. QuoteResearch. (2011, July 22). *When the Facts Change, I Change My Mind. What Do You Do, Sir?.* Quote Investigator. https://quoteinvestigator.com/2011/07/22/keynes-change-mind/

**Chapter 11: Execution Gaps and How to Nip Them in the Bud: X-Gaps Meetings**

35. Churchill, Winston. (n.d.). *Winston Churchill Quotes.* Brainy Quote.

36. *Hotel & Rooms - Rydges Perth Kings Square.* Rydges. (n.d.). https://www.rydges.com/accommodation/perth-wa/perth-kings-square/hotel-rooms/

37. Stone, B. (2013, October 15). *The Everything Store: Jeff Bezos and The Age of Amazon.* Amazon. https://www.amazon.com/Everything-Store-Jeff-Bezos-Amazon/dp/0316219266

**Chapter 12: Strategy**

38. Rometty, Ginni. (n.d.). *Ginni Rometty Quotes.* Brainy Quote. https://www.brainyquote.com/quotes/ginni_rometty_487303

39. Metz, D. R. (1999). *The Air Campaign: John Warden and the Classical Airpower Theorists.* Air University Press. https://www.airuniversity.af.edu/Portals/10/AUPress/Books/B_0065_METS_AIR_CAMPAIGN.PDF

40. De Smet, A., Pacthod, D., Relyea, C., & Sternfels, B. (2020, June 26). *Ready, set, go: Reinventing the organization for speed in the post-covid-19 era.* McKinsey & Company. https://www.mckinsey.com/capabilities/people-and-organizational-performance/our-insights/ready-set-go-reinventing-the-organization-for-speed-in-the-post-covid-19-era

41. Groysberg, B., & Abbott, S. (2020, July 9). *It's Time to Reset Decision-Making in Your Organization.* HBS Working Knowledge. https://hbswk.hbs.edu/item/it-s-time-to-reset-decision-making-in-your-organization

42. Boghani, P., & Malik, K. (2024, March 13). *What Has Happened to Boeing Since the 737 Max Crashes.* PBS. https://www.pbs.org/wgbh/frontline/article/what-has-happened-to-boeing-since-the-737-max-crashes/

43. ChatGPT. (n.d.). https://chatgpt.com/

44. Brewster, F. (2024, January 1). *Airlines Filed 1,800 Reports Warning about Boeing's 737 MAX.* Jacobin. https://jacobin.com/2024/01/boeing-safety-reports-faa-737-max

45. *Updates on Boeing 737-9 Max Aircraft.* United States Department of Transportation. (2024, August 7). https://www.faa.gov/newsroom/updates-boeing-737-9-max-aircraft

46. Valery, V., & Hamilton, S. (2023, January 5). *Outlook 2023: Stabilizing Operations at Boeing.* Leeham News and Analysis. https://leehamnews.com/2023/01/05/outlook-2023-stabilizing-operations-at-boeing/

47. Schonland, A. (2024, January 9). *Boeing 2023 Orders & Deliveries.* AirInsight Group. https://airinsight.com/boeing-2023-orders-deliveries/

48. Losey, S. (2024, February 5). *Boeing pushes back T-7 plans due to faulty parts.* Defense News. https://www.defensenews.com/air/2024/02/05/boeing-pushes-back-t-7-plans-due-to-faulty-parts/

49. *Boeing Company - Boeing Reports Third Quarter Results.* Boeing. (2023, October 25). https://investors.boeing.com/investors/news/press-release-details/2023/Boeing-Reports-Third-Quarter-Results/default.aspx

50. *Airbus Deliveries.* AirInsight Group. (n.d.). https://airinsight.com/?s=airbus%2Bdeliveries

## Chapter 13: The FLEX Cockpit and Our Wings

51. Kemp, Jack. (n.d.). *Jack Kemp Quotes.* Brainy Quote.

52. U.S. Coast Guard. (1978, October 20). *Marine Casualty Report* (USCG I6732/92368). https://www.dco.uscg.mil/Portals/9/DCO%20Documents/5p/CG-5PC/INV/docs/boards/cuyogasantacruz.pdf

## Chapter 14: Building Situational Awareness

53. Burke, Edmund. (n.d.). *Edmund Burke Quotes.* Brainy Quote.

54. Spira, Dan. *Be the Change.* Arcadia Consulting - Architects of Change. (2021, July 15). https://arcadiaconsulting.com/be-the-change/

55. Patton, G. S. (n.d.). *George S. Patton Quotes.* Brainy Quote. https://www.brainyquote.com/quotes/george_s_patton_159766

56. Wikimedia Foundation. (n.d.). *The Wisdom of Crowds.* Wikipedia. https://en.wikipedia.org/wiki/The_Wisdom_of_Crowds

## Chapter 15: The FLEX Way of Thinking

57. Hemingway, Ernest. (n.d.). *Ernest Hemingway Quotes.* Brainy Quote.

58. Page, S. E. (2007). *The Difference.* Scott E Page. https://sites.lsa.umich.edu/scottepage/home/the-difference/

59. Lovallo, D., & Sibony, O. (2013, April 1). *Early-stage research on decision-making styles.* McKinsey & Company. https://www.mckinsey.com/capabilities/strategy-and-corporate-finance/our-insights/early-stage-research-on-decision-making-styles

60. Collins, J. (n.d.). *Blend Creative Intensity*. Jim Collins. https://www.jimcollins.com/search.html?q=blend+creative+intensity+

61. Sorrell, M. (2010, March 1). *How we do it: Three executives reflect on strategic decision making*. McKinsey & Company. https://www.mckinsey.com/capabilities/strategy-and-corporate-finance/our-insights/how-we-do-it-three-executives-reflect-on-strategic-decision-making

62. Beck, K., Beedle, M., van Bennekum, A., Cockburn, A., Cunningham, W., Fowler, M., Grenning, J., Highsmith, J., Hunt, A., Jeffries, R., Kern, J., Marco, B., Martin, R. C., Mellor, S., Schwaber, K., Sutherland, J., & Thomas, D. (n.d.). Manifesto for Agile Software Development. https://agilemanifesto.org/

**Chapter 17: Becoming Flawless—The AD/HDD Version of the Book**

63. Kawasaki, Guy. (n.d.). *Guy Kawasaki Quotes*. Brainy Quote.

64. Wikimedia Foundation. (2024c, November 3). *Zoom Video Communications*. Wikipedia. https://en.wikipedia.org/wiki/Zoom_Video_Communications#:~:text=The%20company%20was%20founded%20in,Zoom%20Video%20Communications%2C%20Inc

65. Levy, A. (2019, April 19). *Zoom's CEO emigrated from China 22 years ago and spoke little English - now he's worth almost $3 Billion*. CNBC. https://www.cnbc.com/2019/04/18/zoom-ceo-eric-yuan-worth-3-billion-after-ipo-profile.html

# About the Author

**Christian "Boo" Boucousis** is a former fighter pilot turned entrepreneur, keynote speaker, and leadership expert. Boo served as an F/A-18 Hornet pilot in the Royal Australian Air Force and has translated his experiences in high-stakes aviation into successful ventures in the business world. He is the CEO of Afterburner, Inc., a company that has helped thousands of organizations implement the Flawless Execution model to achieve their goals. Boo's leadership has guided Afterburner in transforming businesses worldwide, including NFL teams like the New York Giants.

www.ingramcontent.com/pod-product-compliance
Lightning Source LLC
Chambersburg PA
CBHW042314210326
41599CB00038B/7124